Multiplying Divisions

Multiplying Divisions

The Fractious Nature of Israel, God's Elect People

FRANK ANTHONY SPINA

CASCADE Books · Eugene, Oregon

MULTIPLYING DIVISIONS
The Fractious Nature of Israel, God's Elect People

Copyright © 2024 Frank Anthony Spina. All rights reserved. Except for brief quotations in critical publications or reviews, no part of this book may be reproduced in any manner without prior written permission from the publisher. Write: Permissions, Wipf and Stock Publishers, 199 W. 8th Ave., Suite 3, Eugene, OR 97401.

Cascade Books
An Imprint of Wipf and Stock Publishers
199 W. 8th Ave., Suite 3
Eugene, OR 97401

www.wipfandstock.com

PAPERBACK ISBN: 978-1-6667-0613-0
HARDCOVER ISBN: 978-1-6667-0614-7
EBOOK ISBN: 978-1-6667-0615-4

Cataloguing-in-Publication data:

Names: Spina, F. A. (Frank A.) [author].

Title: Multiplying divisions : the fractious nature of Israel, God's elect people / Author Name.

Description: Eugene, OR: Cascade Books, 2024 | Includes bibliographical references and index.

Identifiers: ISBN 978-1-6667-0613-0 (paperback) | ISBN 978-1-6667-0614-7 (hardcover) | ISBN 978-1-6667-0615-4 (ebook)

Subjects: LCSH: Social conflict. | Interpersonal relations—Biblical teaching. | Deuteronomistic history. | People of God—Biblical teaching. | Bible.—Old Testament—Theology. | Church—unity. | Bible—Criticism, interpretation, etc. | Typology (Theology).

Classification: BV600.2 S68 2024 (print) | BV600.2 (ebook)

In loving memory:

Betty Marie Ehmann Spina
(November 13, 1940–October 23, 1993)

Contents

Acknowledgments ix

Introduction: Multiplying Divisions—One God, One People 1

1. The Jordan River: Bridge or Barrier? 9
2. Deborah's Difficulties: A Reluctant General and Israelite Defectors 23
3. The Abimelech Story 32
4. Jephthah's Tragic Vow: A Doomed Daughter and a Divided Community 50
5. Multiplying Divisions: The Story of the Levite's Concubine 62
6. The First Divided Monarchy in Israel 77
7. Absalom's Revolt: King David Flees and Israel Divides 91
8. Sheba's Revolt: Quickly Generated, Immediately Quashed 112
9. The Great Schism 118
10. Israel's Division in Prophetic Perspective 136
11. Israel as a Figure for the Church: Conclusions and Reflections 152

Bibliography 187

Index of Biblical References 191

Acknowledgments

The idea for this book was generated as I was preparing to deliver the 2008 Weter Lecture at Seattle Pacific University. The first part of the title of that lecture became the first part of the title of this book. I was humbled and honored to be selected that year by the university's Faculty Status Committee. To my colleagues I express my deepest gratitude for selecting my topic.

Over my many years at Seattle Pacific University and Seminary I have been blessed with colleagues who were always ready to discuss various interpretations of what we liked to call "the holy books." A number of these exchanges were not for the faint of heart. At the end of the day, however, though one had to gird one's loins, to use a biblical metaphor, to enter into this fray, the outcome typically allowed for the sharpening of one's hermeneutical strategies. I remain grateful for having such competent, engaging conversation partners, many of whom became lifelong friends.

Though our marriage has since dissolved, I would be remiss not to thank (Dr.) Jo-Ellen Watson for her support not only of this most recent project but for her persistent support of my career as a professor, scholar, and priest generally for over more than twenty-five years of marriage. As well, Jo-Ellen saved my life twice, quite literally. No words are adequate for expressing my appreciation for both her intentions and competence.

I completed about half of this manuscript while living with my daughter, Stephanie Taylor, my son-in-law, Zakary Taylor, and my three grandchildren, Grace, Isaac, and Malcolm. This precious family provided me with a loving and affirming environment, as well as wonderful distractions that I not only did not resist but eagerly welcomed. I could never thank them enough.

There is no one on this planet with whom I have discussed topics related to biblical interpretation more than Dr. Stanley D. Walters (d. March 4, 2024). For my continuing conversations with him I give thanks to God.

Finally, thanks are due to Michael Thomson for encouraging me to "shop" my manuscript to Wipf and Stock in the first place.

Introduction

MULTIPLYING DIVISIONS—ONE GOD, ONE PEOPLE

Arguably, one of the most famous features of the Old Testament is its claim that the Israelite God is the only deity who actually exists.[1] Deuteronomy 6:4 is the classical text for this unique belief: "Hear O Israel, the LORD our God is one." A comparable conviction is that this sole existing deity elected one and only one people not only so God could bless them but also in the process make them a blessing for all others (Gen 12:1–3). This people would eventually be called *Israel*. The interactions between this one God and this one people constitute the primary story narrated in the Bible.[2]

Though originally a unified community, unfortunately Israel had difficulty maintaining their unity. Israel's tendency to divide was hardly desultory or ephemeral. Throughout their history, in one way or another, and for a variety of reasons, Israel succumbed to various centrifugal forces. Sometimes this affected only factions within the community. At other times, though, all Israel had to grapple with this propensity to divide. Plus, these

---

1. The designation *Old Testament* is a distinctively Christian term, required when the church recognized a *New Testament* as well. Jews, however, refer to their sacred book variously as the Bible, the Hebrew Bible, the Jewish Scriptures, or TANAK. The latter is an acronym in which the *T*, *N*, and *K* are the first letters in transliterated Hebrew standing for the three main sections of the Jewish Bible: *Tôrāh* (Law, Story, Instruction, etc.), *N^{e}bî'îm* (Prophets), and *K^{e}tûbîm* (Writings). Though the Protestant Old Testament follows the order of the books of a Greek version (= Septuagint) it is essentially congruent with the shorter Hebrew canon recognized by Judaism.

2. Israel's story is not confined to the Old Testament. Jesus, whose story is narrated in the four Gospel tradition, is Jesus the Christ/Messiah. According to the New Testament, Jesus was Israel's Christ/Messiah. This is why the apostle Paul later argued that non-Israelites, or gentiles, had to be either grafted onto the olive tree, which symbolized Israel, or adopted into the Israelite family. This is why I take seriously Israel as a figure for the church, which is further explicated in the final chapter of this book.

divisions were substantial and fundamental, sometimes getting at the heart of what it meant to be Israel, the elect people of God. The sheer number of stories that depict Israel struggling with a penchant to divide underscores how prominent this feature is in the biblical tradition.

Consequently, narratives that focus on divisions plaguing Israel invite scrutiny. Before Israel ever enters Canaan, the land of promise, Israel has to determine whether the Jordan River is a bridge or a barrier between eastern and western tribal units (Josh 22:1–34). In the very next biblical book, Judges, four episodes treat the motif of disunity: Deborah, Barak, and Jael (Judg 4–5); Abimelech (Judg 9); Jephthah and his daughter (Judg 11–12); and the Levite and his concubine (Judg 19–21). After Israel established a monarchy, subsequent to the death of Saul, their first king, the House of Saul and the House of David ruled over differing segments of Israel (2 Sam 1–5). Once David became king over all Israel, afterward his own son, Absalom, fomented revolt, creating a serious rift in Israel (2 Sam 13–19). Immediately after this revolt was quelled, a man by the name of Sheba tried his hand at overthrowing David, something that was possible because of continuing fissures in the body politic (2 Sam 20). The classic instance of Israel's division is narrated when the people are divided into a northern kingdom (Israel) and a southern kingdom (Judah), which never again achieved unity (1 Kgs 12). As one might expect, the prophets had something to say about Israel's disunity and the hope for reunion in the future (this is treated in chapter 11). This book treats these significant passages.

In a final chapter, I will reflect on this study from two different perspectives. One has to do with what the New Testament says about the unity of God's people. Obviously, this will include not only what New Testament authors had to say on the subject but, more significantly, what Jesus said about this subject according to the Gospel traditions. A second perspective derives from the conviction that canonical Israel should be seen as a figure of the Christian church.[3] That means that everything that the Bible says about Israelite unity, or its lack, is immediately and vitally applicable to the church. The question is: What does Israel's seemingly perpetual disunity say about the church's seemingly perpetual disunity throughout her history?

ISRAEL'S ANCESTORS (GEN 12–50)

The story of Israel as a *people* begins in the book of Exodus (e.g., Exod 1:9; 2:11, 23, 25; 3:7). Prior to their becoming a people, though, they were

---

3. It goes without saying that canonical Israel is also a figure for the synagogue (= Judaism) in that God's promises to Israel are irrevocable.

basically an extended family. Granted, there are intimations that this family would eventually become a *people* (Gen 17:16; 28:3; 34:16, 22; 35:6; 48:4, 19) or even a *great nation* (Gen 12:2). But for the most part the narratives of Israel's precursors concentrated on them as individuals and members of a large family. At the same time, examples of division in this family adumbrate later divisions that obtained once Israel had become a people. That datum makes relevant a survey of division as reflected in the ancestral stories narrated in Genesis 12–50.

Soon after arriving in Canaan at God's behest, Abraham had to deal with strife that had developed between those taking care of his flocks and those taking care of Lot's flocks (Gen 13:7). Lot was Abraham's nephew. Abraham settled this minor dispute by allowing Lot to choose an area to accommodate his business interests (Gen 13:8–12). Right after this transaction, God appears to Abraham and reiterates the promise of numerous progeny and the land of Canaan. Implicit in what God said, however, is a criticism of Abraham for his permitting Lot to make the first choice of favorable land. What if Lot had opted for Canaan? Fortunately, though Lot's selection did not eventually end up well (Gen 19:1–38), at this point it did not have a deleterious effect on God's ultimate plan. Though this was little more than a dustup, it did indicate that the family's unity could not be taken for granted.

Much later in the ancestral narratives, God is responsible for a future rift in the extended family. The LORD had responded to Rebekah's seeking out the deity because of distress she was experiencing in her pregnancy. Rebekah was married to Isaac, who was in turn the son of Abraham and Sarah, thus making him the child of promise (Gen 17:15–21). In this communication, God told Rebekah that she was carrying twins, each one of which would become a *nation* (Gen 25:23). These two *peoples* would subsequently be divided. Technically, this is not an adumbration of a later division in Israel, since the elder twin was not slated to inherit God's promise. Still, it does represent a division in the family that God had elected and some of whose descendants would later constitute the *chosen people*.

This divinely predicted division is manifested in the very next episode when Rebekah's twins are grown. The younger twin, Jacob, managed to trick his older brother, Esau, into signing away his birthright. Esau had been hungry and thought he was at death's door. So, he squandered his future for a bite of lunch (Gen 25:29–34). This transaction eventuated in a significant division in the family, for it meant that one part of the family, the part that would later be represented by Esau (later identified as Edom), though enjoying divine benefits (Gen 36:6–8, 31; Deut 2:4–8, 22; 23:7), would never be considered part of elect Israel. From one perspective one might implicate

God in fostering this division. Still, the deity had never provided Rebekah with any specifics about how this turn of events would come to fruition. Only human beings act in this drama. This may be an example of an implicit providence and ordinary human behavior somehow meshing and eventuating in God's inexorable will and predictable family dynamics coming simultaneously into play.[4]

The rift between Jacob and Esau is exacerbated when Isaac, their father, becomes old and decides it is time to bestow on his older son a blessing. While Esau is out hunting for food that he and his father will eat to commemorate the occasion, Rebekah and Jacob spring into action. They plot to deceive Isaac so that the patriarch will instead bless Jacob. This is possible because Isaac is elderly and cannot see well. The scheme works perfectly, so that Esau does not receive the primary blessing (Gen 27:1–45). It is hardly surprising that this tear in the family fabric will increase exponentially. As one would expect, Esau was furious about this outcome and planned to kill Jacob as soon as circumstances allowed it (Gen 27:41).

This immediate crisis is averted when Jacob flees to live with his uncle Laban (Gen 28:2). It turns out, however, that division seems to be in the DNA of this family, for Jacob first struggles with his Uncle Laban, Rebekah's brother, and then later with the four women in his life. Again, these are family squabbles, not major social or political crises. At the same time, they suggest a fair amount of disharmony in this clan.

At first, Jacob's difficulties are with Uncle Laban. Initially, Laban is kind, even gracious, to his nephew (Gen 29:13–14). After all, when the uncle offered Jacob a job, he allowed his nephew to name his wage (Gen 29:15). The conflict soon comes to the fore, however. Because Jacob had been romantically smitten with Rachel, Laban's younger daughter, the wage he requested from his uncle was to have Rachel's hand in marriage in exchange for seven years of labor (Gen 29:18). Uncle Laban agreed with this proposal, but when the time came for the wedding he substituted the elder daughter, Leah, for her sister (Gen 29:23). Naturally, Jacob was irate about this switch, but he had already consummated the marriage without his realizing it! Jacob did manage to get Rachel as his wife, too, but it cost him another seven years of labor (Gen 29:25–30). Though Jacob only desired the one woman, he ended up with four, because each of the sisters had handmaidens who became secondary wives to Jacob. Soon, the conflict between uncle and nephew will spill over into conflicts between wives and their husband.

Because Jacob loved Rachel and hated Leah, God decided to even the score a little, the result of which was Leah bore four sons immediately (Gen

---

4. See Spina, "'Face of God,'" 3–25; *Faith of the Outsider*, 14–34.

29:31-35). Rachel was incensed about this and demanded that Jacob father a child by her at once. When he protested that he was not God, Rachel insisted that he sleep with her handmaiden, which resulted in the birth of two sons (Gen 30:1-8). Leah figured that she could play the same game. Two more sons were born to Leah's handmaiden (Gen 30:9-13). It is almost comical to see these dynamics in a supposed patriarchal culture, for the *patriarch* in this instance is being ordered around by his wives. Indeed, this situation verges on absurdity in an episode in which Leah gave some special plants to Rachel in exchange for having Jacob sleep with her (Gen 30:14-21). This trade eventuated in Leah's bearing two more sons and a daughter. After Jacob's having fathered ten sons and one daughter, Rachel finally got pregnant and bore him another son (Gen 30:22-24). Once again, these marital jealousies and relational conflicts in the grand scheme of things are relatively insignificant. But they do provide some insight into this extended family's persistently disharmonious relationships. When that tendency is extrapolated into Israel as a people, the conflicts do transcend interpersonal and familial squabbles.

The tension between Laban and his nephew comes to a head when Jacob finally decides to go back home with his family and the considerable wealth he has acquired, primarily from outsmarting his devious uncle (Gen 30:25-43). This time Jacob will make good on his effort to leave his mother's kin, encouraged as well by the LORD's explicit instruction to do just that (Gen 31:1-3). God had even helped Jacob to increase his holdings at Laban's expense (Gen 31:9-13). While Laban was distracted with business, Jacob, his four wives, his children, servants, and his numerous flocks took off for home, enjoying a three-day head start (Gen 31:17-19). As expected, when Laban found out what was going on he took off in hot pursuit. Any malice he had in mind, though, would be tempered by God's intervention (Gen 31:22-24). Rachel did not make this tense situation any better, for she had stolen her father's household gods (Gen 31:19).

Rachel's reason for this odd theft remains a mystery, but since Laban was unable to discover that his own daughter was the culprit a potential crisis was averted (Gen 31:33-35). After Jacob's diatribe about his uncle's shabby treatment of him over the years, Laban decided to mend the relationship somewhat (Gen 31:36-50). The two groups made a solemn agreement and had a meal together (Gen 31:51-54).

However, once Jacob solved the problem with his angry uncle, he had next to confront the problem of an even angrier estranged brother. In the story's chronology, Esau has had at least twenty years to seethe about how he had been cheated. Everything Jacob did as he anticipated Esau's likely response was calculated to mollify his aggrieved brother. Though Jacob sought God's help with a foxhole prayer (Gen 32:9-12), he hedged his bets by preparing a huge bribe that he figured not even a justifiably outraged brother could refuse (Gen 32:13-20). By all accounts, Jacob did not do this out of the kindness of his heart, for he thought that Esau's coming to meet him with four hundred men in tow surely presaged conflict (Gen 32:3-8). However, though Jacob had not had a change of heart, Esau certainly had. The moment Esau saw Jacob, he ran to his brother, embraced him, and kissed him (Gen 33:1-4). Before a single word was exchanged, the brothers had a good cry. Arguably, this is one of the most profound examples of reconciliation not only in the ancestral stories, but in the whole Bible. Amazingly, Esau initially refuses the bribe that his brother had prepared, finally accepting it only at Jacob's insistence (Gen 33:9-11). However, though this remarkable incident is a paradigm for reconciliation, the very fact that Jacob remained reluctant to go with Esau to his home suggests perhaps an uneasy truce. In time, unfortunately, Edom (= Esau) would become a sworn enemy of Israel (= Jacob).

Once he was back in Canaan, Jacob seemed to have no difficulty relating to his wives. But he was at odds with his adult children. For instance, he complained that two sons, Levi and Simeon, had been too drastic in their violent response to the rape of Dinah, Jacob's daughter and their sister (Gen 34:30-31). Though briefly mentioned almost as an aside, we are also informed that Reuben, Jacob's oldest son, had sex with his father's concubine, something about which the patriarch was aware (Gen 35:22). To say that this puts family disunity in bold relief is to state the obvious. Add to this Jacob's shameful display of obvious partiality toward his sons by Rachel, namely, Joseph and Benjamin, and once again we have a formula for dysfunctional family dynamics (Gen 37:3-4; 42:36-38). Father and sons were antagonistic, and siblings were antagonistic with each other. This made family unity precarious.

Disunity among brothers also was manifest when they were deciding what to do with Joseph, who had dreams predicting his superiority over his brothers, and even over his parents (Gen 37:5-11). It surely did not help that Joseph earlier had told his father an *evil word* about his brothers (Gen 37:2). That, and Jacob's blatant favoring of Joseph, eventuated in the brothers' inability to speak civilly to their younger sibling (Gen 37:4). Yet, despite their common disdain, they did not agree with what to do to Joseph when an opportunity arose. All of them seemed to agree at first to kill Joseph outright when he arrived at Dothan where they were pasturing (Gen 37:17-20). But one of the brothers, Reuben, thought this was extreme. He talked his brothers into placing Joseph in a pit, in hopes of rescuing him when he got a chance (Gen 37:22). Unfortunately, before Reuben was able to pull off the rescue the other brothers sold Joseph to a caravan on the way to Egypt (Gen 37:25–28). Reuben came back to the pit too late to do Joseph any good (Gen 37:29). This failure to act in concert would later haunt the brothers as they quarreled about how they had previously conducted themselves (Gen 42:21–22; 44:16).

This proclivity toward disunity even plagued the smallest family units. When Judah leaves his immediate family and marries a Canaanite woman, soon circumstances evolve that underscore this tendency (Gen 38:2).[5] Judah fathers three sons to this woman: Er, Onan, and Shelah (Gen 38:3–5). When Er was grown, Judah procured a wife for him: Tamar (Gen 38:6). Er died prematurely, though, because of divine judgment (Gen 38:7). The cultural practice that backgrounds this episode is that when a brother dies before having children, it is the obligation of the next oldest brother to father children in the deceased brother's behalf. However, because Onan protested this practice, he saw to it that Tamar did not get pregnant (Gen 38:8–9). God was unhappy with this, so Onan also died prematurely (Gen 38:9–10). Though this episode is strange to moderns, it nevertheless indicates a rift in the family. One brother refused to honor his deceased brother by seeing to it that his sister-in-law became pregnant. As well, Judah also contributed to these family dynamics by promising Shelah, who was still too young to impregnate Tamar, to his daughter-in-law when the time came (Gen 38:11). But Judah did not keep his promise (Gen 38:14). That reneging led to more disunity. Tamar deceived Judah by pretending to be a prostitute and became pregnant by him (Gen 38:15–19, 24). Though her cleverness in being able to implicate Judah as the father of the child she was carrying (Gen 38:20–23, 25–26) saved her life, this was one more instance of family members being at each other's throats.

The motif of disunity is replete in these ancestral stories. Even Jacob's outlining the future of his sons intimates at several points that common parentage did not guarantee a unified family (Gen 49:4, 7, 8, 27). Unfortunately, these examples adumbrate the fissures that will plague Israel once they become a full-fledged people.

THE GROUND RULES

In this book I execute a close reading of texts pertinent to Israel's tendency to succumb to centrifugal divisive forces. I am interested in the final editing of the canonical biblical text. When necessary, I am not averse to discussing

---

5. See the fuller treatment of this story in Spina, *Faith of the Outsider*, 35–51.

critical issues that have influenced the final editing process. Still, the canonical text will be the primary focus in this study.

Though I personally appreciate well-footnoted biblical scholarship, given the audience I have in mind for this book I will instead use a minimum of notes. I believe the argument will be clear without any recourse to copious footnotes. However, a few notes will provide information that non-specialists may find helpful. Of course, the notes I do have are to credit those scholars whose insights I have followed or with whom I have debated. Since, however, most of the observations of the biblical texts in these studies are my own, I am able to keep the number of notes to a minimum. Obviously, not all my observations are unique, for other scholars observing the same texts have also seen what I have seen. Still, the primary thrust of this study has to do with my appraisal of the relevant texts.

A few remarks about terminology are in order. When mentioning the distinctive name of the Israelite deity, I will use the un-pointed consonants of the *Tetragrammaton*, or four-letter name: YHWH. Otherwise, I will use the ordinary substitutes, such as *God*, *LORD*, and the like. Translations of the Hebrew or Greek text are my own. Otherwise, any direct biblical quotes are from the 1952 Revised Standard Version (RSV).

Chapter 1

The Jordan River: Bridge or Barrier?

INTRODUCTION

The episode recounted in Josh 22 portrays Israel being threatened by division in two ways. One threat involved a natural boundary: the Jordan River. One part of Israel saw the river as a bridge while another part saw it as a barrier. A second threat had to do with a large altar. One segment of Israel insisted the altar was a unifying symbol while another segment protested that the structure was divisive. Thus, before all Israel is settled in Canaan—the promised land—they are faced with a serious conflict that might eventuate in their becoming a divided people.

This dual threat is not obvious at the outset. The chapter begins by reporting that Israel was in the process of settling the remaining territory that would be their home. No difficulties whatsoever seem to be on the horizon, and certainly nothing that might compromise Israel's unity. Indeed, compared to the rest of the book of Joshua, this episode starts off as completely unremarkable. Most of the second section of the book of Joshua describes the location of the various tribal units in Canaan (Josh 14–21). At the conclusion of this section, there is a summation that is so positive and comprehensive (Josh 21:43–45) that it asserts that, despite earlier challenges and a reversal or two, Israel according to the book of Joshua has enjoyed a satisfactory outcome.[1]

---

1. As for these challenges and reversals, twice Israel put themselves in a bind dealing with Canaanites. They spared Rahab, a Canaanite prostitute, and her family when they attacked Jericho (Josh 2). Also, they were duped into allowing the Gibeonites to become part of their community (Josh 9). Both of these incidents involved disobeying the clear rules of engagement (Deut 20:16–18). Also, Achan, an Israelite descended from Judah,

This summary asserted unequivocally that YHWH had fulfilled *every* promise made to Israel: *all* the land had been given (Josh 21:43); the people were given rest *on every side* (Josh 21:44); *not one of the enemies* had withstood Israel; and, as noted, not a single one *of all the good promises* that God made had failed (Josh 21:45). Although this totalizing statement is contradicted by other texts in the same book, suggesting that some land remains to be conquered (Josh 13:1–7; 23:4–5), one hardly anticipates anything unmanageable after this summary. In this light, just as we encountered the undramatic description of allotments to the nine and a half tribes of Israel on the western side of the Jordan, we now expect an uneventful settling of the remaining two and a half tribes on the river's eastern side.

As mentioned, the very first paragraph of Josh 22 (vv. 1–6) is consistent with this expectation. Nothing requires rethinking the rosy summary at the end of chapter 21. The great leader, Joshua, summoned the tribes who had not yet taken possession of their own territory: the Reubenites, the Gadites, and half of Manasseh (the other half had settled on the western side). He applauded them for obeying him just as they had obeyed Moses himself and emphasized that at no time had they abandoned their fellow Israelites who had settled on the western side of the Jordan; further, he pointed out that these actions constituted complete obedience to YHWH's orders (Josh 22:2–3).

Having affirmed these two and a half tribes and having repeated that the western groups had already taken up residence in Canaan, Joshua announced that it was time for the eastern groups to go to their own homes in the areas Moses had personally given to them (Josh 22:4; see also 13:8–12, 15–32; 18:7). He concluded by encouraging the eastern tribes to remain faithful and by blessing them, after which they repaired to their homes (Josh 22:6). The final settlement of the remaining tribes appears a fitting conclusion to Israel's taking over the promised land, in spite of the fact that the event itself is hardly remarkable.

At the same time, it is curious that the account of the settling of the eastern groups comes *after* such a totalizing summary. In fact, a subsequent paragraph supplies more details to what Joshua initially communicated to the two and a half tribes. But before we get to these extra details of Joshua's remarks, the narrator has already informed the reader that *Moses* had given half of Manasseh their possession in Bashan (east of the Jordan) whereas *Joshua* had given the other nine and a half tribes their possession on the western side (Josh 22:7). What is the purpose of revealing that datum? The

---

violated the *ban* and thereby exposed all of Israel to ultimate divine sanction (Josh 7–8). See Spina, *Faith of the Outsider*, 52–71.

answer to that question may be discovered in the extra details of Joshua's initial speech.

When Joshua blessed the two and a half Israelite tribes, it turns out that he also encouraged them that upon their getting to their new homes they should share their lavish holdings ("much wealth"; "very many livestock"; "silver, gold, bronze, and iron"; and "much clothing") with their fellow Israelites (Josh 22:8). It is unclear whether this sharing was to extend to the rest of Israel.

In any case, once we learn everything that Joshua had said to these tribes, we realize that they did go home. But there is one more significant detail: the eastern group left the western group at Shiloh which, the narrative stresses, is in *the land of Canaan,* and settled itself in *the land of Gilead.* As well, the western group is referred to as *the people of Israel* (literally: "the sons/children of Israel") while the eastern group is referred to as *the people of Reuben, the people of Gad, and Half-Manasseh* (literally: "the sons/children of Reuben, the sons/children of Gad, and Half-Manasseh"). Then, at the conclusion of this paragraph, we are reminded that this territory was allotted by virtue of YHWH's command through Moses (Josh 22:9).

These details raise some questions. First, what purpose is served by revealing that *Joshua* had given the nine and a half tribes the western side of the Jordan while *Moses* had given the tribe of Manasseh Bashan on the eastern side? Typically, Moses and Joshua spoke with a single voice.[2] Does this statement reveal that, at least on this matter, there had been a dispute? Second, why is Manasseh singled out in relationship to Bashan? Reuben and Gad are included in the eastern group in the same context (Josh 22:9), but not at the beginning of the paragraph. Is this significant? Third, what are we to make of the additional details of Joshua's blessing? Joshua told the eastern group to go back home while calling attention to their substantial wealth (Josh 22:8). But why was he not more explicit about the beneficiaries of the sharing he had ordered? Fourth, after Joshua's blessing we see that not only Half-Manasseh but also Reuben and Gad left their relatives at Shiloh, expressly called *the land of Canaan.* Does this suggest that *the land of Gilead* is being differentiated from Canaan proper? Fifth, what, if anything, are we to make of the naming of the eastern tribes? At first, they were called Reubenites, Gadites, and Half-Manasseh (Josh 22:1), but later are called "the sons/children of Reuben, the sons/children of Gad, and Half-Manasseh" (Josh 22:9). Is this merely stylistic, or something more? Finally, why are we told three separate times that Moses was responsible for allowing these two and a half tribes to occupy territory east of the Jordan (Josh 22:4, 7, 9)?

---

2. See Spina, "Moses and Joshua," 65–92.

Before attempting to answer these questions, we need to ask a more fundamental one: How did it happen that the two and a half tribes ended up settling east of the Jordan in the first place? Had this area ever been considered part of the land which YHWH had promised to Israel? If not, is there more to this story than we had assumed? The answer to that question is provided by narratives preceding the book of Joshua. To those we now turn.

THE BACK STORY OF THE EASTERN TRIBES

Central to the biblical story is YHWH's election of Israel (Gen 12–50). A crucial feature of this election was the divine promise that this community would be granted a land: Canaan (Gen 12:5–7; 15:18–21; 17:8).[3] Canaan's inhabitants are, quite predictably, known as Canaanites, but this is also an umbrella term. Other residents of the same territory are called Hittites, Girgashites, Amorites, Perizzites, Hivites, and Jebusites (Deut 7:1; Josh 3:10; 24:11).[4] Even more significant than the identity of the residents is Canaan's location.

There are a handful of passages mentioning the boundaries of Canaan. Some passages are idealistic. For example, in Gen 15:18 the promised land extends from Egypt's Nile River to the Euphrates River. Deuteronomy 1:7 indicates that in addition to Canaan proper—the hill country of the Amorites, their neighbors in the Arabah, the hill country, the lowland, the Negeb, the seacoast—the promised land included Lebanon and an area in the environs of the Euphrates. Similar dimensions are found in Deut 11:24. These descriptions correspond to territories that Kings David and Solomon were said to have controlled (2 Sam 8:3–4; 1 Kgs 5:1 [Eng. 4:21]; 8:65).

---

3. The promise of land is found throughout TANAK/Old Testament: e.g., Exod 3:17; 6:4; 13:5, 11; Lev 14:34; 18:3; 25:38; Num 13:2; Deut 1:7; 7:1; 11:30; 32:49; Josh 1:1–3; 24:3; Ps 105:11; Neh 9:24.

4. Only these three references include all seven groups. The order of the lists, however, is inconsistent. In Josh 3:10 the order is Canaanites, Hittites, Hivites, Perizzites, Girgashites, Amorites, and Jebusites. The order in 24:11 is Amorites, Perizzites, Canaanites, Hittites, Girgashites, Hivites, and Jebusites. There is no discernible reason for preferring one order over another. Besides these three references there are combinations of smaller lists, from at least six groups to no more than three (Gen 15:18–21; Exod 3:8; 12:8, 17; 13:5; 23:23, 28; 33:2; 34:11; Deut 20:17; Num 13:28–29; Josh 9:1; 11:3; 12:8; Judg 3:5; Neh 9:8). Ezra 9:1 mentions these same residents of Canaan (excepting Hivites and Girgashites) along with Ammonites, Moabites, and Egyptians. But this listing is confined to people with whom Israelites who had avoided being exiled intermarried. Finally, 2 Chr 8:7 includes five of the seven nations (excepting Canaanites and Girgashites) who were subjected to forced labor by Solomon.

A more specific (and modest) depiction of Canaan's southern, northern, western, and eastern borders occurs in Num 34:1–15. According to this passage, Canaan's western border extends to the *Great Sea* (the Mediterranean), its southern border goes as far as Kadesh-barnea, its northern border reaches Hamath (but excludes Canaanite cities on the Lebanon coast), and its eastern border is the Jordan River. Obviously, the eastern border is primarily of interest in dealing with the episode recounted in Joshua 22.

If Canaan *is* the promised land, and if Gad, Reuben, and Half-Manasseh plan on living *outside* Canaan, how would this be permissible to the rest of Israel or, for that matter, conform to YHWH's promise?[5]

Moreover, considerable territory on the eastern side of the Jordan River had already been allotted by YHWH to people distantly related to Israel. Though distinct from elect Israel, YHWH has not left these relatives to fend for themselves, so to speak. Edom *is* Esau and, of course, Jacob's/Israel's older twin (Gen 25:24–26; 32:28; 35:10; 36:1, 8, 19, 42; Deut 23:7). YHWH has seen to it that Esau/Edom occupies land east of the Jordan River (Deut 2:4–5, 12, 22). Likewise, Moab and Ammon were children of Lot, Abraham's nephew. Infamously, these children were conceived when Lot's daughters got him drunk and had children by him (Gen 19:30–38). Despite the incest, YHWH granted Moab's and Ammon's descendants areas east of the Jordan and also made them off-limits to future Israelite aggression (Deut 2:9–19). While this Transjordan territory was appropriate for Israel's kin, was it also suitable for Israelites? Clearly, Reuben, Gad, and Half-Manasseh thought so. Even Moses thought so. What is the source of the conviction that the territory east of the Jordan River could be considered part of the promised land?

Answering that question requires asking a more basic one: Why had Israel initially engaged the Canaanites by crossing the Jordan River? In light of Israel's previous *southern strategy*, why was Jericho the first Canaanite city to be encountered (Josh 2)? Remember that YHWH had instructed Moses to send men to spy Canaan when Israel was in the Wilderness of Paran, which was southwest of the Jordan River (Num 13:1–2). Presumably, had the spies been optimistic about their prospects for victory, Israel would have entered from that southern vantage point. However, having taken stock of the land and even bringing back some produce, all but two of the spies were pessimistic about Israel's chances to take on the formidable Canaanites. Only Caleb and Joshua urged Israel to attack (Num 13:17–33; 14:6–10).

Most Israelites accepted the negative report, with tragic results. In the process, they challenged Moses' (and Aaron's) authority and determined,

---

5. Throughout Deuteronomy the Jordan River is Canaan's eastern border. Israel must cross the river to get to the land YHWH is offering as a gift (Deut 4:26; 11:31; 12:10; 27:2, 4, 12; 30:18; 31:13; 32:47). See Hulst, "Der Jordan," 167.

incredibly, to return to Egypt, the very nation that had enslaved them (Num 14:1–3). When Caleb and Joshua countered the negative report and instead argued that divine power was available to Israel and, therefore, they should proceed, the people were not only unimpressed but threatened to kill their leaders (Num 14:4–10a).

YHWH's reaction to this perfidy was serious. The deity threatened not only pestilence as judgment but something more frightening: dispossession. As had happened earlier during the wilderness trek, YHWH was so angry that the deity opted to begin anew, starting with Moses (Num 14:11–12; cf. Exod 32:7–10). Fortunately for Israel, Moses intervened in Israel's behalf by reminding YHWH of the ancestral covenant and the fact that the Egyptians would gloat that the Israelite God brought the people out of Egypt with the cynical purpose of destroying them in the wilderness. Though YHWH gave in to Moses' pleas (Num 14:20), punishment was not averted. Indeed, YHWH condemned everyone who was at least twenty years old to die in the wilderness, now lengthened to a forty-year sojourn (matching the forty days of spying the land). This meant that no Israelite who had witnessed YHWH's power executed against Egypt would live to see, let alone enter, the promised land. Caleb and Joshua were the exceptions. The wilderness had just become a burial site for every Israelite twenty years and older; the spies who were behind the negative assessment perished at once (Num 14:21–38).

Despite the severity of divine judgment, Israel insisted on adding insult to injury. Over Moses' strenuous objection, Israel resolved to engage the Canaanites. This was a futile attempt to atone for their sins. The result—just as Moses predicted—was disastrous (Num 14:39–45).[6] After this stinging defeat, entering Canaan from the south was no longer an option. Israel would head in another direction and eventually cross the Jordan River from the east into the promised land (Num 14:25; 20:1, 22–23; 21:4).

But this maneuver only explains Israel's entry into Canaan by passing through its eastern rather than its southern border. The dimensions of Canaan had nothing to do with Israel's point of entry. However, the dimensions were affected by another turn of events. Keep in mind that Israel was on a divine mandate not to possess any of the territory in the Transjordan. As we noted above, YHWH had made provisions for Edom, Moab, and Ammon to reside in this area. Israel had no designs for this territory. In fact, when Israel encountered anyone on the way to Canaan, Israel was obligated to pay for any provisions they used. Unfortunately, avoiding hostile contact became impossible when those on the east side of the Jordan River balked

---

6. There is another tradition about Israel's confronting the Canaanites prior to the actual conquest—this time with better results (Num 21:1–3).

when Israel requested safe passage and offered compensation for resources used.

The Amorites were the first ones to resist Israel's efforts to traverse peacefully. Israel had made it clear that it had no interest in Amorite land, fields, vineyards, or even water on the way to Canaan (Num 21:21–22). But Sihon, the Amorite king, immediately took up arms against Israel (Num 21:23). This battle eventuated not only in an Israelite victory, but their confiscating Amorite cities and dispossessing the Amorite population (Num 21:24–25, 31–32). Consequently, a portion of Transjordan became Israelite territory. The same thing happened when Israel encountered Bashan. Their king, Og, fought Israel, with similar results (Num 21:33–35). In both cases, Israel did to these people what they were supposed to do to the inhabitants of Canaan. Virtually overnight the extent of the promised land had increased.[7]

Once the promised land was expanded to include parts of the Transjordan, inevitably some Israelites expressed an interest in settling there. That happened when the Reubenites and Gadites approached Moses, Eleazar the priest, and other leaders to ask permission to live in this eastern sector rather than cross the Jordan River to live on the western side. These two tribes—Half-Manasseh is not at this point mentioned—had noted that this area was especially conducive for raising livestock, which they had in abundance (Num 32:1–5).

In a way, though, the rationale for the Reubenites and Gadites wanting to live in Transjordan because they had extensive holdings in livestock seems a tad odd. Many Israelites owned livestock.[8] Still, since the narrator affirmed that Gad and Reuben indeed possessed many animals and that the land was especially suitable for this business their request made sense.

However, though seemingly reasonable, what the Reubenites and Gadites asked for did not sit well with Moses. In fact, his first response was to accuse these tribes of desertion! How dare Reuben and Gad remain on the east side of the river while the rest of Israel engages the inhabitants of Canaan on the opposite side of the river (Num 32:6–7)? Moses even goes so far as to compare Reuben's and Gad's request to the response of the pessimistic

---

7. Even Moab and Edom will eventually be victims of Israelite aggression according to Num 22–24. In that narrative, Balak, the king of Moab, hired a man, Balaam, to curse Israel on their way to Canaan. But Balaam ended up blessing Israel instead! In the last part of Balaam's oracle, he predicted future victory over not only Moab, but Edom, Amelek, and others (Num 24:17–24).

8. Famously, there was strife between Abraham and his nephew Lot over livestock and the available grazing land (Gen 13:7). Joseph explained to the pharaoh that his family's business was livestock (46:32). In the exodus story, Israel's livestock was exempted from a plague that afflicted Egyptian livestock (Exod 9:7).

spies that had prompted divine judgment (Num 32:8–13; 13:17—14:38). As Moses saw the matter, Reuben and Gad—a "brood of sinful men"—had with this ill-advised petition once again provoked YHWH to withdraw from Israel while they were still in the wilderness (Num 32:14–15). This Moses could not tolerate.

At first, the reaction of Reuben and Gad to Moses' recalcitrance and indictment appears little more than doubling down on their original request, thus rendering it more of a demand. They let it be known in no uncertain terms that they would build structures for their animals and cities for their children (Num 32:16). But they continue by arguing that they had no intention whatsoever of sitting on the sidelines while the other Israelites take on the Canaanites. Reuben and Gad are even willing to become a vanguard for the rest of Israel. Under no circumstances will those on the eastern side settle down until their kin have occupied the area on the western side. Though their children will in the meantime take refuge in fortified cities, Reuben and Gad gladly offer their services to the rest of Israel as they confront the Canaanites (Num 32:16–19).

Moses accepts this response so enthusiastically that it makes one wonder why he had not thought of it himself. How could one fault what Reuben and Gad offered? The eastern segment of Israel would help the western segment deal with the Canaanites. Once the Canaanites were dealt with, both could occupy their respective territories. Nine and a half tribes would take up residence in Canaan proper whereas the remaining two and a half tribes would take up residence in Transjordan. Reuben and Gad had come up with a win-win solution, which Moses immediately adopted.

Moses reiterates the terms of the agreement, including warning about reneging (Num 32:20–23), and then issues a command congruent with what Gad and Reuben had originally proposed. The eastern group accedes to Moses' orders and repeats the promise to accompany the Israelites about to embark on the western campaign (Num 32:24–27). At this point, Moses briefs Eleazar the priest, Joshua, and various leaders of the particulars, prompting Gad and Reuben to assure everyone that they had every intention to keep this promise (Num 32:28–32). This incident concludes with Moses granting the three tribes—for the first time, Half-Manasseh is identified as the third member of the Transjordan contingent—the eastern territory, including Sihon's and Og's kingdoms and their numerous cities (Num 32:33–42). Just as Joshua would affirm later, Moses himself had allotted this eastern land to these two and a half tribes (Josh 22:4); the narration too confirmed what Joshua had said (Josh 22:7, 9). In sum, we now have the answer about the extent of the promised land and how it came about that two and a half tribes settled on the eastern side of the Jordan River.

THE BIG ALTAR

We return to the passage that transforms a mundane report of a straightforward settlement into an account of a crisis in which Israel verges on civil war. This segment of the story sheds further light on the questions raised by Josh 22:7-9, as mentioned above.

As the episode unfolds, there is some geographical ambiguity. The two and a half eastern tribes come to a *region around the Jordan* (*'el-gᵉlilôt hayyardēn*), that is situated in *the land of Canaan*, and then builds a large altar *by the Jordan* (*'al-hayyardēn*). The ambiguity derives from the fact that typically *Canaan* refers to the western side of the Jordan River. However, we explored previously texts indicating that the promised land had been expanded to include some segments of the eastern side of the river. Does the *land of Canaan* at this point refer only to the original land of promise on the western side of the Jordan or does that designation now include the newly acquired eastern side? And, is the ambiguity incidental or purposeful? If the latter, might the ambiguity reflect a situation in which some Israelites insisted on the original boundaries of Canaan whereas others had no difficulty with expansion?

The ambiguity remains unresolved by the text. Whatever area is being referred to spatially, the first collective action on the part of the eastern Israelites was not only to build an altar, but a conspicuously large one (*mizbēaḥ gādôl lᵉmar'eh*). No reason for building this altar, let alone a large one that presumably ensures it will be visually prominent, is given. One may infer that the altar was designed for religious activity. What other purpose would obtain in erecting an altar? An altar is presumably a sacrificial site.[9] Was this large altar to be used for sacrifices being offered by the eastern Israelites? If not, what was the reason for its erection? We remain for now in the dark about two things: the precise location (is it on the western or eastern side of the Jordan?) and the reason it was constructed (for sacrifices for the eastern Israelites, or all Israelites, or for some other religious reason for one or both groups of Israelites?).

---

9. Noah sacrificed on an altar after the flood (Gen 8:20). But Abraham built an altar three different times (Gen 12:7-8; 13:4, 18) without mentioning sacrifice. Yet, some sort of religious activity is implied in that each time he also *pitched his tent* and *called on YHWH's name* (in Gen 13:18 there is no indication that Abraham called on YHWH's name). Abraham did build an altar for the purpose of sacrificing Isaac (Gen 22:9). Isaac likewise *built an altar, pitched his tent,* and *called on YHWH's name* (Gen 26:25), with no explicit mention of sacrifice. Jacob similarly erected an altar but did not sacrifice (Gen 33:20). He did this again at YHWH's command, but again there is no specific mention of sacrifice. Every time an altar is constructed religious activities are presumed but not necessarily sacrifice.

However, there is no ambiguity whatsoever about the reaction to the large altar on the part of the western Israelites. Once they *heard*—as opposed to *saw*—that Reuben, Gad, and Half-Manasseh had constructed this large altar the ambiguity about location is resolved, at least according to their allegation. The western Israelites protested that the altar had been erected in *front of the Land of Canaan* (*'el-mûl 'ereṣ K^{e}na'an*), which they further designated as *the region about the Jordan* (see Josh 22:10) and, perhaps more crucially, as territory belonging to the Israelite people (*'el-'ēber b^{e}nê Yiśrā'ēl*; Josh 22:11). Does this contention intimate that only the western Israelites could claim to be the only true Israelites? Instead of waiting for an answer to this bold accusation, the western Israelites gathered at Shiloh and prepared to go to war with the other eastern Israelites who had erected the large altar (Josh 22:12). Still, it remains to be seen whether the primary issue is the altar's location, for nothing so far has been expressed about either its size or potential use.

Prior to attacking, however, an impressive delegation representing the western Israelites—including Phinehas ben Eleazar the priest and ten officers from each of the tribal units but excluding Joshua—is sent to the eastern tribes in the land of Gilead (Josh 22:13–14).[10] This is when we learn what had so disturbed the western Israelites. Not only does the delegation incriminate the eastern Israelites for being apostates but compares their behavior to the notorious sin at Peor which triggered YHWH's wrath (Num 25) and Achan's infamous violation during the sack of Jericho which made Israel as a whole subject to the very *ban* to which the Canaanites were subjected (Josh 7:1–12; 22:16–18, 20). In the eyes of the western Israelites, when the eastern group built the large altar, this was an egregious act that had made all Israel liable to YHWH's judgment. The only mitigating factor in this indictment is that the western Israelites considered the eastern residents as still belonging to Israel.

But there is another extremely important issue brought up by the western delegation which, if true, would be critical, even fatal, for the eastern Israelites. This issue involved the charge that the east side of the Jordan River was an *unclean land* (*ṭ^{e}mē'āh 'ereṣ*) and consequently unworthy of being considered part of the promised land. This assertion is not only extreme, but flies in the face of Moses' allowing the occupation of select areas on the eastern side by Gad, Reuben, and Half-Manasseh, not to mention as well Joshua's blessing of that occupation. Apparently undaunted by Moses' actions and Joshua's benediction, the delegation goes so far as to invite

---

10. Eleazar was Aaron's son (Exod 6:25). Phinehas, his son, was instrumental in lessening YHWH's wrath against Israel when they *yoked* themselves to Baal at Peor (Num 25:7, 11).

(demand?) that the two and a half eastern tribes return to the territory in which YHWH's tabernacle stands, thereby taking up residence in the west (Josh 22:19). Otherwise, *all Israel* would be condemned just as they were in the Peor and Achan incidents, respectively. Is this invitation a thinly veiled way of letting the eastern groups know that without their compliance war is inevitable? Is Israel about to be ripped apart at the seams by a civil war prior to their settlement in the land that YHWH had promised to them?

The eastern tribes respond to this charge with a resounding denial of any wrongdoing. After invoking the divine name with a string of epithets— Mighty God (*'ēl 'ĕlôhîm*); YHWH; Mighty God (*'ēl 'ĕlôhîm*)—they insist that the Israelite deity knows—YHWH doubtlessly *knows!*—and now the rest of Israel should *know* that rebellion against the Israelite God is not only a slanderous accusation but the last thought in their collective minds. Had they been guilty of such a scurrilous charge, then they would willingly submit to YHWH's just punishment (Josh 22:22). The erection of the altar had nothing to do at all with rebelling against YHWH, or any breach of faith, or, for that matter, even using it for offerings (Josh 22:23). Gad, Reuben, and Half-Manasseh vehemently protest that the western Israelites had jumped the gun in taking this extreme position.

The eastern group maintained that they had built the altar with completely different aims from those of which they felt they had been so unfairly accused. Though the western group threatens Israel's unity based on their assumption of the altar's purpose, the eastern group counters this aggressive move by explaining why they had built the altar. The eastern group ignores the demeaning characterization that the land that it was about to occupy was *unclean*. Indeed, since the eastern Israelites were about to settle in this land, they clearly believed it was perfectly *clean*.[11]

In an effort to rebut the western delegation's claims, the eastern group first off notes that it had been originally afraid of a future circumstance that would have dire implications for Israel's unity. Might a time come when subsequent generations—*your children* speaking to *our children*—complain about the religious devotion of their counterparts in the east? Was it such a stretch to think in these terms given the presence of the Jordan River as a boundary between the two parts of Israel? Could a situation conceivably arise in which one part of Israel no longer recognized another part as

---

11. These counter assertions that the eastern territory was either *unclean* or *clean*, depending on who was making the claim, probably has to do with being *ritually* unclean or clean. Israel believed that certain religious practices, attitudes, or particular objects could render a place (or person) unclean (e.g., Lev 5). Given such a belief, declaring something generically as unclean functions as more than an insult. It is a serious charge.

perpetual members of the elect people of God? The eastern group envisions a situation in which a future western generation declares, "What have you to do with YHWH, the God of Israel? For YHWH has made the Jordan a boundary between us and you, you Reubenites and Gadites; you have no portion in YHWH." In sum, the eastern tribes were concerned that a future generation of western Israel—*your children*—might decide to prevent a future generation of eastern Israel—*our children*—from worshipping YHWH (Josh 22:26–27). In the vivid imagination of such a future reaction on the part of western Israel to eastern Israel, even the omission of Half-Manasseh from the text at this point may not be dismissed as simply incidental.

From the perspective of the eastern Israelites, it was precisely this fear of a future rift that gave them the idea of building an altar. Though commonly a site for sacrificial rites, eastern Israel had not built the altar with that purpose in view. Instead, the altar was to be a *witness* (*'ēd*) between the west and the east, not only now but in the future as well. Contrary to the accusation of false worship, the altar was meant to symbolize the proper worship of YHWH *in his presence* (*lᵉpānāw*), presumably referring to the place where *all* Israel was to worship. This altar, with its symbolism as a witness as well as the proper worship in which the eastern tribes plan to participate, should dissuade any future western generation from asserting that "you [i.e., the eastern group] have no portion in YHWH" (Josh 22:26–27). Interestingly, not only do the Transjordanian Israelites insist that the altar that they made was not to be used for actual sacrifices they maintain as well that it was merely a *copy* (*tabnît*), which was intended to be a *witness* (Josh 22:28). At this point, the eastern group makes it abundantly clear that they have no trouble accepting that the altar which stands before YHWH's tabernacle is the only licit place for various sacrifices (Josh 22:29).

The argument put forward by the eastern Israelites seems suspiciously weak. Why build an altar, the express purpose of which normally is for offering sacrifices, as a *witness*? Plus, to what does the altar witness? Equally, why was a large altar necessary? Then again, what accounts for the paranoia that was the basis for believing that the western Israelites would eventually denounce and even dispossess their eastern counterparts? Finally, why would the eastern Israelites justify their actions *after* they built the altar when they could have prevented a confrontation at the outset by explaining beforehand what they were planning to do?

Whether these questions are apt or not, they appear not to have occurred to the western delegation. For this group, the proffered explanation was sufficient (Josh 22:30). Indeed, the priest, Phinehas ben Eleazar, announced to the Reubenites, the Gadites, and Half-Manasseh that YHWH had surely been in the midst of these deliberations which concluded that no treachery against YHWH had taken place. The priest went on to say that the eastern side had saved Israel as a whole from divine judgment (Josh 22:31).

Subsequently, the western delegation returned to its territory and informed the remainder of Israel, which led to most positive results. Western Israel foreswore any actions against their eastern sisters and brothers, including destruction of the land (Josh 22:32–33). The episode concludes with the Reubenites and Gadites—curiously, once again Half-Manasseh is not mentioned at this point—naming the altar *Witness* in that the structure was a testimony that YHWH is God (Josh 22:34).

CONCLUSION

On the surface, at least, the story related in Joshua 22 seems to end on a positive note. The boundaries of the promised land, originally confined to Canaan proper, have been extended to include some territory on the eastern side of the Jordan River. From Israel's perspective, surely that is a positive development. As well, this expansion enabled Israel to accommodate Gad, Reuben, and Half-Manasseh, who had requested to live in Transjordan as this area was so conducive to raising flocks and herds. That, too, could only be viewed as a plus.

Even the dynamics between the western and eastern tribes appeared to conclude positively as well. After all, the eastern group succeeded in mollifying an upset Moses, then later denied that the western delegation's charges of apostasy were true. In short, they had persuaded Moses of their sincerity in offering the western group all the help it needed in taking over the Cis-Jordanian area. And, they subsequently convinced the western delegation that the construction of the big altar would unify rather than divide Israel. Since this episode finally portrays the Jordan River as a *bridge* instead of a *barrier*, Israel deserves kudos for dealing with this contentious issue, forging a workable compromise, and averting an outcome that could have been disastrous.

Still, a question lingers: Is there more to this episode than the surface meaning, which by all accounts is on the plus side of the ledger? There are hints, howbeit subtle, that just below the surface potential problems are lurking. For example, though it had happened some time ago Moses' rush to judgment that the eastern group was planning to abdicate its responsibility to join the western Israelites in settling Canaan is disquieting. Why was that Moses' first thought? What was it about Israelite behavior that he had no trouble believing that two and a half tribes would abandon their brothers and sisters in such a crucial endeavor? Then again, the eastern group's rejoinder to Moses' accusation was so readily accepted that it made Moses look rash. Why had Moses not given the eastern group the benefit of the doubt in thinking that they would settle in the eastern territory only after the western group was able to settle in the west?

Difficulties of this sort are also evident in the big altar story. As soon as the western Israelites were aware of the big altar that the eastern Israelites had constructed, they believed the worst. The western delegation did not first ask for an explanation. Its first salvo was to accuse the eastern Israelites of rebelling against YHWH and committing sins that were comparable to what had happened at Peor and what Achan had infamously done, therefore making all Israel a target of YHWH's judgment. Why did the western group not take an intermediate step? Why not ask questions before making such serious accusations?

Finally, how did the eastern group get by with such flimsy counter arguments? Why did the altar have to be large and, therefore, conspicuous? Why construct an altar upon which no sacrifices would be offered? Why had the eastern group hypothesized a time when a western generation might denounce them of no longer being part of Israel or believing in Israel's God? Yet, these facile reasons were immediately accepted by the western group as though they were the epitome of unassailable logic.

If we have interpreted these hints correctly, then the peace that was negotiated in the matter of the big altar was a fragile peace. Unfortunately, several stories in the next narrative section, the book of Judges, seem to confirm that the peace achieved by these two Israelite factions would not hold for long.

Chapter 2

Deborah's Difficulties: A Reluctant General and Israelite Defectors

In the previous chapter, it was difficult to determine whether the unity that Israel achieved in the incident involving the *Big Altar* was likely to be permanent or temporary. I suggested that the accusations of the Israelites on the western side of the Jordan River were so abrupt and extreme, while the justifications offered by the Israelites on the eastern side of the river were so anemic and facilely accepted, that this did not bode well for a lasting unity. The book of Judges seems to confirm this assessment. No fewer than four stories accenting division in Israel are found in this book. The story featuring Deborah (Judg 4–5) is the first one.

THE CONTEXT OF THE STORY

The first part of the book of Judges depicts Israel acting as separate tribal units, but only minimally intimating that this suggests division in the community. Right after Joshua's death, Israel asks YHWH *collectively* who should initiate the battle with the Canaanites (Judg 1:1). God says Judah should go first. Then Judah asks for Simeon's help, and together they engage the Canaanites. The outcome was successful, with one exception (Judg 1:2–19). Various other tribes engaged the Canaanites in differing places, but this time with mostly negative results (Judg 1:21–36). Does this hint that Israel does better when acting in concert rather than individually? Perhaps, but Israelite division is hardly a prominent motif at this juncture.

But that is about to change. When YHWH's angel denounced Israel for failing to deal appropriately with the Canaanites due to its religious infidelity, all of a sudden Israel *as a whole* comes into sharp focus. The angel thundered against *all the Israelites*, and the *people* lifted up *their* voices and wept (Judg 2:4; *'el-kol-benê-Yiśrā'ēl wayyiśᵉ'û hā'ām 'et-qôlām wayyibᵉkû*). From now on, Israel brought troubles on themselves when they sinned, and YHWH sent an enemy to oppress them (Judg 2:11). They sinned as a unit and were punished as a unit.

Indeed, Israel's sinning was the first element of a pattern that typified the narration in Judges until chapter 17. The pattern has six elements: (1) Israel sinned; (2) YHWH got mad and gave them over to enemies; (3) Israel cried out because of their oppressors; (4) YHWH raised up a deliverer (often called a *judge* or *deliverer*); (5) the deliverer rescued Israel from the oppressive forces; (6) the Israelites lived in tranquility for a season (Judg 2:11—3:6). It is in this context that we encounter Deborah's story.

ENTER DEBORAH

Deborah emerges because Israel had behaved evilly, which prompted YHWH to give them over to Jabin, the king of Canaan. Sisera was a military commander in the Canaanite army, whose power came in the form of nine hundred iron chariots. With strength of that magnitude, the Canaanites were able to mistreat Israel for two decades. Naturally, this led Israel to *cry out* (*wayyiṣ'ăqû*) to YHWH (Judg 4:1-3). Breaking the pattern slightly, Deborah, who was also a prophetess, was already judging Israel when the Canaanites became a problem. Indeed, she is the only one of the judges who engages in any judicial activity (Judg 4:4-5). Her counterparts in the Judges narration seem to be exclusively military operatives.

But Deborah has no difficulty in assuming a military role herself. She summons a member of the Naphtali tribe in Israel, Barak ben Abinoam, who is a military officer. Apparently, because of her status also as a prophetess, she knows what YHWH has in mind. YHWH wants Barak to enlist 10,000 troops from two tribes, Naphtali and Zebulun, and prepare to engage Sisera's formidable chariot forces. YHWH will actually participate in the ensuing battle by drawing out Sisera's army, at which point God will ensure an Israelite victory (Judg 4:6-7). This is a straightforward plan and, since it comes from YHWH's mouth, should be easy to implement. Given God's involvement, the outcome is all but guaranteed.

But there is a snag. Barak apparently has cold feet. He refuses to obey a direct order from YHWH unless Deborah accompanies him. Up till now, there has been no indication that Deborah was planning to participate herself. Faced with Barak's refusal, however, she accedes to his demand and lets him know that she will indeed go with him to battle. But she has a caveat.

Though she agrees to fight side by side with Barak, she wants him to know that he has forfeited any claim to glory after a victory. Instead, she insists, YHWH has shifted the plans such that Sisera will be dispatched by a woman (Judg 4:8–9). Surely, the obvious assumption is that this statement refers to Deborah herself. In any case, she accompanies Barak to Kadesh, where they enlist the 10,000 troops (Judg 4:10). So far, nothing seems untoward that only Naphtali and Zebulun are conscripting troops.

SCREEN FLASH

If this were a movie rather than a text, we would see a screen flash providing information crucial to the continuing story. In a movie, we might encounter something like, "Two weeks earlier," or, "Brazil, 1936." That would help us understand the story on the screen or "fill in the blanks." When dealing with literary art, such information is called a *frame-break*. This frame-break introduces us to Heber the Kenite, who was kin to people who were related to Moses' father-in-law. It is important for us to know that Heber lived near Kedesh, where the Israelite troops had been drafted (Judg 4:11).

SISERA'S DEFEAT AND DEATH

When Sisera realized that Barak's troops were by Mount Tabor, he engaged the Israelites with his impressive iron chariots. Deborah responded by issuing a battle cry, and by urging Barak to meet the challenge confidently in that YHWH was ensuring Israelite victory (Judg 4:12–14). Obviously buoyed by this charge, Barak led his 10,000 troops into the teeth of the battle. And, just as Deborah had promised, YHWH routed the chariots and the Canaanite army, including Sisera, who was forced ignominiously to abandon his chariot and flee on foot. He was not around to witness Barak's pursuit of the chariot force or the annihilation of the Canaanite forces (Judg 4:15–16).

What takes place next is one of the most lurid episodes in all of the Old Testament. Sisera ran into what he thought was friendly territory. The area was inhabited by Kenites, who at the time were in an amicable relationship with Jabin, the Canaanite king. As Sisera fled, he happened by the tent of Jael, none other than the wife of Heber himself (Judg 4:17). It is impossible to know whether Sisera knew who lived in that tent, or whether he was operating on the adage, "any port in a storm."

It may be presumed, however, that when Jael took the initiative by approaching Sisera and invited him into the tent, he had to be greatly relieved. He was, after all, running for his life. Not only did Jael calm Sisera by telling him not to worry, when he entered the tent she covered him with a blanket or a rug (Judg 4:18). Was he exhausted, or cold, or both? Was this ordinary or extraordinary hospitality extended to an ally? Sisera had said nothing so far. Jael had done all the talking. At this point, all her actions were consonant with someone willing to go out of the way to harbor a military fugitive. Keep in mind that the Kenites were in a good relationship with the Canaanites (Judg 4:17). However, we cannot forget that the Kenites were also shirttail relatives with Israelites. Which relationship would trump the other? Only time will tell.

Once in the tent and covered, Sisera finally speaks. His request is natural: he would like a drink of water. He had been on foot, presumably traveling at breakneck speed. Who knows how long he had been running at this pace? Of course, he would be thirsty. Asking for a drink was hardly surprising. But Jael's response was odd. He requested water; instead, she gave him milk to drink (Judg 4:19). Why? Was milk considered more gracious? Did she want him to think that there were no bounds to her hospitality? Was this a maternal gesture? Was there any ulterior motive? Did she believe milk would relax him, even making him sleepy? If so, why did she want him to fall asleep? Did Jael even know with whom she was dealing? Sisera had never identified himself. She had not asked him who he was. She had called him "my lord," but that was an ordinary honorific for addressing a strange man (Judg 4:18). Had Sisera been dressed in a manner so that she would realize he was a soldier? No answers to these questions are forthcoming. For now, we can only speculate.

Also, when she gave him the milk, once again we are told that she covered him (Judg 4:19). Why that detail? Had he gotten up to drink the milk, thus uncovering himself? One way or another, the narrator wants us to remember that he remained covered even after consuming the milk.

After being covered again, Sisera had something more to say. Jael had told him not to be afraid, but Sisera was still a little leery. He was not afraid of his hostess, but he did express some concern about anyone else who might be on the search for him. For this reason, he ordered her to stand at the door just in case someone came inquiring about him by asking, "Is anyone here?" Should that happen, she needs to say, "No." What is curious about Sisera's order is that he uses the masculine form of the imperative, "Stand." It is as though he were issuing orders to one of his soldiers (Judg 4:20). Was this just a grammatical slip? We learn that he was exhausted and soon fast asleep (Judg 4:21). Did fatigue make him slur his words or forget the niceties of Hebrew grammar? For whatever reason, Sisera had gone from requesting a drink of water to ordering Jael to stand guard at the door of the tent. He had sought refuge but had reverted to being a military commander.

As it happens, Sisera would have been wise to suspect his hostess instead of anyone coming to the tent in the hopes of finding him. No one came, so Sisera was safe on that score. Instead, danger was lurking in the tent. Sisera had fallen asleep because he was so tired, which left him completely vulnerable. At that point, Jael took a tent peg and a hammer and sneaked up on the slumbering and helpless fugitive. She drove the peg into his temple and hammered it into the ground. In one of the great understatements in the Bible, we then are informed that *he died* (Judg 4:21)!

Only then does someone appear at the door of the tent. It was none other than Barak, hot in pursuit. Deborah was not with him. In fact, it seems that Deborah had opted out of participating in the battle at all, which was unique for an Israelite judge. Upon seeing him, Jael invited Barak in and immediately showed him Sisera's corpse. Somehow, she knew that this was the man for whom Barak was searching (Judg 4:22). When Deborah declared toward the beginning of the episode that YHWH would eventually lead Sisera into the hand of a woman, it was natural to think she was referring to herself (Judg 4:9). But it turned out to be Jael, the wife of Heber, distant relative of Moses' father-in-law, who got the glory that otherwise would have gone to Barak. In the end, Israel pressed its advantage over the Canaanites—with YHWH's help, of course—until Jabin, the king, was eliminated (Judg 4:23–24).

DEBORAH'S AND BARAK'S SONG

Before we address the nature of the song that appears in Judges 5, we need to pay attention to the manner in which it is introduced. The introduction is somewhat problematic. As expected, we encounter a verb indicating a female subject: "Then Deborah sang" (Judg 5:1; *wattāšar*). That makes perfect sense in Hebrew, except for the fact that Barak sang as well. Does this mean that Barak was something of an afterthought? Or, does the feminine form in this case anomalously cover both subjects? With Barak as one of the singers, one expects a third person plural verb here: "Deborah and Barak [*they*] sang." This enigma stands, even though it is not hard to see why Barak might have gotten second billing in light of his behavior in the previous chapter. Still, in the song Barak is praised just as Deborah is praised (Judg 5:12). At the same time, in the very next verse the Hebrew states that YHWH's troops "went down for *me* against the warriors" (Judg 5:13).[1] Almost surely the *me* in this instance is Deborah (most translators follow the Greek version here, translating *him*). But that itself is odd in that there is no indication

---

1. In Hebrew the word meaning *people* (*'am*) often signifies *troops* when in a military context.

that Deborah was on the field in this battle. Perhaps she is nevertheless viewed as ultimately responsible for Israel's forces whether she took part in the actual fight or not. Unfortunately, Judges 5 is replete with grammatical, syntactical, and even vocabulary problems, making it impossibly difficult in places. Some of the anomalies cannot be solved. So, we have to be content with the *possibility* that Barak is being presented in a slightly less flattering light given the way in which the song was introduced. The feminine form of the verb notwithstanding, Barak sang along with Deborah, even if he were something of a second fiddle.

In dealing with the song itself, two separate but related issues come to the fore. Relative to the song's genre, the question is whether it is exclusively a victory song. Sometimes, the song is compared to Exodus 15, since that song also follows a prose account covering the same basic story line.[2] Is that an apt comparison, and if so, does that suggest that Judges 5 should be deemed a victory song, plain and simple? At the very least, in light of their canonical placement, both of these songs probably should be seen as popularly received, an indelible part of the communal memory, enhancing the importance of the event itself, and eminently repeatable, as poetry set to music would surely be. These songs are not incidental but consequential.

However, despite the comparison to Exodus 15, there are aspects of Deborah's (and Barak's) song that render it somewhat different from an ordinary victory song. To be sure, the narrative in the previous chapter recounts a resounding defeat of the Canaanite army and its dreaded iron chariots. Would not a victory song subsequent to such an impressive win be completely natural? The answer seems obvious. At the same time, there are elements in the song that sound not a victorious but a censorious note. Does that fact transform the song into something other than a victory anthem?

Indeed, even though the song celebrates Israel's astounding victory by praising YHWH, Deborah and Barak, Jael, and Israelite soldiers, it also contains a blistering criticism of those Israelites who refused to join their fellow Israelites in the battle. This denunciation seemingly comes out of the blue since the only division occurring previously was between Deborah and Barak. Granted, only troops from Naphtali and Zebulun were involved in confronting the Canaanite troops, but no overt criticism emerges about any other segments of Israel deciding to sit out the battle. How should we regard the song with its accent on division plaguing Israel when the previous narrative appears to ignore any hint of widespread division? The answer to that question may be sought in the fact that the division between Deborah and Barak reflects the rift that obtained later in Israel, which the song rehearses.

2. See Hauser, "Two Songs," 270–73.

This perhaps explains why Judges 5 is a mixed genre, containing elements of a victory song as well as imprecations against those parts of Israel who were nowhere to be found on the day of the fateful battle.[3]

As just mentioned, the prose and poetic accounts of the Deborah story may not be as far apart in content as a surface reading leads one to believe. As noted above, the prose section only deals with an altercation between Deborah and Barak, whereas the poetic segment is about a rift in Israel's body politic. Surely, these two examples of division are hardly comparable. As far as that argument goes, that is a cogent point. But as it turns out, throughout the book of Judges divisions occurring in smaller Israelite social or political units are later mirrored in Israel as a community. In this particular story, there is a division between Deborah the Judge and Barak the Officer. Elsewhere we will witness rifts between father and son (Gideon), siblings (Abimelech; Jephthah), and even a married couple (a Levite and his concubine). Each of these seemingly small-scale examples of division eventuate in much larger and more serious divisive events in Israel as a community. That is, micro-divisions of various sorts in Israelite social or political life devolve into macro-divisions which threaten the unity of *all Israel*. That is a constant in this biblical book.[4]

If this is a correct reading, it is not surprising that the song in effect magnifies the tension between Deborah and Barak as though it had spilled over into much more serious discord among Israelites as a people. According to the song, only parts of Israel engaged the Canaanites: Ephraim, Benjamin, Zebulun, Issachar, and Naphtali (Judg 5:14–15, 18). Those who did not heed the call to arms were Gilead, Reuben, Dan, and Asher (Judg 5:15de, 16–17). Gilead is not technically a name of one of the standard twelve-tribe Israelite units, but in this case seems to indicate Israelites living in the Transjordan area. A little later in the song an angel of YHWH curses Meroz and its inhabitants for failure to rally to the Israelite deity in the battle (5:23).[5] Unfortunately, there are no details supplied about why these tribes did not deploy. Or, for that matter, we are not told when or whether they were summoned. Still, the curse of a city or a village indicates that the refusal of some parts of Israel to take part in this battle left an extremely bitter taste.

All we can know for certain from the song is that a significant segment of Israel, for reasons impossible to ascertain, did not join their confreres in the battle against the Canaanites. It does not help to speculate. However, since division in Israel is so prominently described in the rest of Judges,

---

3. Wong, "Song of Deborah as Polemic," 1–22.
4. Oeste, "Butchered Brothers," 295–316.
5. Meroz's location is not known.

perhaps the lack of detail in this initial story does not matter. Indeed, it may be the case that only intimation of division is necessary at the outset. As the narrative unfolds, the story progressively emphasizes how badly division was besetting Israel. What begins as a mere hint in the Deborah story, is described in excruciating and lurid detail at the end of Judges (as we shall see).

Toward the end of the song, Jael is treated as a veritable heroine in Israel's defense. She gets even more press than Deborah. She is called *more blessed* than any other women (Judg 5:24). Even her husband gets credit. Details are provided about her giving Sisera milk when he requested water (Judg 5:25). Even her murderous act is described in grisly detail (Judg 5:26). Sisera's death is, at it were, transmitted as though in literary slow motion:

> Between her feet, he sank, fell, went down;
>> between her feet he sank, went down.
> where he sank, there he fell, mortally wounded. (Judg 5:27)

It should not be lost on us that this celebration of the risk Jael took when she assassinated Sisera comes immediately after Meroz is cursed for failing even to show up when the battle was enjoined. Meroz, of course, was not alone in skipping out of its obligation. How is it that Jael, someone so distantly related to Israel, did more in their behalf than several tribes who were AWOL on that fateful day? The answer would scarcely be flattering to Israel. It was divided when unity was desperately required.

The song ends with a taunt and an imperative addressed to YHWH. The taunt involves Sisera's mother. She is envisioned looking out the window while awaiting her warrior son's chariot (Judg 5:28). This anxious mother cannot fathom why the chariot has been delayed. Her attendants try to calm her by offering reasons which are left unspoken. Whether they did any good or not, the mother supplies her own explanation for the delay. A victorious army, led by her son, would by all means take longer on the return trip because their chariots would be laden with loot. Women slaves would be brought back as well as fine clothing for Sisera and the womenfolk (Judg 5:29-30). The mother had every expectation that she would be especially lavished with gifts. However, in effect, Sisera's mother and her attendants are left gazing out of the window as they look forward to dividing spoil. They would be before too long sorely disappointed. The soldiers would not be hauling loot to be shared; indeed, many of them would not be returning at all. Alas, those killed in action would include Sisera.

The final verse is appropriate to a victory song, notwithstanding the inclusion of imprecations for certain Israelites who had abandoned their brothers and sisters:

> May all your enemies perish, YHWH,
> while all His friends be powerful as the rising sun. (Judg 5:31)

Right after this sentiment, the concluding element in the six-pattern structure of the book of Judges is narrated. The land rested (Judg 5:31).[6]

CONCLUSION

The Deborah story in both its prose and poetic forms tantalizes in terms of dealing with Israel's propensity to divide. It sets the stage by describing initially the debate between Deborah and her military officer, Barak. His refusal to obey her explicit command, itself an example of division between the two most prominent Israelites in the narrative, is later reflected when several Israelite tribes do not participate in the battle against the Canaanites. We will observe this same pattern throughout the book of Judges.

At this point, however, were we reading Judges for the first time we would have no way of knowing that Israel's maddening tendency to divide is on the horizon. We might lament that Israel did not enjoy unity in the Deborah era while anticipating its solving that problem as the story develops.

---

6. In the book of Judges, the time that Israel *rested* was always longer than the preceding period of oppression.

Chapter 3

The Abimelech Story

INTRODUCTION

The protagonist of the story recounted in Judges 9—Abimelech, the son of Gideon/Jerubbaal—sticks out like a sore thumb. This is because he managed to get himself appointed as a *king* over Israel (Judg 9:6, 22) in a period which features *judges* rather than kings. God designated these judges to rescue Israel from an enemy's oppression, even though initially that hostility had been orchestrated by the deity (Judg 2:11–16). Prior to Abimelech, there were five judges; subsequent to Abimelech there were seven.[1] The question is: How did a king seemingly come out of nowhere when judges were the designated leaders of Israel and how did Abimelech manage this feat? More importantly, how did Abimelech's kingship affect Israel's unity?

Answering these questions requires setting the stage on which Israel's judges acted. Normally, the word *judge* in English connotes some sort of legal activity. We think that judges typically preside over law courts. But in the book of Judges the only judge that engages in judicial procedures of any sort is Deborah, who is also called a prophetess (*'iššāh nᵉbî'āh*). There is a brief description of Deborah's judging Israel in the ordinary sense of the word (Judg 4:4–5). But Deborah is an exception; no other judge in this book is involved in jurisprudence.[2] What, then, do the other judges do and,

---

1. Othniel (Judg 3:7–11); Ehud (Judg 3:12–30); Shamgar (Judg 3:31); Deborah (Judg 4–5); Gideon (Judg 6–8), were all prior to Abimelech. Afterward, there were Tola (Judg 10:1–2); Jair (Judg 10:3–5); Jephthah (Judg 10:17—12:7); Ibzan (Judg 12:8–10); Elon (Judg 12:11–12); Abdon (Judg 12:13–15); Samson (Judg 13–16).

2. There are numerous examples of judging in the ordinary sense of the word found in the Old Testament (e.g., Deut 1:16; 16:18; 17:9, 12; 19:17, 18; 21:2; 25:2).

if they do not figure in any legal system, should this nomenclature even be applied to them?

Judges are referred to in the book of Judges by two synonymous terms: *šōpēṭ* and *môšîaʿ*.[3] Taking the second word first, the activity suggested by this word involves rescuing or saving Israel from foreign subjugation usually by using military force (e.g., Judg 3:15–30; 4:1–16). Thus, a judge is Israel's *rescuer* or *savior*. That is precisely what a *môšîaʿ* is said to do throughout the book, namely, rescue or save the people from political distress (Judg 2:16, 18; 3:9, 31; 6:14, 15, 31, 36; 7:2, 7; 8:22; 10:1, 12, 13, 14; 12:2; 13:5). The first term, *šōpēṭ*, also connotes rescuing or saving Israel from an enemy's tyranny even though this has been translated conventionally as *judging* (Judg 3:10; 4:4; 10:2, 3; 15:20; 16:31). In what sense is *judging* to be equated with rescuing or saving? It might be helpful to think of a judge as executing justice under the aegis of a sovereign entity, like a king, a state, or even a deity. A judge would normally do this in a decidedly legal context, but more broadly a judge does what is necessary to ensure carrying out a sovereign entity's will to bring about justice. It is this nuance that is behind the judges as described in this biblical book. These are people who engage in saving, rescuing, and *judging* Israel by implementing YHWH's sovereign wishes.

But how did a *judge* become a *judge* in the first place? The answer to that question is simple: God acted. Whenever Israel was suffering at the hands of a foreign power, YHWH raised up a savior/judge (Judg 2:16, 18; 3:9, 15). In each case, the judge operates at YHWH's initiative and with YHWH's empowerment (Judg 3:10; 6:34; 11:29; 13:25; 14:6, 19; 15:14). These people were chosen according to God's inscrutable will. A judge's selection had nothing to do with age, status, tribal affiliation, gender, or location.[4] Even though the judges stopped Israel's persecution and ushered in a period of tranquility (Judg 3:11, 30; 5:31; 8:28), they were not necessarily moral stalwarts; indeed, each judge was morally inferior to his or her predecessor.[5] Nevertheless, the judges saved Israel from oppression, just as God had wanted. The pattern depicted in Judges is that first God providentially inflicted Israel with punishment as a result of their evil deeds—mostly idolatry (Judg 2:11–15, 17, 19; 3:7, 12; 4:1; 6:1; 8:33–34; 10:6; 13:1)—and after a season of misery that same deity provided for their rescue by raising up judges.

With regard to Abimelech, however, perhaps the most significant datum regarding the judges was that God's selection, as mentioned, had nothing to do with age, status, tribal affiliation, gender, or location. This means

3. *Šōpēṭ* (Judg 2:16, 17, 18, 19); *môšîaʿ* (Judg 3:9, 15; 12:3).
4. See Malamat, "Charismatic Leadership," 162.
5. Deborah, perhaps, being an exception to this rule.

that Abimelech was the quintessential *anti-judge*.[6] Abimelech was not compelling as a moral man. He was no improvement over his own father, Gideon, who had promoted idolatrous worship (Judg 8:27). But Abimelech's fundamental sin had to do with bypassing God's selection procedure and arrogating to himself political power.[7] This explains my contention that Abimelech sticks out like a sore thumb in Judges. Surrounded by judges summoned by God, he aspired to be a king using naked power devoid of divine activity.

ABIMELECH'S INTRODUCTION

Abimelech's introduction is innocuous at first. We learn that his father, Gideon/Jerubbaal, had seventy sons by virtue of having many wives (Judg 8:30). Curiously, the only child that is named at this point is Abimelech, whose mother was an unnamed concubine who resided in Shechem (Judg 8:31). This is straightforward. At the same time, this seemingly ordinary introduction poses some interesting questions. One, was this concubine one of Gideon's many wives, or are we to see her as distinct from this group? Two, was Shechem an Israelite city or a Canaanite city? Three, was there any significance to Gideon's naming his son Abimelech, which means "My Father is King"? We will deal with these questions in order.

In the Old Testament a concubine (*pîlegeš*) normally is a spouse whose status is somewhat lower than that of a primary wife. Famously, for example, Solomon's harem consisted of three hundred concubines to go with his seven hundred wives (*nāšîm*) and princesses (*śārôt*) (1 Kgs 11:3). But it is difficult to determine how absolute any lesser status was in every instance. Keturah, for example, is called Abraham's wife (*'iššāh*) in Genesis (25:1) but his concubine in 1 Chronicles (1:32). Even prominent Israelites had concubines as a mother, as evidenced by Dan and Naphtali (Gen 30:1-8). Their mother's name was Bilhah, who is referred to variously as a *maid* (*šipāh*) and a *concubine* (Gen 29:29; 30:3-8; 35:22). Equally, Gad and Asher were born to Zilpah, who was Leah's maid. Zilpah is never referred to specifically as a concubine in spite of the fact that she had the same standing as Bilhah. Both Bilhah and Zilpah were called *wives* in Gen 37:2; indeed, in a genealogical listing of Jacob's children no differentiation is made depending on the status of the respective mothers (Gen 35:22-26).

---

6. Malamat, "Charismatic Leadership," 163.

7. Not every judge was explicitly said to have been called by YHWH. A few so-called *minor judges* are cryptically described only in terms of their exploits (Judg 3:31; 10:1-2, 3-5; 12:8-10, 11-12, 13-15).

In the case of Abimelech, therefore, it is hard to know whether we should view his mother as occupying a different station than Gideon's other wives. For that matter, the text is not clear that Abimelech's mother should be distinguished from the *many wives* who had given birth to Gideon's seventy sons (Judg 8:30). Was Abimelech one of the seventy? That this concubine lived in Shechem is not decisive because we are not told where the other wives lived. Did they all live in one city or were their residences dispersed? We are perhaps being told of the concubine's location merely because the narrator is in the process of introducing the Abimelech episode. Obviously, Gideon's seventy sons would involve a number of half-brothers, of whom Abimelech was one, his mother's status notwithstanding. In any case, Gideon's concubine should not be considered as automatically occupying an inferior position.

What about Shechem? Was this Israelite territory or did it belong to Canaanites who had not yet been subdued? Recall that Judges continued the story of the occupation of the land, the first stage of which had been narrated in the book of Joshua. Even though Israel continued to have success in taking possession of the promised land (Judg 1:1–20), it also suffered reverses (Judg 1:21, 27, 29, 30, 31–32, 33, 34–36). This circumstance was not due to military weakness; instead, it was a direct result of divine judgment (Judg 2:3, 11–15, 21–23). Israel's sinfulness meant that Canaanites were still found throughout what was supposed to be exclusively Israelite territory (Josh 1:2–5; 21:43–45). Thus, it is perfectly legitimate to inquire about the makeup of Shechem's population.

During the ancestral period Shechem's identity was most definitely Canaanite (Gen 12:6). The relationship between the city and a person of the same name is harder to determine, however (34:2).[8] At the same time, since Shechem (the man) had violated Jacob's daughter, Dinah, her two brothers, Simeon and Levi, eventually killed all the males of the city and subsequently plundered it by capturing flocks, herds, asses, whatever else was in the city and nearby fields, including wives and children (Gen 34:25–29). Whatever the name of the actual city was in this incident, it was by all means a city (Gen 34:20, 24, 25, 27). Might the name of the man and the city have been the same? Interestingly, though it is impossible to know how much narrative time passed after this, in the next two stories involving Jacob and his family the city of Shechem seems either completely pacified or at least amenable to contact with this sojourning family (Gen 37:1). In one instance, Jacob was

---

8. Shechem the man is identified as a Hivite, which was one of the sociopolitical groups that were sometimes included with the generic group named Canaanites (Gen 36:2; Exod 23:23, 28; 33:2; 34:11; Deut 7:1; 20:17; Josh 3:10; 9:1–2, 7; 11:3, 19; 12:8; 24:11; Judg 3:3).

attempting to purify his family's religious practices, which led him to hide their foreign gods and earrings under an oak near Shechem. Right after this, Jacob's sons have no trouble pasturing their flocks close to Shechem (Gen 35:4; 37:12–14).

Shechem is never mentioned as one of the cities occupied during Israel's taking over the promised land, but twice it is listed (Josh 20:7; 21:21) as one of the cities of refuge (*'ārê hammiqlāṭ*). These were sites designed to protect people who had killed someone unintentionally and were escaping from people seeking vengeance (Josh 20:1–6). Certainly, this would make such cities Israelite by default. Thus, it should occasion no surprise that Joshua gathered all Israel and their representatives in Shechem for a covenant ceremony (Josh 24:1, 25, 32). In that ceremony, Israel finally pledged their loyalty to Israel's God YHWH (Josh 24:19–24). The fact that people who lived in Shechem later betrayed their pledge and worshipped Canaanite deities is hardly shocking given the numerous times when Israel was accused of apostasy in this turbulent period (e.g., Judg 2:1–5, 11–13). In that sense, the residents of Shechem were worse than Canaanites in that they were Israelites who had adopted foreign gods as their own by breaking their original word never to do that. Israel had managed to blur the distinction between themselves and the Canaanites. What did it mean to be Israel when promising fealty to Canaanite gods? Shechem was, in fact, Israelite in identity, howbeit an identity that had been compromised by idolatrous loyalties.

This brings us to the matter of Abimelech's name. One way of understanding its meaning could not be less controversial. *My Father Is King* is a typical Israelite name meaning simply *My (Divine) Father Is King*. Such a name evokes a belief about God and God's sovereignty. The name is similar to *Elimelech*, which means "My God is King" (Ruth 1:2, 3; 2:3; 4:3, 9), or *Malkiyyah*, which means "My King is YH(WH)" (Jer 21:1; 38:1). In this light, Gideon gave a fine orthodox name to his son. God is often depicted throughout the Old Testament as having the characteristics of a king or ruling as one (e.g., Pss 47:9 [Eng. v. 8]; 93:1; 96:10; 97:1; 99:1; 146:10).

But there is an incident involving Gideon that suggests a touch of irony in his naming his child Abimelech. After his successful time as Israel's judge, the Israelites decided to alter the very nature of the office. Previously, a judge came to the fore only at God's bidding and according to God's enabling. That pattern had worked so far. The Israelites who approached Gideon figured that they could improve on the divine plan. They ordered—there was nothing interrogative in their tone—Gideon by saying, "Rule over us" (*mᵉšol-bānû*). They in addition insisted that Gideon's son and grandson also rule when the time came (Judg 8:22). Their rationale was that Gideon had saved

Israel from the Midianites. They said nothing whatsoever about God's role either in raising up Gideon or helping him in any way.

Gideon's response to this demand was perhaps his finest hour. Without equivocation, he refused to comply and for good measure insisted that no one in his family would go along with this demand either. Moreover, he made abundantly clear that it was not his prerogative to rule; instead, only YHWH would rule over Israel (Judg 8:23). Gideon would not allow the *ad hoc* manner in which God had selected judges previously be replaced by what amounted to the establishment of a dynastic system.

Unfortunately, Gideon went immediately from his principled rejection of a new dynastic arrangement to engaging in idolatrous behaviors that jeopardized Israel's religious commitments (Judg 8:23–27). We do not know whether Abimelech had already been born and named when Gideon behaved so shamefully. By all means, the order that Gideon and his son(s) and grandson(s) rule intimates that at least some of his sons were already around. But beyond that we can only speculate. Still, the very fact that Abimelech used a power play to become a king right after his father's death is noted indicates that his name indeed had an ironic cast to it. Had Abimelech been alive when Gideon refused to rule, or had he heard this story from others in the family, he might have gone to Shechem to promote himself politically thinking about the opportunity that his father had missed. Abimelech could have easily deluded himself into believing that his father *should* have been king, which would have put him at least in the running to succeed, in which case he might have entertained the delicious irony of his given name, "My (Biological) Father is King," contemplating all the while, "Why should I not make the most of this opportunity that my dad foolishly squandered?"

ABIMELECH'S RISE TO POWER

Abimelech wasted no time in making a move to promote his political ambition. Even though there was no precedent for Israel's having a king, Abimelech was not deterred. He went directly to Shechem, his mother's residence, and appealed to his maternal relatives (Judg 9:1). He was hardly subtle in his effort to get his kin to present the lords of Shechem (*ba'ălê šᵉkem*) with two diametrically opposed choices.[9] Did they prefer to be ruled by an oligarchy comprised of all seventy sons of Jerubbaal or did they want to be ruled by only one man? Just in case there was the slightest doubt about the identity of this man, Abimelech reminded those to whom he was speaking, that "I am

---

9. The RSV translates this term as "the citizens of Shechem." The NRSV translates in this instance more literally as the "lords of Shechem," suggesting some sort of ruling council in the city. This nuance, it seems to me, is correct.

your bone and flesh" (Judg 9:2). Equally telling, Abimelech referred to his father exclusively as Jerubbaal rather than Gideon. Even though this name was itself ironic—it means: "Let Baal Contend"—Abimelech construes the name in this instance as being more or less positive regarding the Canaanite deity.

This stunning power grab was dubious for several reasons. One, there had never been a situation where a judge was succeeded by a family member or, for that matter, from someone from the same tribal group. No dynastic relationships were developed in spite of the fact that the land had rested for a long time under the aegis of the respective judges (Judg 3:11, 30; 5:31; 8:28). The text gives no details about a judge's everyday activities, concentrating exclusively on military exploits. This is presumably why Gideon turned down the possibility of establishing a dynasty for his own family (Judg 8:23). Even later on when this situation must have changed, neither Eli nor Samuel was able to preserve dynastic succession given the corruption of their respective sons (1 Sam 2:27–34; 4:11, 18; 7:15; 8:1–9). Two, even if Gideon were to have a son as successor, nothing suggests that Abimelech would have been the son selected. Indeed, given the sheer number of Gideon's sons, the chances of succession were remote at best for any one of them. Three, God was in the business of raising up judges when Israel was in crisis. Abimelech's self-aggrandizing efforts were not in response to an Israelite crisis. Instead, Abimelech *created* a crisis in Israel rather than responded to one. Four, no oligarchy had ever been in charge in Israel before then and no oligarchy ruled afterward. That was a false choice. Finally, God was most conspicuously absent in every deliberation that eventuated in Abimelech's political elevation.

Nevertheless, Abimelech's ploy paid off handsomely. His maternal kinfolk relayed his offer to Shechem's lords, who promptly threw their support to him. There is some ambiguity as to which group said, "He is our brother" (Judg 9:3). Was this Abimelech's maternal kinfolk pulling out all the stops to garner support? Or, was this what the lords said to his maternal relatives as a way of showing that they were also, not literally but politically, in Abimelech's family? Regardless, the pledge of support was not limited to verbal assent. The lords also bankrolled Abimelech with funds from the temple of Baalberith, which obviously demonstrated Israel's persistent idolatrous ways (Judg 8:33; 9:4). Abimelech used the money to fund his personal militia, who are ominously referred to as a vain and reckless lot (*'ănāšîm rêqîm ûpōḥăzîm*). A semantic English equivalent might better be translated as *thugs* and *hoodlums*. In any case, Abimelech had used the money to ensure enough muscle to support his efforts to seize and consolidate power.

Abimelech's attempt to govern immediately mutated from being legally dubious to being the essence of banal evil. Not willing to risk any counter maneuvers, Abimelech cynically decided to eliminate any potential rival, in spite of the fact that not a single one of his half-brothers revealed an iota of interest in exercising political power.[10] To accomplish this diabolical scheme, he went to his father's home at Ophrah and slaughtered all seventy of his half-brothers *upon one stone* (Judg 9:5). How he managed to carry out this gruesome massacre is not described. The text does not explain how it was that all seventy were at their father's home, or how Abimelech managed to round them up, or whether the goons who accompanied him did the dirty work, or what the stone symbolized. All we are told is that Abimelech monstrously made himself one of the greatest fratricidal murderers of all time. Only one half-brother, Jotham, was able to hide and avoid the carnage. Unaware of Jotham's escape, Abimelech returned to Shechem and was made king by its lords and Beth-millo (a section of the city). Though his deeds were beyond abominable, Abimelech's strategy had worked to a tee.

JOTHAM'S PARABLE

How or where Jotham was able to hide as his brothers were being butchered, the story never mentions. Yet, as soon as he heard about Abimelech's becoming a king Jotham came out of hiding and addressed the new situation in a loud voice from a mountain top (Judg 9:7). He targeted his remarks to the officials who were responsible for Abimelech's new position. What Jotham had to say took the form of a parable, which he introduced in a peculiar way: "Listen to me, oh lords of Shechem, so that God might listen to you." What Jotham implied by that is hardly transparent, but at least he was invoking God in some sense. This is the first time God is brought up at all since the whole Abimelech episode began.

The parable itself is simple. Jotham told a story about trees who were trying to appoint a king. Their first choice was to ask an olive tree. But the olive tree declined by noting that there were better things to do than holding sway over the trees, like producing fatness (oil?) which honors God and people (Judg 9:8–9). The trees went to their second choice: the fig tree. Once again, they were turned down—the fig tree was content to continue producing sweet fruit. That was a better vocation than lording over the trees (Judg 9:10–11). A third time the trees tried to convince the vine to rule. The vine

---

10. Schneider argues that Abimelech's murder of the seventy sons is "more evidence that Gideon's children established a dynastic house." But nothing in the text suggests this. This is a reading *behind* not *of* the text. See Schneider, *Judges*, 137.

likewise refused their offer, deciding instead to support a wine industry that delights people and even gods (Judg 9:12–13).

After these embarrassing rejections, the trees finally succeed when they find an amenable candidate: a bramble bush. Though the bramble accedes to their request, the response is bizarre. In accepting the offer, the bramble makes a very thinly veiled threat. It offers shade on the condition that the trees are acting in good faith. Otherwise, their selection will be disastrous, causing the bramble to combust, thereby burning down even the mighty cedars of Lebanon (Judg 9:14–15). The trees looking for a king will also fall victim to this blaze. The bramble does not clarify either its ability to provide shade or how it will determine whether the request was made in good faith. Nor, does it explain how it will light the Lebanon forest on fire. Still, the threat is unmistakable.

Jotham's parable flattered neither the process in which the trees were engaged nor their ultimate selection. Three productive forms of vegetation were totally uninterested. Only an unproductive, indeed worthless, shrub was willing to take the job, and at that its acceptance speech was menacing. Clearly, the bramble represented Abimelech, something that Jotham made explicit just in case the parable's meaning was lost on those who had been responsible for establishing a king in Israel for the first time (Judg 9:16).

But Jotham was not finished. After telling this parable, the point of which could scarcely be missed, he left nothing to chance. If the parable was somehow too subtle for dense listeners, Jotham made his accusations crystal clear. With tongue planted firmly in his cheek, Jotham point by point denounced the lords of Shechem for their outrageous actions. If the lords had behaved in good faith when they made Abimelech king—which Jotham manifestly believed was not the case—and if they had taken into account all that his father had done for Israel—which Jotham did not accept for a minute—then all was well. However, since the lords had completely ignored Gideon's risking his life to take on Midian in Israel's behalf, and in fact had risen against Gideon's house as made evident in looking the other way when Abimelech carried out his assassinations, there would be no mutual joy in this arrangement. To the contrary, destruction would rear its ugly head between the new king and his subjects (Judg 9:16–20). After his blistering denunciations, Jotham had no choice but to flee (Judg 9:21).

Had Abimelech been a local monarch in a lone city, perhaps Jotham's *prophecy* would have been soon forgotten. However, whereas Shechem might have been his headquarters, Abimelech's rule was not confined to that city. He reigned over *Israel* (Judg 9:22). Plus, he had been ruling for three years. Shechem had gotten the ball rolling, but the rest of Israel was living with the results. It would not be long to wait to see whether Jotham's predictions had any truth to them.

GOD'S INTERVENTION

So far in this episode Jotham is the only character who has even mentioned God. Doubtlessly, he had in mind the Israelite deity, though he did not use God's distinctive name (YHWH). Now, though, the narrator lets us know that God is not sitting idly by as these events unfold. To the contrary, God intervened by sending an *evil spirit* (*rûaḥ rā'āh*) between Abimelech and Shechem's citizens. As a result, the latter took it upon themselves immediately to withdraw their support for Abimelech, primarily to avenge the murder of his half-brothers. As well, these residents of Shechem sought to punish the city lords who had backed Abimelech in this whole sordid affair (Judg 9:22–24). The text is a little confusing in employing the same vocabulary—the lords of Shechem (*ba'ălê Šᵉkem*)—to indicate both those who had initially supported Abimelech and the general citizenry of the city (Judg 9:23). This might also be the narrator's clever way of saying that morally there was little difference between these two groups. God's *evil spirit* apparently induced bad blood between Abimelech, his supporters, and those now arrayed against him. God was not pitting *good* people against *bad* people! In any case, those disposed against Abimelech set up ambushes in the mountains to rob those who were supportive of him. Israelites were systematically waylaying other Israelites in reaction to King Abimelech's rule. It was not long before Abimelech realized what was taking place (Judg 9:25). Three years ago, the people in Shechem had rallied behind their new king. Now, they were at each other's throats. Abimelech's self-aggrandizing efforts and God's response in sending an evil spirit to create chaos had put Israel in an intolerable situation.

What should we make of this evil spirit sent from God? Was this a spirit of discord and antagonism? Was this a spirit of chaos and disorder? Was this God's effort to punish only Abimelech and his backers through the instrumentality of those who had suddenly come to their senses and realized their error in making Abimelech king? Was God trying to pass judgment on *all* the Shechemites for their initial complicity in making Abimelech king by subjecting them to civil war? The only verb detailing divine action was the sending of the evil spirit. God orchestrates no other actions. Once the evil spirit is sent, somehow the people involved in this mess have no trouble in making matters exponentially worse.

There are a couple of other examples in the Old Testament that might provide some insight into God's dispatching an evil spirit. When Samuel anointed David as the king to replace Saul, the spirit of YHWH came mightily on David and simultaneously left Saul (1 Sam 16:13–14). Making matters worse, however, Saul was not merely bereft of the divine spirit; instead, an evil spirit *from* YHWH afflicted him (*ûbī'ătattû rûaḥ-rā'āh mē'ēt YHWH*). This circumstance led to Saul's hiring David not only as an armor bearer but as a musician who would play soothing music when the evil spirit struck (1 Sam 16:21–23). Surely this should be understood as a punishment issuing from YHWH on Saul. A couple of other times the evil spirit prompted Saul to move aggressively against David (1 Sam 18:10–11; 19:9–10). This was less of a punishment and more an inducement to reckless behavior. Nevertheless, the divine spirit functions providentially somehow in these incidents. In one way or another, the evil spirit that was *from* YHWH was making Saul's life miserable.[11]

Another example is found not with an evil spirit either sent by God, as in the Abimelech story, or an evil spirit *from* YHWH, as in the Saul episode, but with a *lying spirit* (*rûaḥ šeqer*), which YHWH used to compel King Ahab's prophets to persuade him to go into battle where he would supposedly be victorious. Instead of winning, however, an archer *accidentally* and *providentially* shot the Israelite king, mortally wounding him (1 Kgs 22:19–23). In all these cases, God acts providentially, to be sure, but not in such a way that human free will is completely suspended. In the Abimelech account, it as though God's sending an evil spirit between two main factions did not need to do much to upset what little equilibrium there had been in this politically charged and toxic environment. God's evil spirit in this situation was simply the proverbial straw that broke the camel's back.

GAAL'S ENTRANCE

At this point, another character is introduced. Seemingly emerging out of nowhere, a man named Gaal ben Ebed shows up with his brothers (or kin) and is at once favorably received by Shechem's citizens (Judg 9:26). A number of questions are raised by this sudden appearance. First, was Gaal ben Ebed a resident of the city? He intimates as much a little later (Judg 9:29), but the text is somewhat ambiguous. In any case, for reasons that are not stated, this man at once enjoys Shechemite trust as though he were a favorite son.

---

11. For an explication of David's rise and Saul's fall, see Spina, "The Son of Jesse," 171–95.

A question is: how are we to interpret his name? The root (*gʻl*) from which it derives means in its verbal form *abhor* or *loathe*. If the name has been shortened by omitting a divine appellation, the name might mean that a particular deity (YHWH; El; Elohim; Baal, etc.) *abhors* or *loathes*. But abhors or loathes what? Most names say something positive about people or a deity. Even Gaal's father's name is almost certainly also a shortened form. The name means *servant*. Typically, it would involve being the servant of some god (e.g., *ʻAbdā* [Servant of YH{WH}], *ʻAbdᵉ ʼēl* [Servant of El]).[12] Of course, *ʻebed* also means *slave*. If that is how we should take the name here, then we have the possibility of a name made up to fit this story. A parallel would be the name Nabal, which means *fool* (1 Sam 25:3). No parent would ever saddle their child with such a terrible name. If Gaal's name is appropriate only for this narrative, then it means something like *Loathsome Son of a Slave!*[13] In that case, it might be an ironic denigration of Abimelech's singularly lofty name: *My Father Is King*. Unfortunately, though this is suggestive in light of the story's theme, we cannot be certain.

A third question begging for an answer is why Gaal arrives in Shechem with his brothers. Are these literal brothers, or members of an extended family? Is this entourage a way of mocking Abimelech's shameless appeal to the lords of Shechem by underscoring his relationship to his mother and her relatives? Is Gaal demonstrating that two can play the familial card? Or, does the fact that Gaal is accompanied by a band of brothers expose Abimelech for not having any brothers to accompany him because he had murdered them? The answers to these questions likewise remain elusive.

Then again, why did the Shechemites put their trust in Gaal immediately? Gaal garners support from Shechemites before any campaigning. But support for what? What did Gaal have in mind when he rode into town and why did the people of Shechem think it would to be their advantage by so blithely expressing confidence in him? Had the Shechemites concluded that Gaal was an obvious candidate to lead their rebellion against Abimelech, or take over once the king was ousted? Once more, we can at this point only speculate. At the same time, perhaps the answers to most of these questions may have to do with the *evil spirit* God had sent to roil the whole situation.

We are on firmer ground when we ask about Abimelech's whereabouts when Gaal entered Shechem. There are three indications that Abimelech was not at the time in the city. One is that Gaal and the support he quickly received could hardly have happened right under the nose of the putative king. That would have been a suicidal move, especially in light of Abimelech's

---

12. The name appears in this form in Ezra 8:6.
13. Schneider, *Judges*, 143.

slaughtering his own half-brothers without compunction. A second indication is that Shechem's citizens had already put men on the mountain tops to ambush everyone who came by. Perhaps this involved innocent people too; however, the implication is that they targeted mostly those who had sided with Abimelech. This is what had alerted Abimelech to the fact that he could no longer count on Shechemite loyalty (Judg 9:25). Third, a man named Zebul, who was second in command (he is called a *śar*), suggested that he was in charge of day-to-day administrative matters. This allowed Abimelech to leave administration in someone else's hands. Still, Zebul's presence notwithstanding, Gaal stepped into a vacuum apparently created by Abimelech's absence.

Right after the text states that Gaal won Shechemite allegiance, we learn that *they* go to the vineyards—the location is unspecified—and harvest grapes, which *they* turn into wine for a festival in the temple of *their* god, from which location *they* formally revile Abimelech (Judg 9:27). To whom did *they* refer? Were these people exclusively from Shechem or were other Israelites included in this ceremony in which folks drank, so to speak, to a denunciation of Abimelech? It is difficult to know. Still, it appears that this was no isolated random group expressing usual gripes about a king's administration. This was a more or less formal gathering that afforded Gaal an opportunity to press his claims.

Thus, we are hardly surprised that Gaal took the bull by the horns to promote himself at Abimelech's expense. First off, Gaal identifies himself *with* Shechem and casts doubt on Abimelech's own credentials as a Shechemite (Judg 9:28). Gaal demands to know why *we* should serve Abimelech given that he (i.e., Abimelech) and Zebul, Jerubbaal(/Gideon)'s officer, once served Hamor, the father of the man from whose name Shechem is derived. How could someone who had served Shechem turn around and make the Shechemites his servants? Regardless of the cogency of this argument, Gaal now puts all his cards on the table. Were he to be Shechem's leader he would engage Abimelech militarily and easily defeat him (Judg 9:29).

In his efforts to get Shechem to switch loyalty from Abimelech to himself, Gaal insults not only Jerubbaal(/Gideon)'s son (i.e., Abimelech) but Zebul. Gaal calls Zebul a *pāqîd*, which in a military context is a captain or lieutenant. But why bring up this particular officer at this time? It does not take long to discover the reason, for, as noted above, it turns out that Zebul is an official of some sort (*śar-hāʿîr*) in Shechem. Again, Zebul's presence and function in the city explains Abimelech's absence. Zebul is Abimelech's deputy. Upon hearing about Gaal's attempt to undercut Abimelech and by implication himself, Zebul blows his stack (Judg 9:30). He also gets word about what has happened in the city to Abimelech and encourages him to muster his troops and attack the very next morning (Judg 9:31–33). A military confrontation is brewing.

But it is important to inquire about this Zebul character. The narrator never says a word about him until Judg 9:30. Prior to this, we only have Gaal's testimony about him (Judg 9:28). A narrator always tells the truth. A character may dissemble. Why did the narrator not say anything at all about Zebul before? Was he, in fact, allied to Jerubbaal(/Gideon) as a military officer? If he was, what circumstance led him to occupy a leadership role in Shechem? Plus, how was it that he was in Abimelech's camp when the latter had put Jerubbaal(/Gideon)'s sons in such bad light? Or, had Gaal concocted a fabrication about Zebul's relationship to Jerubbaal(/Gideon) and to the latter's son, Abimelech, as a way of inciting further the citizens of Shechem? Answers to these questions are elusive, too. But we do know—as the narrator informs us—that he was, indeed, a governor or mayor of Shechem, that he was in cahoots with Abimelech, that he had gotten angry upon learning about Gaal's efforts to dislodge the king, and that he had apprised Abimelech of the situation, including advising him to prepare for battle against the city that had initially made him king.

Abimelech took Zebul's advice, and that very night deployed four battle groups against Shechem (Judg 9:34). Gaal had stationed himself at the city gate prior to Abimelech's forces approaching the city. Apparently, Gaal knew nothing of Zebul's secretly helping Abimelech to forge a counter strategy, which is why Gaal seemed to be surprised to see troops storming from the mountaintops. Also, Zebul fooled Gaal into thinking that he had mistaken mountain shadows for troops (Judg 9:35–36). When Gaal took a second look, he realized that, indeed, he had actually seen soldiers, at which point Zebul mocked the rebellious leader's former bravado (Judg 9:37–38). In the ensuing battle, Abimelech and Zebul together routed Gaal, inflicted numerous casualties, and made it impossible for Gaal to remain in Shechem (Judg 9:39–41).

But there was more to come. On the very next day, troops from Shechem went out to the fields, presumably to recover from the previous day's defeat. Abimelech, who was living in Arumah at this time, heard about this counter maneuver.[14] Unfortunately for the Shechemites, they were no match for Abimelech's forces. Eventually, Abimelech defeated not only those who had come out of the city but also those who had remained in the city. Of those who had tried to engage Abimelech and of those who had stayed

---

14. The location for Arumah is not known. Context suggests that it was near Shechem.

in the city, the narrator tells us cryptically and somberly that Abimelech *slew* them (Judg 9:42–44). This may indicate as well that Abimelech in addition killed his family, something he had already done to his half-brothers.[15] For good measure, Abimelech killed yet more people, razed the city, and sowed it with salt (Judg 9:45). Gaal must have been the one who ran away and was chased by Abimelech, even though Gaal's death is not explicitly cited (Judg 9:40). In light of this dreadful destruction, Jotham's parable ended up being an apocalyptic but nevertheless quite literal prophecy (Judg 9:15, 20).

DEATH AT THE TOWER

In spite of the extent of the slaughter, a few in Shechem had somehow survived. These lords/citizens who were connected to a tower in Shechem fled for their lives to the temple of Elberith (Judg 9:46). The name of the temple suggests that Baal was not the only Canaanite deity who was worshipped in Shechem—the god El also could boast Israelite worshipers. Again, news traveled fast. Abimelech quickly heard that the lords/citizens had gathered to escape his wrath (Judg 9:47). To prepare for taking out those who remained alive in Shechem, Abimelech and his men went to Mount Zalmon where they procured enough brush to use fire as their weapon of choice in attacking the tower (Judg 9:48–49). The fire was brutally effective in that everyone in the tower perished, about a thousand in number, including women (Judg 9:49). The population of Shechem had been totally destroyed.

Inexplicably, once Abimelech annihilated the population of Shechem and rendered the city inhabitable—at least temporally (see 1 Kgs 12:1)—he moved on Thebez and captured it (Judg 9:50). All we know about this city is that it was less than ten miles northeast of Shechem. As it turns out, however, this city also had a tower. When assaulted, men, women, and citizens/lords of the city went there to save themselves (Judg 9:51). Pointedly, a group identical to those who had tried to resist Abimelech in Shechem are mentioned. Once again Abimelech decided to use fire against this tower as well. This makes good military sense in that Abimelech had used fire so effectively against the tower in Shechem (Judg 9:49). This time, though, Abimelech failed. Before a match was struck, a *certain woman* (*'iššāh 'aḥat*) who was not named managed to throw down a millstone (*pelaḥ rekeb*) that cracked Abimelech's skull when he was at the door (Judg 9:53). Knowing he was soon to die Abimelech ordered his armor-bearer to finish him off so that he could avoid having it said in the future that he had been killed in battle by a woman. The armor-bearer complied with the king's request (Judg

---

15. Schneider, *Judges*, 146.

9:54). Ironically, however, that is precisely how Abimelech's ignominious death was remembered in Israelite lore (2 Sam 11:21).

Upon Abimelech's death Israel's experimenting with kingship also died. At the end of the day, this was God's doing. The divine judgment fell directly on Abimelech, who not only usurped power that only God could bestow but used his naked political ambition as the rationale for the degenerate murder of his seventy half-brothers (Judg 9:56). Those who backed Abimelech in this vile effort were also subjected to God's censure (Judg 9:57). Jotham's parable was transformed from a potential curse to an actual one.

CONCLUSION

At first blush, the story which features Abimelech and his nefarious efforts to be made a king seems more or less local in its extent. Only three named cities are mentioned: Ophrah, Shechem, and Thebez (Judg 9:1, 5, 50). Is it appropriate to conclude that this narrative has at least one of its themes, division in Israel? Or, does the episode speak only to the issues of kingship versus judgeship and the God of Israel versus Baal or other Canaanite gods?[16] By all means, these two issues are important to the Abimelech episode. But the motif of Israel's unity versus its disunity is also in play.[17]

The Abimelech episode needs to be seen in the context of the book of Judges generally, in which Israel is in focus even if not every tribal group or every city is explicitly mentioned in every episode. For example, in the preceding story, which features Abimelech's father, Gideon/Jerubbaal, Israel is certainly central. Though Gideon resided in Ophrah, his summons to act was a function of Israel's misery due to Midian's oppression (Judg 6:1–6). This oppression was, of course, brought about by YHWH (Judg 6:1), the very deity to whom Israel cried out for help (Judg 6:7). Before remedying their situation, YHWH sent a prophet to *the people of Israel* to remind them of their idolatry (Judg 6:8). When YHWH prepared Gideon for his task, the goal was delivering Israel (Judg 6:14). Gideon did not think he was fit for this enterprise, but there was no question what it was, namely, delivering Israel (Judg 6:15). Not every tribe would participate in saving Israel from Midian's oppression—only Manasseh, Asher, Zebulun, and Naphtali were

---

16. On Baal versus Israel's deity, see Endris, "Yahweh versus Baal," 173–95; Bluedorn, *Yahweh versus Baalism*; Clements, "Baal-Berith of Shechem," 21–32.

17. In spite of its provocative title, Hauser deals primarily with various organizational theories relative to George E. Mendenhall's and Norman K. Gottwald's views about the validity of Martin Noth's amphictyony thesis. See Hauser, "Unity and Diversity," 289–303.

mustered at first (Judg 6:35)—but there was no doubt that delivering Israel was the aim (Judg 6:36). YHWH pares down Gideon's forces so that *Israel* did not get conceited and believe that they had saved themselves (Judg 7:2). A little later the narrator refers to Gideon not as Ophrah's favorite son and potential war hero, but as a *man of Israel* (*'îš Yiśrā'ēl*) (Judg 7:14). Even Gideon's headquarters is called the *camp of Israel* (Judg 7:15). The troops who were to play a decisive role in this endeavor were pointedly referred to as the *men of Israel* (Judg 7:23). After Gideon's victorious campaign it was the *men of Israel* who asked him to rule perpetually (Judg 8:22), just as *all Israel* (Judg 8:27) committed idolatry in response to Gideon's shameful behavior. Regardless of the number of cities or tribes who actually had a part in this particular episode, at every turn the story was about Israel (Judg 8:28).

Likewise, in the narration prior to the Gideon material Israel remains the focal point. The very first deliverer YHWH raised up after *Israel* had behaved sinfully (Judg 3:7) and after *Israel* had cried out to YHWH (Judg 3:9) was Othniel. Equally, Ehud operated as *Israel's* savior once more after they had sinned (Judg 3:12), had been mistreated by Eglon, King of Moab (Judg 3:14), had cried to YHWH (Judg 3:15), and enjoyed a period of rest after the judge's success (Judg 3:30). The same holds true during Deborah's time. *Israel* did evil in YHWH's eyes (Judg 4:1) and protested their punishment at the hand of Jabin, the Canaanite king (Judg 4:3). As mentioned, this was a period when Deborah was judging *Israel* (Judg 4:4). When she enlisted Barak, a military man, to confront the Canaanite king, she couches her appeal in terms of YHWH's summons: "The Lord, the God of *Israel*, commands you" (Judg 4:6). The narrative portion of the Deborah story concludes with the notation that God subdued the king of Canaan before the people of *Israel* (Judg 4:23).

Without missing a beat, the narrative emphasizes that Israel continues to be spotlighted *after* the Abimelech story. Tola delivered *Israel* (Judg 10:1) after which he judged *Israel* for twenty-three years (Judg 10:2). He was followed by Jair, who did his work for twenty-two years in *Israel* (Judg 10:3). In the next story, *Israel* once again sins (Judg 10:6), engenders God's anger and suffers from divine punishment (Judg 10:7-9). This circumstance leads to *Israel's* crying out to YHWH and repenting of their sins (Judg 10:10-15).[18] *Israel* is central to the Jephthah story also (Judg 11:4-5, 13-27; 12:7). *Israel* is still highlighted when Ibzan (Judg 12:8), Elon (Judg 12:11), and Abdon

---

18. There is at least a whiff of special pleading in Israel's confession in that, while they concede to their being justly punished, they also ask God to deliver them immediately (Judg 10:15). See Polzin, *Moses and the Deuteronomist*, 178.

(Judg 12:13) were judges. Finally, *Israel's* persistent sin introduces the story of Samson, the last judge (Judg 13:1, 5; 16:31).

The point of this survey is to demonstrate that regardless of the judges, cities, or tracts of real estate involved, the narratives all cast Israel in a leading role. This is also the case for the Abimelech story. Even though only Ophrah, Shechem, and Thebez are mentioned, Israel is in view. Abimelech was made king in Shechem, but he did not confine his rule or even his residence there. The narrative could not be more explicit: "Abimelech ruled over *Israel* for three years" (Judg 9:22). To be sure, this is an account treating principally Abimelech's grab for power, his abominable murder of his brothers, Jotham's scathing parable, and the final conflict between Abimelech and those who turned against him. But the backdrop of every single event that makes up this story is Israel. We are not told that Abimelech exercised control over Shechem, or Ophrah, or Thebez, or other cities close by; instead, he ruled Israel. Indeed, right after the narrative asserts this, we learn that at that precise point God sent an evil spirit to roil the situation (Judg 9:23). Similarly, it was the *men of Israel* (*'îš Yiśrā'ēl*) who witnessed Abimelech's death, not the citizens of this or that city (Judg 9:55). After they had seen Abimelech's death, each went home, presumably to unspecified places that were part of Israel. Whatever else we might make of this narrative, it has a pan-Israelite dimension, just like the rest of the book of Judges.

This is the context in which the Abimelech story should be evaluated. To be sure, Israel's disunity is not the only issue that the story addresses. It also deals with judges as opposed to kings as YHWH's preferred way of leadership in Israel during such a volatile period. Also, the matter of YHWH's sovereignty over that of Canaanite deities is treated. But Israel's unity, or in this case, disunity, is, if not central, certainly prominent. Abimelech fostered Israelite disunity in pitting his maternal relatives against Gideon's extended family. He created a situation which eventually pulled apart Shechem at the seams. He ruled Israel on the basis of his ill-gotten power base, complete with a personal militia funded with tainted money. He personally showed no regard for a judge who had answered God's call. He killed his half-brothers gratuitously, in that there was no reason that any one of them had an expectation of succeeding their father. His attack on Thebez demonstrated that his rule was not confined to Shechem. And, finally, his outrageous actions induced God to send an *evil spirit* which only exacerbated Israel's disunity. From beginning to end, Abimelech multiplied divisions among God's elect people, Israel.

Chapter 4

Jephthah's Tragic Vow: A Doomed Daughter and a Divided Community

THE PRELUDE TO THE EPISODE

In the book of Judges, just prior to the story featuring Jephthah, we learn that Israel had committed evil deeds in YHWH's eyes (Judg 10:6). Of course, this is a veritable refrain (Judg 2:11; 3:7, 12; 4:1; 6:1; 8:33). But in this instance, there is a twist. This is because when announcing Israel's failures, specifics replace generalities. We are told that Israel was serving a variety of gods resident in various places: Syria, Sidon, Moab, Ammon, and Philistia. No details are given to describe the effects of these worship patterns. Nevertheless, we will come across at least one of these effects when we get to the episode concerning Jephthah. Almost as bad as acknowledging these other deities, Israel seems not even to have included YHWH in their pantheon. Indeed, Israel *forsook* YHWH, thus making no pretense of serving the God who had elected them (Judg 10:6). Israel's punishment is thus hardly surprising: the people are given over to oppression, this time at the hand of Ammon and Philistia (Judg 10:7–9). For eighteen years Israel was under the thumb of these enemies.

Despite this sorry state, Israel managed to aggravate the situation. At first, though, it appears that Israel had come to their senses not only by crying out, as they had done previously (Judg 3:9, 15; 4:3; 6:7), but also by admitting to their idolatry (Judg 10:10). YHWH was not impressed! Instead of absolving, the LORD condemned them. YHWH reminded them of the gracious acts that had been done on Israel's behalf, namely, rescuing them from the Egyptians, Amorites, Ammonites, Philistines, Sidonians,

Amelekites, and Maonites (Judg 10:11–12). There was no mistaking the extent of YHWH's gracious actions since the time of the exodus. Yet, that had not induced Israel to pay attention to the very deity who was responsible for saving them repeatedly. Rather, Israel worshipped the gods of the very people from whom YHWH had freed them. YHWH resolved to get out of the rescuing business, at least for a while. Therefore, YHWH announced that Israel should not expect any more divine deliverance (Judg 10:13). In case future rescue was needed, Israel should *go and cry out* (*lᵉkû wᵉzaʿăqû*) to the deities whom they were currently worshipping (Judg 10:14). This is the same vocabulary that previously characterized Israel's appeal to YHWH when they were desperate for rescue. They will now have the opportunity to find out whether that language would work on their newly adopted gods. YHWH's decision seems final: "I will deliver you no more" (Judg 10:13).

YHWH's pronouncement, however, got Israel to reconsider. That reconsideration led them to reiterate their confession and likewise submit to divine punishment (Judg 10:15). Though at first that seemed a step in the right direction, their next statement gives us pause. This is because they immediately put limits on their submission to divine discipline. Having invited God to punish them appropriately, in the next breath they implore that God "deliver us this very day" (*ʾak haṣṣîlēnû nāʾ hayyôm hazzeh*). This plea for immediate clemency casts doubt on the sincerity of their initial confession. That assessment might be too generous. Did their asking YHWH to relent from suitable punishment render their confession completely null? While we ponder that question, the narrator lets us know that Israelite behavior, in fact, headed down a more positive path. They spurned foreign gods and began serving YHWH (Judg 10:16).

Regardless of whether Israel was hedging their bets, YHWH responded graciously. The Israelite deity had declared in Judg 10:13 that the day of divine rescue had come to an end. By v. 16 YHWH relented and got angry instead about the misery Israel was experiencing because of Philistine and Ammonite oppression (Judg 10:7). It took all of three verses for YHWH's graciousness to trump YHWH's anger. This had nothing to do with Israelite behavior and everything to do with the nature of their God.

Though God was once more willing to rescue the people, Israel had not yet come completely clean. Typically, in Judges when Israel was needing help because of foreign harassment, YHWH summoned someone to save them (Judg 2:16, 18; 3:9–10, 15; 6:11ff.). But that did not happen in this instance. Rather, Israel deployed forces in Gilead as the Ammonites approached (Judg 10:17). At that point, Israelite leaders determined it was up to them to find someone to deal with this threat (Judg 10:18). No prayers were offered, and no religious personnel were consulted. The fact that Israel took these steps on their own was concerning.

JEPHTHAH INTRODUCED

Jephthah appears on the scene after we learn that Gilead's leaders were looking for someone to take the military reins as the Ammonites encroached (Judg 10:18). The first thing said about Jephthah potentially made him an excellent candidate. He was described as a *gibbôr ḥayîl*, a *substantial man* or *a mighty warrior* (Judg 11:1). However, the second thing said about him is as disparaging as the first is flattering: He was a son of a *zônāh*, that is, a prostitute.[1] Whether this designates a woman who sells her body or one who was promiscuous is difficult to tell. Nevertheless, in this context Jephthah's siblings, who shared the same father, a man named Gilead, ostracized him due to his relationship to the unnamed *zônāh* (Judg 11:2). These half-brothers wanted to ensure that Jephthah was not able to execute inheritance claims. His mother, according to their way of thinking, had no legal rights. Because of this, Jephthah fled, settled in Tob, and attracted a crew who *went out* (*wayyēṣᵉ'û*) with him (Judg 11:3). The nature of this group is a bit of a mystery, though the terminology used to describe them—*'ănāšîm rêqîm*—is scarcely becoming: *idle* or *worthless men*. Were they mercenaries to provide muscle for a fee or opportunistic troublemakers? Ironically, it appears that Jephthah lived in a *Good* place, for that is what *Ṭôb* means, but was surrounded by men who did not enjoy the best reputation.

As the Ammonites approached, the elders of Gilead seek out Jephthah in Tob (Judg 11:4). It remains unclear why they wanted him to lead Israel in the pending battle. Was it due to his status as a *gibbôr ḥayîl*, however we are to understand that title? Or, was it because the people who were with him were notorious enforcers? It is hard to know. Regardless, Jephthah is reluctant to accept their offer. He seems to blame them for what his half-brothers did to him, therefore accusing the elders of hating him and ousting him from his father's house (Judg 11:7). Did he think that the elders were implicated in his siblings' actions? Was he looking for redress? Was he merely lashing out because he had been treated so shabbily by members of his own

---

1. See Schulte, "Beobachtungen," 255–62. Schulte argues, unconvincingly in my judgment, that the negative connotation of this word only developed in later periods. In pre-state and pre-monarchic periods the term refers primarily to an independent woman who lives in a matriarchal structure. This conclusion violates the plain meaning of several narratives, certainly from a literary point of view.

family? For some reason, Jephthah wants to know why, all of a sudden, they are enlisting his help.

Sidestepping Jephthah's direct question, the elders repeat their offer (Judg 11:8). Had they also sweetened it? At first, they wanted Jephthah to be a *qāṣîn*, a word that connotes *chief* or *ruler*, perhaps with a military nuance (Judg 11:6). But the second time around they suggested that, should he accept their offer, Jephthah would become a *rō'š*, *head*, over all of Gilead's inhabitants (Judg 11:8). It is conceivable that the two terms are equivalent. It is just as possible that the elders are inviting Jephthah to lead Gilead into battle and subsequently rule in a political capacity. Jephthah certainly seems to construe the second offer as an enhancement. In an abrupt about face, he agrees to become their *head* (= *rō'š*; Judg 11:9). It is significant that the narrator tells us that when the Gilead elders sealed the deal they set Jephthah up as head (*rō'š*) *and* ruler (*qāṣîn*), thus reversing the order of the two terms (Judg 11:11). Again, a little textual ambiguity remains but the reversal of the two terms is suggestive.

Two other features of the terms of this arrangement are worth mentioning. Jephthah put forth a couple of conditions that had to be met for him to comply. One involved something Gilead's elders had to do. Another required something for YHWH to do. What Jephthah wanted of Gilead's elders was that "you bring me back" or "bring me home" (*'im-mᵉšîbîm 'attem 'ôtî*) (Judg 11:9). That is not a geographical reference but a sociopolitical one. Does Jephthah's wish to be brought back/brought back home mean that Tob will no longer be where he resides?[2] Or, does this desire indicate that Jephthah will once again be in Israel's good graces, his siblings' protestations, and efforts to marginalize him notwithstanding? The latter option seems more likely.

The second condition has to do with Jephthah's willingness to become head over Gilead's inhabitants only if YHWH enables him to be victorious (Judg 11:9). This is the first invocation of YHWH on anyone's part since the deity had become incensed about Israel's being so severely oppressed (Judg 10:16). Typically, in Judges YHWH's becoming upset at foreign oppression—which, it should be recalled, had been orchestrated by YHWH in the first place—would prompt the deity to summon a deliverer. That does not happen here. Instead, the Israelites, represented by Gilead's elders, seek

---

2. There are other geographical complexities in this passage. Jephthah recites the elements of this agreement first at Mizpah, a location to be distinguished from the more famous town with the same name. Later on, when Jephthah is on the way home, the town mentioned is again Mizpah. Is this part of or close to the Land of Tob (Judg 11:3)? Perhaps, but it seems odd to name a *land* as part of Gilead. See Arnold, "Mizpah," 879–81.

out their own deliverer. They make no appeal to God whatsoever. After they told Jephthah what they had in mind, *he* brings YHWH into the picture. Whether YHWH was pleased with the elders' choice at this juncture is not expressed. Still, Jephthah agrees to become Gilead's head after God ensured victory over the Ammonites.

Jephthah's invocation evidently had a positive influence on the Gileadite elders in that they call on YHWH to witness the arrangement that had just been concluded (Judg 11:10). Though this seems to be a step in the right direction, we still have no indication about what YHWH thought about these proceedings. The last thing the narrator had told us about YHWH was that the deity had become angry that Israel was being mistreated (Judg 10:16). Yet, even before engaging the Ammonites, and therefore knowing whether YHWH would bring about an Israelite victory, Jephthah went with the elders to Mizpah where they installed him as head (*rō'š*) and chief/ruler (*qāṣîn*) over Gilead (Judg 11:11). While at Mizpah, Jephthah recited *his words* to YHWH, which presumably refers to the terms of the agreement. However, we still have no idea what YHWH's reaction was either to the elders or to Jephthah.

Once Jephthah is in charge, he initiates a discussion with the king of the Ammonites by sending messengers to get an explanation for their aggression (Judg 11:12). Presumably, Jephthah wants to avoid bloodshed. With this tactic, he is conducting himself as a political leader just as much as a military figure. The Ammonite king had a ready response to Jephthah's inquiry. The king accused Israel of taking large swaths of Ammonite land when they were in the area after escaping from Egypt (Judg 11:13). Naturally, the Ammonites want this territory restored peaceably (*bᵉšālôm*). If Israel wants to avoid violence, they will have to accede to the Ammonite demand.

Jephthah counters by sending a second set of messengers, who explain why Israel is not guilty of the Ammonite charges. Via these messengers, Jephthah put forward his own take on Israelite history (Judg 11:14). First, Jephthah maintains that Israel had not confiscated land from either Moab or Ammon during the wilderness trek (Judg 11:15). Second, he insists that Israel made a good faith effort to pass by peaceably the various territories that needed to be traversed, including Edom and Moab. Unfortunately, the kings of Edom and Moab balked (Judg 11:16-17). In light of this negative response, Israel decided to go around (Judg 11:18). Third, the Israelites made a similar offer to go through Amorite lands peaceably, but that offer was also rejected. This time hostilities ensued (Judg 11:19-20). Fortunately for Israel, YHWH enabled a victory, allowing them to take possession of Amorite territory, not only of the area "from the Arnon to the Jabbok" (Judg 11:13), but also including "from the wilderness to the Jordan" (Judg 11:21-22). Fourth, because YHWH was behind this operation Israel has every right to hold on to this territory (Judg 11:23). Because YHWH was responsible not only for Israel's win but the resulting appropriation of the conquered territory, the matter should be viewed as settled.

The elaboration of the fourth point above is interesting. Not only do Jephthah's messengers underscore the finality of what had happened due to YHWH's actions, they appeal to the logic of their position. But this is curious. Would not the Ammonites have used a similar rationale had their deity, Chemosh, made possible possession of the territory in question?[3] Likewise, according to the messengers, since Israel's deity was responsible for the Israelite victory and subsequent confiscation, why should that be determinative (Judg 11:24)? Considering the question rhetorical, the messengers appeal once more to the past, citing the time of Balak, former king of Moab (Judg 11:25). Balak had hired Balaam to curse Israel (Num 22–24). When that ploy failed, Balaam simply went home (Num 24:25). According to the chronology mentioned by Jephthah's messengers, that was three hundred years ago (Judg 11:26). Since no one had attempted to retake the territory during these three centuries, it made little sense to demand land to be returned now. From an Ammonite point of view, the Israelite logic was hardly cogent, not to mention transparently special pleading. It therefore comes as no surprise that the Amorites rejected the premise (Judg 11:28). Without question, war was on the horizon.

For the first time since Judg 10:16, the narrator makes first order statements about YHWH. Before this, only characters in the story have said anything about YHWH, but the narrator had not confirmed what the Israelite deity thought about what others had said. That changed in Judg 11:29, when YHWH's spirit came upon Jephthah. In spite of the breaking of the pattern since Israel's putative confession and the deity's announcing that Israel's crying out would not be effective (Judg 10:13–15), YHWH had decided to participate once again in Israel's affairs. That happened when YHWH's spirit came upon Jephthah. YHWH's spirit was often instrumental in enhancing the actions of a deliverer who had been summoned by the same deity (e.g., Judg 3:10; 6:34; 13:25; 14:6, 19; 15:14). Jephthah was no exception, even though he had not been selected for duty by YHWH. Nevertheless, YHWH's spirit was on him as he was about to take on the Ammonites.

---

3. Jephthah's messengers referring to Chemosh as the Ammonite deity is odd. That was Moab's god. Were the messengers being deliberately inaccurate as a way of denigrating the deity? Was it an honest mistake? Or, had the Ammonites included Chemosh in their pantheon? Milcom/Molech was usually identified as the Ammonite deity (1 Kgs 11:5, 7).

JEPHTHAH'S VOW

YHWH's spirit empowering Jephthah surely has to be viewed as a positive development. This was good news, especially in light of YHWH's having declared just recently that no more divine deliverance would be forthcoming (Judg 10:13). With Jephthah now possessing (or, being *possessed by*!) YHWH's spirit, Israel is not only once again in God's good graces but as well may legitimately anticipate deliverance from the enemy. Yet, Jephthah inexplicably managed to ruin the moment. Ironically, he did so by doing something that would ordinarily have been praiseworthy. All other things being equal, making and keeping a vow to YHWH would be a good thing. Unfortunately, that was not true in this instance.

Not only was Jephthah's vow extraordinary in terms of its repugnant content; it was completely unnecessary. Once YHWH's spirit had endowed a deliverer, nothing more was needed—a vow would be extraneous. YHWH had already indicated without question divine intentions with the movement of the spirit. Sadly, Jephthah thought otherwise or, had not thought at all, but acted impulsively and foolishly.

As though having YHWH's spirit was insufficient, Jephthah promised a burnt offering to YHWH on the *condition* that the Ammonites suffer defeat. Promising a burnt offering to YHWH if the deity comes through in the battle exposes Jephthah's implicit belief that the Israelite God needs to be induced. That thinking was at best presumptuous and at worst heretical. As though Jephthah's twisted thinking about YHWH's needing an inducement was not bad enough, the inducement itself is mind-boggling. Jephthah offered to sacrifice the first one emerging from the doors of his house when he arrived at home after the battle (Judg 11:30–31). Can there be any question that he had a human being in mind? Any animal—and several would have been suitable—would not have come out of the doors of his *house*.[4] Usually, in the biblical world only people reside in houses. By what odd logic would Jephthah have expected an animal to emerge from his home and come out to greet him? In any case, as promised, YHWH made Jephthah victorious over the Ammonites (Judg 11:32–33). YHWH had not abandoned Israel despite the earlier threat to do precisely that (Judg 10:13). At the same time, YHWH's willingness to rescue Israel once more did not by any means signal that Israel had repented and amended their ways. Indeed, Jephthah's vow only underscored Israelite heresy and depravity. Though a burnt offering

---

4. See the study of Alexandra Rottzoll and Dirk U. Rottzoll comparing critical and Jewish interpretation in the pre-critical era: "Die Erzählung," 210–30. They deal extensively with the debate over the centuries of whether Jephthah had in mind an animal or a human being when he made the vow.

was entirely superfluous in this situation, Jephthah's vow was more than rash. It was diabolical.

Though it was tragic for Jephthah personally that his daughter was the first one to come out of *his house*, not to mention how tragic it was for the unlucky daughter, it would have been no less despicable had someone else appeared. Our initial impulse might be to sympathize that Jephthah had taken a chance that would put his own daughter at risk because he had failed to consider this possibility. But we cannot lose sight of the fact that Jephthah promised a human being as an offering to YHWH. Jephthah does not deserve a smidgen of sympathy. He had blithely orchestrated a circumstance in which *someone* would be sacrificed. Such abhorrent behavior for an Israelite father is not mitigated by the happenstance that his daughter became the victim. Would Jephthah be off the hook, morally and religiously speaking, had his mother or father, uncle or aunt, cousin, or any servants had appeared instead? The issue here is human sacrifice, not the relationship to the contemptible person who made the vow in the first place.

Indeed, it would be a grave mistake to see YHWH's rescuing Israel from Ammonite oppression as the deity's giving Israel a pass for their idolatry, or not caring about the failure of Gilead's elders even to consider waiting for God to select the next deliverer and instead going ahead with their own choice or viewing Jephthah's countenancing human sacrifice as a minor moral lapse. On the latter issue, human sacrifice was not only expressly forbidden but regarded as an abomination (Lev 18:21, 24–30; Deut 12:31; 18:9–10; Ps 106:37–38). YHWH remained committed to Israel, to be sure, but was hardly willing to ignore Israel's egregious behavior. Israel's election was grounded in YHWH's promise, and therefore irrevocable, but that did not exempt them from episodic judgment, especially when it came to depravity on this level.

Though Jephthah was horrified when he saw his daughter, his only child, who was dancing and playing music as she came through the doors of the house to greet joyfully her father, he responded by complaining that he had no choice but to fulfill the vow. After all, he had "opened his mouth to YHWH" (*wᵉʾānōkî pāṣîtî pî ʾel-YHWH*) and thus thought he could not nullify the vow (Judg 11:35). Ironically, the Hebrew verb, *pātaḥ*, to *part* or *open*, is the basis for Jephthah's name: "He Opened." Though another word for *open* is used when he remarked in this manner, this would have been an instance where he should never have opened his mouth! In addition, Jephthah displayed not a whit of parental concern. Even if he had to endure punishment for making a vow to YHWH and then not keeping it, that would have been preferable to a loving father instead of callously allowing his sole child to suffer for his stupidity, rashness, and heresy. In terms of Israelite tradition, human sacrifice is never to be countenanced.[5]

In fact, Jephthah's creating the conditions for any human sacrifice let alone his own child, and his daughter's willingness to comply with this deplorable practice, despite the personal price she was about to pay, illustrates how far Israel had departed from orthodox Israelite religious tradition.[6] Despite the natural sympathy one might express for the daughter's plight, though she laments her misfortune she seems not to be aghast at the prospect of human sacrifice itself. She asks only for time to bewail that she will die as a virgin (Judg 11:37). Plus, the daughter comes close herself to attributing the victory which the Lord allowed Jephthah to achieve to his having made the vow (Judg 11:36). Instead of reacting with horror about this unspeakable act, the Israelite response was to ritualize this awful event by an annual gathering of the daughters of Israel for four days to lament Jephthah's daughter (Judg 11:40). However, they seemed only to have lamented her dying as a virgin, ignoring the horrible reality that a judge in Israel had sacrificed his own daughter, thinking that YHWH would be pleased (Judg 11:39).

DISUNITY IN ISRAEL

The story featuring Jephthah is not the first time in the book of Judges that dysfunction and division in smaller social units, even families, spills over to dysfunction and division in the community at large. It is thus hardly surprising that Ephraim, a tribal unit, confronted Jephthah in Zaphon. Ephraim's posture was hostile at the outset—they challenged Jephthah after preparing to fight (Judg 12:1). Their complaint was that Jephthah had not summoned them to fight against Ammon. This complaint was accompanied by a threat to burn down Jephthah's house. This is the second time that Ephraim lodged a complaint like this. They were also bent out of shape after Gideon had defeated Midian (Judg 8:1). Gideon managed to placate the tribe at that

---

5. The story in Genesis 22 about God's testing Abraham by ordering him to offer his son, Isaac, is not an exception to the prohibition of human sacrifice. That episode emphasizes God's making sure that Abraham's trust in God accords with his relationship to God and is consonant with the blessing that God has in store with the rest of humanity. See Davis, *Opening Israel's Scriptures*, 30–32.

6. See the remark of Baker, that "the gravity of this offense cannot be overstated." In addition to the gratuitous loss of life and the sacrifice of any human being, the shedding of blood in this manner also pollutes the land (Num 35:33–34), making it unfit for the habitation of a holy deity. "Double Trouble," 40.

time, so no hostilities ensued (Judg 8:2–4). But this time around bloodshed could not be averted.

As noted, Ephraim was so upset that they threatened to torch Jephthah's house. But Jephthah did not back down at all. He retorted by pointing out that "I and my people" contended with the Ammonites. Furthermore, though they had in fact been summoned Ephraim had not lifted a finger to help. This is why Jephthah decided to take on the Ammonites on his own (Judg 12:2–3). Jephthah simply does not understand why Ephraim is acting so belligerently.

Jephthah's response requires further comment. First, whom did he have in mind when he referred to "my people"? Is this a reference to the men who had originally surrounded him (Judg 11:3)? Or, does he mean Israelites in general? However, no summons went out to any other Israelites, at least according to the present text. Either there was such a call to Israelite forces and for some reason Ephraim was excluded, or there had been no general call to arms because Jephthah's personal army was up to the task (Judg 11:29). In any case, Ephraim refused to be mollified and prepared for a fight.

Jephthah gathered the men of Gilead to get ready for the battle. That battle was over almost before it started. In a sequence of verbs, Jephthah *gathered* the troops, *battled*, and *dispatched* Ephraim (Judg 12:4). At this juncture, we catch a glimpse of how very fractured the body politic was. Ephraim apparently had taunted the Gileadites by accusing them of being fugitives from Ephraim, intimating a dispute over to which Israelite group Gilead belonged. Gilead had long since been viewed as part of Israelite territory, but evidently under whose tribal aegis was in dispute. Regardless, in this instance Ephraim used the Gileadites and their alleged flight from Ephraim as a pretext for warring against current Israelite authority in the person of Jephthah.

The extent of Israelite division may be observed by what happened in the Jordan fords, where at least part of the battle took place. Gilead's soldiers were able to position themselves in such a way that rival combatants had to go by them as they tried to reunite with Ephraimite soldiers. Of course, since all the soldiers were in fact Israelites and because no one wore distinctive uniforms, the identity of soldiers had to be ascertained. Physical features did not matter, and dress also did not matter. But language did! In this story world, every individual spoke Hebrew. However, Hebrew was a dialect of Canaanite, thus it had dialectical variations of its own. That meant that pronunciation or differing accents might be a way of determining to which group one belonged.[7]

7. Think of the English language, depending on whether it is spoken by an American,

Gilead's forces fighting under Jephthah's leadership were not about to allow soldiers who had survived Ephraim's initial defeat to return home unscathed. When these straggling warriors arrived at the fords, they were met by the victors. When the Ephraimite soldiers asked for safe passage, they were immediately questioned about whether they were, in fact, Ephraimites (Judg 12:5). Obviously, these fleeing troops would reply negatively. At that point, they were asked to pronounce *shibboleth*, a common word meaning an "ear/head of grain." Unfortunately for these soldiers, they had difficulty with the *sh*-sound—they could only manage an *s*-sound. Being betrayed by their own Hebrew dialect, they were slaughtered on the spot when they mispronounced (Judg 12:6). This was no skirmish, for we learn that in the end 42,000 Ephraimites lost their lives in this battle. It is unclear that that was the number of the ones who perished at the fords. More likely, we are to understand that this was a summary of the total losses the Ephraimite army had suffered. Either way, it was not a pretty scene.

CONCLUSION

The story featuring Jephthah illustrates the moral depths to which Israel had sunk. Granted, YHWH had relented from the initial decision not to rescue Israel any longer, even suggesting that they call on the *other gods* that they were currently serving (Judg 10:13–14). That reversal was demonstrated when YHWH's spirit endowed Jephthah when he was about to engage the Ammonites (Judg 11:29). Though Jephthah had not been originally raised up by YHWH, he received all the divine help necessary. That ensured his military success but did little for his moral transformation. Jephthah's deplorable oath, promising a human sacrifice, reflected not only the depravity of a single person but the widespread immorality of Israel as a whole. Jephthah's daughter, who became the victim, lamented that she would die a virgin, but did not protest this horrific violation of the Israelite ethic. Significantly, no one else in Israel cried out in horror at what was transpiring. Israel had apparently become accustomed to abominable behavior.

As though human sacrifice was insufficient to show how far from YHWH Israel had gone, the story concludes with yet another instance of Israelite disunity. The pattern is being developed that disunity is a prime consequence of Israelite sin. Division in this episode was not a minor affair affecting only a handful of people. This involved tribe against tribe. Ephraim experienced dreadful losses. These losses were compounded by the sorry

---

someone from England, or an Australian. Indeed, there are differences of accent, spelling, and pronunciation *within* those countries.

spectacle of Israelites ferreting out other Israelites based on speech patterns in an effort to punish the offenders down to the very last soldier.

It is telling that Jephthah's death and time of rule is not followed by the notation that the land enjoyed a time of rest, which is typical (Judg 3:11, 30; 5:31). The only good news in this episode is found in YHWH's gracious relenting of the divine anger against Israel and rescuing them from Ammonite oppression via Jephthah. Everything else is bad news, including Israel's blithe acceptance of human sacrifice and another sad example of the fractured state of God's elect people.

Chapter 5

Multiplying Divisions: The Story of the Levite's Concubine[1]

INTRODUCTION

The story recounted in Judges 19–21 remains relatively obscure even for people who appeal to the Bible for religious reasons. Almost certainly, this is due to its reprehensible content. A narrative that describes in such lurid detail a gang rape surely deserves obscurity. Why would anyone want to subject himself or herself to such a *text of terror*?[2] Is there any redeeming value to such an abhorrent account? The answer seems to be painfully obvious.

At the same time, despite its repugnant content, the story does occupy a strategic position by virtue of being the conclusion to the book of Judges. From a strictly literary perspective, beginnings and conclusions are always significant, perhaps even essential, for understanding the thrust of the material. The passage in Judges 19–21 is no exception. For that reason, we have no choice but to face this stomach-churning narrative. As it turns out, as I hope to show, this particular text speaks as poignantly as any we will consider to the issues related to Israel's disunity. Indeed, the details are repulsive primarily because the disunity of Israel that is signified by the story is equally repulsive. The narrator appears to believe that only such a horrific account could capture the gravity of Israel's being so hopelessly divided.

---

1. This chapter is a revised version of the 2008 Weter Lecture I delivered at Seattle Pacific University in 2008: "Multiplying Divisions: A Figural Reading of the Story of the Levite's Concubine (Judges 19–21)." Obviously, I have used the first part of the title as the title of this book.

2. See Trible, *Texts of Terror*, 65–92.

A FAMILY AFFAIR

At first, however, there is little in the story that suggests any implication for Israel as a whole. Only two people are initially introduced, neither of whom have any important position in Israel as a community. These people are not even named. This is a story about Mr. and Mrs. Nobody, who happen to be Israelites. The man is identified as a Levite who is visiting territory in Ephraim; the woman hails from Bethlehem in Judah (Judg 19:1). The only other item we are told at the outset is that the woman that the Levite *took* (i.e., married) was a woman who was also a concubine (*'iššāh pîlegeš*).[3] How does this introduction of an unnamed man and woman, who have seemingly no title or religious or political significance, pertain in the least to Israel as a people?

Israel is barely mentioned as an afterthought in the notation that the story that is about to be related took place before Israel had a king (Judg 19:1). By itself, such a temporal indicator seems at best mildly interesting. Is this an effort on the part of the narrator to say that the period of judges is ending while the period of kings is about to begin? If so, how does the story of Mr. and Mrs. Nobody have anything to do with this transition? Were this temporal reference an isolated comment, such a conclusion might be warranted. In fact, however, the footnote, so to speak, that this episode preceded Israel's having kings turns out to occur four times in a short amount of narrative space. The first time the phrase occurs, it is stated in a fuller form: "In those days there was no king in Israel; everyone did what was right in their own eyes" (Judg 17:6). The shorter version appears in Judg 18:1. Once more the succinct rendering begins the story of the Levite and his concubine (Judg 19:1). Finally, the longer statement concludes not only these final five chapters but the whole book of Judges (Judg 21:23).

How should we understand these phrases? First, they govern only the two separate accounts that are narrated in the last five chapters of the book. Episodes involving judges conclude with chapter 16 when Samson dies (Judg 16:31). Second, the literary pattern that was evident in the various stories featuring judges—the people sin; YHWH hands them over to an oppressor; the people cry out; YHWH raises up a judge; the judge delivers; the land is pacified (Judg 2:11–16)—is no longer evident in these last five chapters. Third, the implication of the phrase seems to be that such religious and social depravity as is described in these two stories would have been prevented were Israel to be under a monarchy. For the present, we will leave open the matter of the impact of the Levite and his concubine on Israel

---

3. See the previous discussion about concubine status in my remarks about Abimelech's mother in chapter 3.

generally or on the kingship particularly. We will have occasion to revisit this question, however. For now, we will concentrate on these two individuals whose significance on the rest of Israel remains to be seen.

As soon as we learn that this man and this woman were a married couple, we are told that *she whored against him* (*wattizneh ʿālāw*) (Judg 19:2). This Hebrew verb indicates that she had been unfaithful. Two Greek (Septuagintal) traditions of this story, however, say either that she had left him or gotten angry with him, though no reasons are given to explain either action. It is impossible to know whether the Greek translators were trying to soften the harsher wording or were following another Hebrew tradition. Some scholars have also attempted to soften the Hebrew by citing an Akkadian word (*zenū*) that means *to be angry* or by thinking Hebrew *zānāh* was mistakenly substituted for *zānaḥ*, which means *to spurn or reject*. At a psychological level, almost anyone would prefer anger or leaving rather than committing adultery in light of what happens to this poor woman later in the story. But because of the figural role we believe the woman eventually plays in this account we should retain the word in its plainest and more difficult sense. No details are supplied of her illicit encounter. The concubine merely left her husband and returned to her father's house, where she stayed for four months before anything else transpires in the story. Any response on the husband's part to his wife's infidelity is completely left to our imagination.

After four months the husband has had enough of this separation. So, he decided to speak to her heart (*lᵉdabbēr ʿal-libbāh*), that is, to address her tenderly, and bring her back home (Judg 19:3). The Levite should get high marks for this gesture at reconciliation, especially in light of the circumstance that had triggered the woman's departure. But the woman should get some credit also, because when her husband arrived, she went to meet him and brought him into her father's house. That is what the Hebrew text says, although the RSV and NRSV follow the Greek in this instance. JPS[4] gets the translation right, in my view. The narrator clearly wants to emphasize that both the man and the woman are trying to patch up their differences. Even though we are informed that the woman's father was tickled to see his son-in-law, the woman had said nothing to her estranged husband and, pointedly, the husband had remained silent, too, in spite of his earlier intention to speak tenderly to his wife. Perhaps the husband is waiting for a more opportune time.

---

4. These letters stand for the Revised Standard Version, the New Revised Standard Version, and the Jewish Publication Society Bibles, respectively.

THE FATHER-IN-LAW'S HOSPITALITY

Evidently, to match the joy elicited by his son-in-law's arrival, the woman's father insisted on *him* staying around for three days. Not a word is said at this point about the daughter or the young man who had accompanied the Levite, although the young man might be included in the notation that *they stayed there* (Judg 19:4). It is less clear that the woman was part of the *they* who had eaten and drunk. Did only the father-in-law and son-in-law partake of this meal? Why is there no explicit reference to the daughter's/wife's participation? Is this significant or incidental?

On the fourth day, when *they*, surely referring now to the traveling party *and* the Levite's wife, arose to leave, the woman's father intervened by offering another day of hospitality (Judg 19:5). This time the text is more explicit—only the two men feasted (Judg 19:6). Was the woman even at the table? How had she all but disappeared from the scene when she was the very reason for the Levite's presence in the first place? Then, still ignoring his daughter, the host invited his guest to stay one more night, again promising revelry (Judg 19:6). The Levite accepted the invitation without consulting with or speaking to his wife (Judg 19:7). In fact, it is not lost on us that he has not uttered a single word to the woman. He has not only not spoken tenderly to her; he has not spoken to her at all.

On day five, the father-in-law doubles down on his invitation, which is verging on being more oppressive than gracious (Judg 19:8). Once again the Levite finds it impossible to decline, so he spends another day eating and drinking. Pointedly, once more we are told that only the two of them ate. It is as though the host's daughter and the guest's wife do not exist. As night or perhaps dusk approaches, the father-in-law urges *him* to stay and party some more because the hour is so late. They could then depart early the next day (Judg 19:9). Because the Levite, his wife, and his servant had gotten up to leave, the father-in-law's addressing only the Levite reduces his daughter in effect to the status of a servant.

Nevertheless, the Levite finally declines the most recent offer and takes off despite how late it had become (Judg 19:10). On their trip home, they arrive at Jebus, another name for Jerusalem, a city not yet Israelite (see 2 Sam 5:6–10). For that reason, the Levite is reluctant to book lodging there, even though the young man, his servant, thought that was a good idea. The Levite's reasoning is quite explicit. The inhabitants of Jebus/Jerusalem are foreigners and not Israelites (Judg 19:11–12). The Levite does not believe he will be welcomed in such a city, so he insists that they press on to Gibeah or Ramah, both of which are Israelite (Judg 19:13). After all, he has recently been lavished with hospitality from an Israelite home. Surely, the Levite and his party could count on at least a modicum of hospitality from people who, though not kin, were nonetheless Israelites.

But these hopes were dashed. Having arrived at Gibeah, a town in Benjaminite territory, the Levite, his wife, and servant, not to mention the livestock, were compelled to bed down in the city square because not a single person offered lodging (Judg 19:14–15). This was the reception they thought they would receive had they tried their luck in Jebus/Jerusalem. What a revolting development that they encounter a cold shoulder in an Israelite city. Perhaps the Levite at this point wished he had stayed one more day at his father-in-law's house. Though the hospitality there was over the top, they would have had full bellies and a place to sleep.

THE OLD MAN'S HOSPITALITY

Fortunately for the traveling party, an old man from Ephraim who was himself a visitor in Gibeah was coming from his work in the field when he spotted the Levite (called here a *wayfarer*) in the square and asked him where he had come from and where he was going (Judg 19:16–17). A couple of details are noteworthy in this initial meeting. One, why does the age of the visitor from Ephraim matter? Two, why does the narrator feel the need to remind us that the *men* of Gibeah were Benjaminites—we knew that already (Judg 19:14)? Three, the visitor notices, at least at first, only the wayfarer. The wife and the servant are more or less invisible to this old man's eyes. Are these incidental details or important ones?

Even more questions come up when the Levite responds to the old man. The Levite does use the first personal plural pronoun when he describes the journey underway from Bethlehem to the hill country of Ephraim: "*We* are passing from Bethlehem in Judah to . . . Ephraim" (Judg 19:18). But that is his only concession to either his wife or his servant in that he points out that Ephraim is where *I* am from, and *I* went to Bethlehem in Judah, and *I* am going to the House of the LORD. It is understandable that he cites Ephraim as his home base and that he did go by himself initially to Bethlehem in Judah. That was quite literally true. Still, he barely mentions the others on the return trip, highlighted by his insistence that upon arrival in Gibeah no man took *me* home. Equally odd is his claim that he is going to the House of YHWH.[5] Is the Levite trying to impress the old man with his religious devotion? So far in the story there has been no indication whatsoever of

---

5. RSV and NRSV opt for the Greek text in this case. JPS translates the actual Hebrew text but notes that its meaning is uncertain.

religious commitment on the part of any of the characters in the story. This statement comes out of the blue.

But the matter of the Levite going to the House of YHWH may also evoke Israelite religious practices. The Levite's specifying that his destination is the LORD's House, regardless of what he wanted the old man to think, makes us attend more closely to how a Levite should be regarded in the whole narrative. Levi, the eponymous ancestor of this tribal group, famously earned his father's opprobrium for the violence he and his brother, Simeon, had undertaken in the wake of their sister Dinah's rape (Gen 34; see vv. 25-26). Though the other brothers apparently participated in the subsequent sack of the city (Gen 34:27-29), Jacob singled out Levi and Simeon for making the family's position in the land precarious relative to the indigenous inhabitants (Gen 34:30). Then, when Jacob spoke formally for the last time about the future of his sons, Levi and Simeon were roundly condemned (Gen 49:5-7). However, despite this inauspicious beginning, Levi's descendants later distinguished themselves in zealously punishing the Israelites who had built and worshipped the golden calf in the wilderness (Exod 32:25-28). In the wake of this action, no less a figure than Moses lauded the Levites for what they had accomplished in YHWH's behalf (Exod 32:29). Of course, it cannot be forgotten that the great Moses was himself a Levite (Exod 2:1-10).

Apparently, one of the upshots for the zeal demonstrated by the Levites was their being selected for special sacerdotal duties (e.g., Exod 38:21; Num 1:47, 50, 53; 3:5-10; 18:6, 23; Deut 31:25; 33:8-11; Josh 3:3; 18:7). Another privilege the Levites were accorded was their unique status relative to the allotment of the promised land. Every tribal group in Israel was assigned a particular location. But this was not the case for the Levites. They had no territory of their own. Instead, the so-called Cities of Refuge were reserved for them (Num 35). The inheritance of the Levites was their priestly vocation rather than a particular section of turf (e.g., Num 18:23-24; Deut 10:9; 12:12; 18:1, 6-7). Even though the Levites could consider the Cities of Refuge as their residence as was convenient, in fact they were able to reside virtually anywhere in the other tribal areas.

This ability of the Levites to live throughout Israel was beneficial to them in another way. In effect, when traveling throughout Israelite territory the Levites enjoyed the same benefits as a *sojourner* (*gēr*). Typically, a sojourner was distinguished from someone who was native born (e.g., Exod 12:19, 49). In this sense, in modern terms a *gēr* was a resident alien. But Israelites were admonished to be especially gracious to sojourners (*gērîm*), as is evidenced in Exod 22:20 (Eng. v. 21).[6] Sometimes, other disadvantaged groups are included among those who are to receive Israel's generosity, like widows or orphans (Exod 22:21 [Eng. v. 22]). Most interesting for present purposes is how the Levites are even mentioned along with such marginal groups as particularly deserving of Israelite care and compassion (Deut 16:9-14; 26:11, 12, 13). What this means is that a Levite had double protection, as it were, not only as an Israelite but also as a sojourner in his or her own land. If any Israelite had a right to expect hospitality from other Israelites, Levites would be first in line.

In this light, any Israelite would have been sorely disappointed at the lack of hospitality in Gibeah. For that matter, any ordinary sojourner seeking shelter in the city would have had a legitimate complaint to register about the city's failure to respond. But Gibeon's negligence when a Levite came by seeking sanctuary and sustenance is nothing short of appalling. The Gibeonites were violating not only usual customs and mores by not providing the Levite and his party at least a place to sleep but were neglecting religious obligations as well. This studied neglect is made worse given that the Levite had enough to feed his party and his animals (Judg 19:19). Gibeah, therefore, is not only being culturally insensitive, but religiously questionable as well. Until the Levite mentioned that he was going to the House of YHWH, we had not considered the religious dimension of the story. Now, that dimension has at least been intimated.

The old man compensates for Gibeah's negligence by refusing to allow the travelers to stay outside for the night. Instead, he invites them to come inside and offers them and their animals food, notwithstanding the Levite's insistence that he had no need of provisions. Once feet are washed, the animals provided for, and folks ate and drank, it is as though the hospitality in the father-in-law's house had continued unabated in Gibeah (Judg 19:20-21). The old man made up to a degree for Gibeah's failure to treat this Levite as the sojourner he in fact was.

THE HORRIFIC NIGHT

So far in this story there have been only five characters who have played a role: the Levite, his wife/concubine, his servant, the wife's/concubine's father, and the stranger who extended hospitality in Gibeah. To be sure, Israelites hover in the background. There's the reference this marital rift took

---

6. Though translated with the word *stranger*, the Hebrew word is more literally *sojourner* (*gēr*). For a full treatment of this important word, see Spina, "Israelites as *Gērîm*," 321-35.

place before *Israel* had a king (Judg 19:1), *tribal groups* are cited in a couple of places (Judg 19:1, 14, 16, 18), and we are told that the Levite opted to seek lodging in *Israelite* territory rather than trying his luck with foreigners (Judg 19:12). But for the most part the narrative concentrates on these five people, who have yet to do anything that might potentially have an impact on Israel as a people. This circumstance, however, was about to change, and to change dramatically.

Once again, the Levite finds himself participating in a private party. The *they* who are engaged in this enjoyment is not made explicit, but if the previous expression of hospitality is any indication, we can be quite sure that at least the old man and the Levite were enjoying themselves (Judg 19:22). Whether the wife or the servant had a seat at the table is not indicated. Tragically, however, the festivities are short-lived when they are noisily and alarmingly interrupted by a rabble of base fellows ($b^e n\hat{e}$-$b^e liyya‘al$), translated aptly as *a depraved lot* by JPS, pounding on the door. They did not have juvenile mischief in mind. Instead, they were intent on homosexual rape. As it turns out, someone in Gibeah *had* noticed the Levite and those with him, for these thugs were clearly aware that the old man had given them haven. Instead of offering hospitality to the guests in their city, as enjoined by Torah,[7] this *depraved lot* was determined to engage in the worst form of hostility imaginable.

The old man's initial response to this despicable assault elicits only admiration. He tries to talk these deplorable men out of their execrable demand, calling it both evil and vile (Judg 19:23). Also, he appeals to his ethical obligation in offering the man hospitality, which was a consummately Israelite thing to do. This was a less than subtle dig that hospitality was what the townspeople should have made available in the first place. At the same time, as admirable as was the old man's initial effort to resist this heinous behavior, it is worrisome that he confines the protection he proffered only to *this man* ($h\bar{a}$'$\hat{\imath}\check{s}$ $hazzeh$). What about the servant, another male in the house that might have been a target? At this juncture, we might give the host a pass for not mentioning the Levite's wife/concubine since she was not being sought by these degenerates.

Alas, any admiration the reader might have had for the old man's efforts to ward off this perfidious attack immediately devolves into disgust. Not only does he cave in almost instantly, but also exposes his core misogyny and his own depravity by volunteering two females in his house as a substitute for

---

7. Torah means, literally, *law*, but also *teaching, instruction*, and even *story*. Technically, it refers to the first five books of the Old Testament/Hebrew Bible. But its derived sense has to do with Israel's response to the gracious deity who had elected them and formed them into a people.

this man, a phrase he repeats for a second time (Judg 19:24). Without a shred of decency, he bargains with the mob by enticing it with either his virgin daughter—this is the first time she has been mentioned—or his guest's concubine. The old man is beyond loathsome when he tells these reprobates what to do with these women, one of whom, it cannot be forgotten, is the man's own daughter! Incredibly, he suggests that they ravish them, and do whatever they want to these female victims. Using the idiom of doing to these women whatever is *good in your own eyes* is an echo of the phrase used twice in the formulaic statements that frame the final five chapters of Judges (Judg 17:6; 21:25). Is this the narrator's way of emphasizing that these abominable actions on the part of Israelites would be prevented or at least minimized if Israel was ruled by kings?

No matter how one answers that question, Israelite lawlessness was on full display that dreadful night. When the attackers refused to listen to the counteroffer of overpowering a woman rather than a man, either the old man who had made the offer or the Levite who had overheard it took the matter into his own hands. The text says literally that *the man (hā'îš)* took *his concubine* and put her out to the ravenous mob (Judg 19:25). But which man did this? Did the old man seize *his concubine*, meaning, of course, the Levite's concubine? If so, was this a pathetic attempt on the old man's part to spare his daughter even though he had already suggested that they might prefer her as a substitute? Or, had the Levite inserted himself into the situation by thrusting outside his own wife/concubine? The text's ambiguity at this point might be quite purposeful, in that both men were equally guilty by not only not lifting a finger to protect a daughter or a wife, but also being willing to put one or both women in harm's way as they shamefully looked the other way? The depravity being manifested by the men outside the house is matched by the depravity being manifested by the men in the house! Whoever did the grabbing in this scene—and both men seemed equally plausible—the poor concubine was now in the clutches of men completely bereft of an ounce of decency.

The gang rape lasted throughout the interminable night. Exactly what time the pounding on the door had occurred is not stated. Regardless, the abuse went on *all night until morning (kol-hallayāh 'ad-habbōqer)* (Judg 19:25). Being so explicit about the time that had passed makes the reader almost feel the intensity of this unspeakable violence. At dawn, the men let the woman go. Incredibly, the woman manages to make it back to the door of the house from which she had been so callously discarded (Judg 19:26). Significantly, the terminology used for her husband at this point is altered. He is now not her *husband*, but her *lord* or *master ('ădôneyhā)*. Would a master have even treated a slave in such a manner?

Instead of the old man or the Levite at the first opportune moment reaching out to bring the woman back into the house, she remained at the threshold until light had broken (Judg 19:26). Indeed, instead of either of the men waiting anxiously to rescue the woman once she was released, the text implies that the men had gone to sleep! In the morning, *her master*— there's that term again—got up in the morning. This is the normal way to describe someone waking from slumber (Judg 19:27). When he got to the door to continue his journey, he all but tripped over the woman who was lying there with her hands on the threshold. For the very first time in the story, the Levite speaks to his wife/concubine by saying, "Get up, let's go." He started his journey several days ago to speak tenderly to his wife, but now grunts out his command as though he was irritated that his wife/concubine was delaying an early start and as though nothing untoward had happened. When the woman naturally did not answer, the man put his wife/concubine on the ass and proceeded to return home (Judg 19:28). His wife/concubine has been rendered indistinguishable from luggage! Nothing further is said about YHWH's House. As for the woman, we still do not know whether she is alive or dead.

In fact, we do not whether she was already dead when the Levite, upon returning home, proceeded to cut the woman's body into twelve pieces, which he distributed throughout Israel. Each of the twelve tribal units received a ghastly memento to what had just happened in an Israelite town (Judg 19:29). The Israelite response was appropriate to what they had seen as an unprecedented criminal act. But once more ambiguity inserts itself. Was Israel responding to the brutal gang rape itself or to the Levite's macabre manner of making the crime known? In any case, this is no longer a family story, or a local story involving Gibeah. All of a sudden, Israel as a community is now a player in the drama.

THE ISRAELITE RESPONSE

Significantly, *all* the Israelites responded—*as a single person* ($k^e\tilde{\imath}\tilde{s}$ '$eḥād$)— from Dan to Beersheba (the extreme north to the extreme south) to this tragedy when they gathered to YHWH at Mizpah (Judg 20:1).[8] An episode that initially involved only one man and one woman has now implicated Israel as a whole. As well, Israel was represented by chiefs who were over the people and 400,000 soldiers (Judg 20:2). This was serious business. Ominously, the Benjaminites got wind of this meeting (Judg 20:3). Of course, Benjaminite thugs had perpetuated this outrage. It turns out that *all Israel*

---

8. The geographical location of Mizpah is unknown.

had congregated without one of their tribal groups. The Benjaminites were not participants in this gathering. Surely, this is telling.

The Levite is immediately questioned about what had taken place (Judg 20:3). His testimony predictably leaves out any details that would implicate his sorry behavior during the terrible ordeal. Even the narrator allows an ambiguity to stand by referring to the Levite as the man whose wife was murdered but refrains from specifying whether the rapists or the husband were responsible for her death (Judg 20:4). According to the narrator, the wife was indeed gang raped (Judg 19:25), but we are not told whether she died from that abuse or later when her husband dismembered her. She had survived the rape and crawled to the door when her husband found her (Judg 19:26). Who actually caused her death remains shrouded!

In any case, the Levite accurately reports that he and his concubine got to Gibeah with the intention of spending the night (Judg 20:4). But he says nothing about the sojourner who offered him hospitality. He indicates only that the *lords* of Gibeah rose against him by attacking the house where he was with the intention of killing him (Judg 20:5). He offers not a word about the men from Gibeah wanting to rape him, or about the sojourner's attempt to dissuade them, or about the counteroffer of the man's daughter and his guest's concubine, or that one of them pushed the concubine into the clutches of the attackers (Judg 19:22–25). The Levite also tries to deflect any suspicion over who was responsible for his wife's death. He said simply that the men raped her, and that she died, implying that the rape itself had brought about her death. At this point, the Levite relates that he cut up his concubine into pieces and sent these grisly remains to the rest of Israel to underscore the abomination that had been committed in Israel (Judg 20:6–7). Now, he wants to know how Israel will handle this situation.

Taking the Levite at his word, Israel springs into action. Again, the narrator describes Israel as unified. They arose once more *as one man* (Judg 20:8; see 20:1). Refusing to go home, Israel casts lots to determine who will confront Gibeah; they also prepare provisions for those who will ultimately be asked to right this terrible wrong (Judg 20:8–10). Just to make sure we do not forget that they are acting in unison, the narrator underscores that Israel gathered against Gibeah *as one man* (Judg 20:11).

Though they are bent on administering punishment for this abhorrent crime, Israel tries to be fair in bringing only the perpetrators to justice. Gibeah might have been collectively guilty of not offering hospitality, but only a handful of men had engaged in egregious behavior deserving of much more serious sanction. Thus, Israel asks Gibeah to hand over those who were guilty. Incredibly, Gibeah refused to comply, deciding instead to protect their fellow Benjaminites, notwithstanding their indefensible behavior

(Judg 20:12-13). But the Benjaminites did more than refuse this reasonable request on Israel's part. They were also willing to go to war to defend their tribal interests over the interest of Israel as a body (Judg 20:14). Thus, an incident that once had to do with one man and one woman was about to involve Israel in a civil war. Both groups had ample resources for this engagement, though Israel had more troops than Benjamin (Judg 20:15-17).

Israel certainly had every right to bring this incident to a just conclusion. And, Benjamin was just as certainly in the wrong in their efforts to protect their tribal kin. Given this particular confrontation, one intuitively expects Israel to defeat Benjamin. When Benjamin put themselves in the position of protecting these rapists and perhaps murderers, they automatically implicated themselves. They should, therefore, share in their punishment. Is that what Israel's God also wanted? We are about to see.

A STUNNING REVERSAL

So far in this story the only mention of Israel's God is the odd reference the Levite had made to the old man in Gibeah that he was heading for the House of the LORD (Judg 19:18). Israel, however, at this juncture brings God into the heart of the matter when they *inquired* of God about who should lead the charge against Benjamin (Judg 20:18). To its credit, Israel is asking for divine direction. YHWH answers immediately by saying that Judah should go first. God's response in this setting seems to imply that the deity thought Israel was unquestionably right to exact punishment on Benjamin.

YHWH had all but guaranteed Israel's victory in the response to their question, which makes Israel's subsequent defeat difficult to comprehend (Judg 20:19-21). What went wrong? How did Israel, who was fighting for such a righteous cause, get beaten so badly by a group who was defending its fellow tribesmen despite such indefensible actions?

Instead of posing the question that is on the reader's mind, Israel gathers itself for a second round of fighting. Once again they seek YHWH's favor, this time praying much more fervently as testified by shed tears (Judg 20:22-23). And, once more they receive divine approval when the deity proclaimed, "Go up against them." Perhaps Israel's tears would do the trick this time around. Amazingly, however, Israel suffers yet another defeat, even though they lost fewer soldiers on this second occasion (Judg 20:24-25). Still, losing first 22,000 troops and then 18,000 troops is tough to spin as much of an improvement! Righteous Israel is being thoroughly defeated by unrighteous Benjamin. What gives? Is God playing games?

Two humiliating military reversals notwithstanding, Israel figures the third time might be the charm. When they appeal to YHWH this time around we get some clues about what had gone amiss during the first two battles. Keep in mind the formula that frames these last two stories in the book of Judges, the full form of which is, "In those days there was no king in Israel; each did what was right in their own eyes" (Judg 17:6; 21:25). Even the abbreviated version of this formulaic saying implicitly alludes to the fuller version (Judg 18:1; 19:1). This suggests that even though the men of Gibeah had acted abominably against the Levite's wife/concubine, the rest of Israel had not demonstrated their loyalty and covenant commitments to the deity who had elected them and made them a people. This conclusion is warranted by paying close attention to Israel's approach to God prior to the first two military encounters and then prior to the final encounter, which had a different result.

Initially, when Israel approached the deity we are told that they "inquired of God" (Judg 20:18). To our modern ears, that seems just fine. But Israel's God had a distinctive, personal name: *YHWH*. Israel's inquiry in this first instance was more or less to a generic deity—*'Ělōhîm*. Note that Israel approached *God*, but *YHWH* responded. It is as though Israel had forgotten how to address their own deity. When they approached God the second time, they did a little better. This time Israel wept before *YHWH* all day long and then inquired of *YHWH* (Judg 20:23). But that was insufficient. The third time explains everything. After this second defeat, *all the Israelites* (kol-bᵉnê Yiśrāʾēl) and *all the troops* (wᵉkol-hāʿām) repaired to Bethel, a religious center, and wept as they sat there before *YHWH*. Moreover, they fasted until evening, made various offerings before *YHWH*, and they engaged in these activities with the ark of the covenant in proximity along with the priestly presence of Phinehas, who was part of Aaron's line. As well, when they inquire of *YHWH*, they are much more diffident, asking whether they should once more go against Benjamin or not (Judg 20:26–28). Israel seems to be getting its religious act together.

YHWH's response confirms this. The LORD's fuller response illustrates that it had been some time since Israel had been in contact with God or had heard their God correctly. YHWH now tells Israel to go into battle for "tomorrow I will give them (i.e., the Benjaminites) into your hand" (Judg 20:28). This is exactly how God had first directed Israel at the beginning of the book of Judges (Judg 1:2). Apparently, that was a divine signal that God was behind the Israelite effort. The first two divine responses in this episode that eventuated in Israelite defeat were signals that something was amiss (Judg 20:18, 23). God was saying, in effect, "Go ahead, but you are on your own." The more fulsome appeal on Israel's part elicited a fulsome response from YHWH. Israel's defeating Benjamin was now assured, even though it required deft military maneuvers (Judg 20:29–48).

THE AFTERMATH

This victory notwithstanding, Israel's divisions continued to multiply. What happens next borders on the absurd. Benjamin's destruction was not total because six hundred troops were able to escape and hide for four months (Judg 20:47). In the meantime, we learn that while at Mizpah Israelites had sworn never to let any of their daughters marry Benjaminite men (Judg 21:1). Clearly, this was the result of abominable behavior, namely, the Benjaminite rapists and the later defense of these rapists on the part of the whole tribe of Benjamin. This tribe had become a pariah in Israel. Still, Benjamin was part of Israel. In light of this vow made at Mizpah, the rest of Israel now realized that Benjamin would soon be extinct (Judg 21:2–3). This led Israel to think of other options to save Benjamin from disappearing altogether. After some religious activities (Judg 21:4), they wondered aloud whether there had been anyone in Israel who had not answered the call to arms to go against Benjamin (Judg 21:5). Recall that failing to answer the call to arms or being upset at not being called had been a problem in several accounts in the book of Judges. As it turned out, no one from Jabesh-Gilead had gone to Mizpah to join the Israelite assembly in this cause (Judg 21:8–9). Refusing to serve in this instance was punishable by death (Judg 21:5). That meant that everyone in Jabesh-Gilead was now liable to capital punishment.

This came in the form of slaughtering the whole population. Israelites were now doing to other Israelites what was typically reserved for Canaanites, Israel's perpetual stereotypical enemies (Judg 21:10–11). However, not every inhabitant in Jabesh-Gilead was killed. Four hundred virgins were spared and brought back to Shiloh (Judg 21:12). At this point, the six hundred men who had fled when Benjamin had faced the rest of Israel were informed of the availability of these women (Judg 21:13). However, there were six hundred men and only four hundred women to serve as wives. This was deemed as insufficient. Somehow, it did not occur to anyone that the Benjaminite population could be built up with four hundred marriages and the children this would produce. Two hundred more women needed to be found!

Since Israel had already promised not to allow their daughters to marry Benjaminite men, and because only four hundred women were left from the slaughter at Jabesh-Gilead, another source for women had to be found. One absurdity leads to another! Another plot is hatched. This time it will not involve the military. Instead, an annual feast to YHWH held at Shiloh (Judg 21:19) will provide a solution. The Benjaminite men are instructed to hide in the nearby vineyards and wait. When the daughters of Shiloh come out to dance, the Benjaminite men will have a chance to abduct the women (Judg 21:20–21) and take them back to Benjaminite territory. To be sure, fathers and brothers of these dancing women were likely to object. When they do, the Benjaminites will justify their actions by asking the menfolk to be gracious since the women were not taken as captives in a war and were not given freely, which would have been a violation of the prior oath at Mizpah (Judg 21:22). The Benjaminite men carried out this ridiculous ploy perfectly. Benjamin was saved! It is utterly fitting that this story ends with the now familiar words, "In those days there was no king in Israel; everyone did what was right in their own eyes" (Judg 21:25).

CONCLUSION

It is difficult to describe this story. The content is almost impossible to stomach. At the same time, though the content is repugnant its placement is strategic. The beginning and ending story of any narrative complex will always be strategic. At the same time, even if most of this material is largely metaphorical it brings to the fore this disturbing question: What was it about division in Israel that required a story that was so lurid, so depraved, so downright disgusting that one tries (in vain!) to forget its contents? Even the attempts to deal with the consequences of almost obliterating Benjamin introduce preposterous efforts for solving the problem.

Yet, the objections that one might have to the story make the point. Division in Israel was considered as so problematic and devastating that a story like this was required. Division in Israel was figured by the concubine's being tortured by gang rape, by either dying after this awful ordeal or being killed when her husband butchered her. But a raped woman who was divided into twelve pieces also mirrored division in Israel's body politic. A divided woman mirrored a divided community. Israel's division could only be described with essentially pornographic depictions. As well, Israel's divided state was a function of its distance from God. *One* God had elected *one* people. But that people was no longer one. Throughout the book of Judges Israel was becoming more and more divided. That division finally eventuated in this final story. As sad as Israel's state is at this point in the larger biblical narrative, the expressed belief that things might improve were Israel to have a king turned out to be a hollow promise. Not only did Israelite kings not achieve Israelite unity, arguably they exacerbated Israel's tendency to divide.

Chapter 6

The First Divided Monarchy in Israel

Typically, commentators consider the narrative beginning at 1 Kings 11 as the prime example of Israel's divided monarchy. That is, indeed, a crucial period and will be treated later. However, prior to that infamous episode the material narrated in 2 Samuel 1–5 describes how Israel had already experienced two royal houses ruling over differing sections of its territory. This chapter focuses on that material.

SAUL'S DEATH: SETTING THE TABLE

At the outset, the first segment of this passage reports that Saul, who had been Israel's king for some time (since 1 Sam 10:1) is dead, and that David, who had been anointed as a replacement soon after Saul became king (1 Sam 16:13), had remained two days in Ziklag after enjoying a military victory (2 Sam 1:1). Those are significant details in the ongoing story but seem at this point somewhat prosaic. One expects a little more drama in the next narrative breath in that David will doubtlessly fill the political vacuum resulting from Saul's demise. But that does not happen immediately or, for that matter, anytime soon (in the narrative chronology). Plus, neither the report of Saul's death nor mention of David's military win are as straightforward as it first appears. As it happens, the details not only underscore the story's complexity, but also prompt us to recall how Saul and David arrived at this point. Both Saul's death and David's military exploit turn out to have been substantive events.

The narrative tantalizes by retarding David's reactions to Saul's death and instead merely noting that David had returned to Ziklag after defeating the Amalekites (2 Sam 1:1). This event was hardly business as usual. After all, God had already rejected Saul's kingship long ago precisely because of his failure to *proscribe* the Amalekites (1 Sam 15:10–11).[1] Granted, the prophet Samuel had previously denounced Saul (1 Sam 13:13–14), but it is unclear whether YHWH shared Samuel's perspective. Only Samuel condemned Saul when the king was deploying against the Philistines. To be sure, Samuel was YHWH's specially designated prophetic voice (1 Sam 3), such that what he said often was consonant with the will of the deity who had called him and for whom he spoke. But the overall narrative portrays Samuel as rather more complicated than simply a mouthpiece for God without remainder.

Keep in mind that when Israel's elders requested that Samuel "set up a king who will rule over us like all the nations" (1 Sam 8:5), this did not sit well with either the prophet or YHWH (1 Sam 8:6–7). At that time, the prophet and YHWH were on the same page. However, the elders had made this request because they were worried about Samuel's advanced age and the possibility that his corrupt sons would succeed him (1 Sam 8:3–4). Later on, Samuel tellingly did not mention his sons as one of the reasons for Israel's request for a king. The prophet instead accused Israel of demanding a king in reaction to the threat of Nahash the Ammonite king (1 Sam 12:12). But that was not true. Plus, when Samuel insisted that YHWH had rejected Saul and had already chosen someone else this made the prophet seem prescient even though he did not know whom God had in mind (1 Sam 13:13–14; 16:6–7). Was Samuel guilty of a bald-faced lie?

This ambiguity notwithstanding, there is no question at all about YHWH's ultimate decision regarding Saul in a second incident (1 Sam 15:10, 35). Because the king had failed to carry out the divine judgment directed against the Amalekites, YHWH was through with Saul and already had chosen someone else (1 Sam 15:10; 16:1). *Perhaps* YHWH was also disappointed with Saul's actions against Philistine forces (1 Sam 13), but there is no doubt whatsoever about what YHWH thought when Saul engaged the Amalekites.

Now, the Amalekites were no run-of-the-mill Israelite foe. When Israel was in the wilderness on the way to the promised land it encountered resistance from Amalek (Exod 17:8). Israel, under Joshua's leadership, was victorious in this confrontation (Exod 17:11, 13). YHWH's reaction to this

---

1. The Hebrew root *ḥrm*, whether in nominal or verbal form, has no precise English equivalent. Conventionally, it is translated "annihilate" or "proscribe." The term is virtually never used to describe conventional military activity. In the Old Testament, it refers to the severest form of divine judgment exercised against stereotypical reprobates, such as the Canaanites who resided in the promised land. See the excellent treatment from a biblical theological perspective by Earl, *Joshua Delusion* and *Reading Joshua as Christian Scripture*. See also Spina, "Irony," 27–43.

incident demonstrates Amalek's status as an extraordinary enemy—the deity was determined to erase from memory any recollection of this people (Exod 17:14). Right after YHWH's chilling pronouncement, Moses erected an altar, named it, and then pronounced that YHWH would war against Amalek in perpetuity (Exod 17:15). Amalek was special in that it inhabited the southern part of Canaan (Num 13:29) and thus was targeted as susceptible to proscription. Even Balaam predicted Amalek's eventual destruction (Num 24:20). Animosity against Amalek was enshrined by Moses' words the last time he spoke to Israel (Deut 25:17, 19).

Samuel had commanded Saul to finish the job of proscribing the Amelekites, but the king had failed. This was because Saul spared Agag, the Amalekite king, and also kept precious booty for Israel's own use (1 Sam 15:1-9). Both those actions were forbidden by the rules of engagement (Deut 20:1-20) for those residing in Canaan proper. This led to YHWH's ultimate denunciation and removal of Saul (1 Sam 15:10). In addition, Saul's disobedience allowed Amalek to stay in the land and be around for other Israelites to face (1 Sam 27:8). When David dealt with Amalek later, he was in effect taking care of Saul's unfinished business (1 Sam 27:8-9). Given this, what could be more ironic than that the messenger who reported about Saul's death was none other than an Amalekite (2 Sam 1:8, 13)?

Without question, this Amalekite, who does not identify himself as such immediately, lies to David that he was responsible for Saul's death. The actual manner of Saul's death—suicide after being gravely wounded—had already been made explicit by the narrator (1 Sam 31:4-6).[2] Almost certainly, the man reporting to David in this episode is attempting to ingratiate himself to a man for whom Saul's death would prove to be most convenient. When he arrives, he makes a public display of his sorrow for the news he is about to offer and is appropriately deferential to David (2 Sam 1:4). This man reveals that he has just come from the Israelite camp and therefore has firsthand knowledge. His alleged eye-witness account is that Israel has suffered a terrible reversal, made even worse by the deaths of Saul and Jonathan, his son (2 Sam 1:3-4). David then inquires how the man was sure that Saul and Jonathan had been killed. The man answers by noting that by chance (*niqrō'*) he happened to see Saul leaning on his spear after the king had been wounded and as enemy soldiers were fast approaching. Upon

---

2. When there is a discrepancy between the implied narrator and a character in a story, the former is always to be presumed as truthful. Without this assumption, no narrative could ever work at a literary level. Contrary to older commentaries that in this case we have contradictory sources about how Saul died, a literary perspective requires that we believe the account in 1 Sam 31, because it derives from the narrator, and disbelieve the account from the Amalekite.

being noticed by the king, the man reports that Saul asked who he was. He admitted that he told Saul that he was an Amalekite, whereupon the king went on to request that the man put him out of his misery. This, the man explained, he did, after which he stripped Saul of his crown and armlet to bring them to David (2 Sam 1:5–10).

The Amalekite badly misjudged in thinking his account would endear him to David. David's immediate response to the report of Saul's and Jonathan's deaths, which he obviously believed, was to mourn formally for the rest of the day, as did David's men (2 Sam 1:11–12). Even though the man had already said that he had identified himself to Saul as an Amalekite, David put the question to him again, as though he were doubting the man's story. When the man repeated that he was, indeed, an Amalekite, David asked another, more penetrating question: How did he have the temerity to take the life of YHWH's anointed (2 Sam 1:13–14)? It needs to be kept in mind that David himself refused to harm Saul twice when he had the chance (1 Sam 24:3–7, 8–15; 26:9–12, 13–16, 23). In both instances David expressed his conviction that it was not up to him to harm someone whom YHWH had anointed (1 Sam 24:6, 10; 26:9, 11, 16). Consequently, for his efforts in seeking favor with David, doubtlessly surmising that he would be rewarded with treasure or office, he was summarily executed on David's orders (2 Sam 1:15). It did not make any difference that David had no way of knowing that Saul had killed himself. The Amalekite had implicated himself with his own false testimony (2 Sam 1:16).

DAVID'S LAMENT

Having dispatched the offending Amalekite, David turned to composing a lament over Saul and Jonathan (2 Sam 1:19–27). Though the Hebrew text is difficult, it appears that David provided for the lament to be widely published, as it were (2 Sam 1:18). Three times in the dirge, David grieves that the "mighty have fallen" (2 Sam 1:19, 25, 27). He deplores the possibility that the Philistines will gloat over this tragic news (2 Sam 1:20) and underscores climatic reactions to Israel's defeat (2 Sam 1:21). David praises both Saul and Jonathan as heroic soldiers who fought in tandem and whose physical prowess was unmatched (2 Sam 1:23). While David urges Israel to weep over Saul for his efforts in the people's behalf, he reserves his most personal comments for his deep friendship with Jonathan (2 Sam 1:24, 25b–26).

On the surface, David's lament appears to be straightforward. But appearances can be deceiving. Some scholars have argued that there are subtle hints in the poem that laud Jonathan at the expense of Saul, who was, after all, the king.³ Instead of entering that debate, let alone settling it, there is sufficient material in the larger narrative to suggest that David's lament may indicate mixed emotions. From the beginning, Saul looked askance at David. Saul took issue with the women praising David while diminishing the king's reputation (1 Sam 18:6-9). The monarch was so incensed at this sleight, that he threw a spear at David (twice!) while playing the lute—as he had been appointed to do (1 Sam 16:14-23)—when God's evil spirit afflicted Saul (1 Sam 18:10-11). Saul also realized that YHWH was *with* David, and therefore aiding him (1 Sam 18:12-15). It did not help—from Saul's point of view—that *all* Israel and Judah loved David (1 Sam 18:16). Twice Saul used the pretext of offering his daughters to David in marriage in the hopes that the Philistines would kill him in battle or later when asking absurdly for one hundred Philistine foreskins as a bridal price (1 Sam 18:17-30).

Saul even put out a contract on David (1 Sam 19:1). Fortunately, Jonathan let David know of this plot and later pled to his father to give up these nefarious schemes. Though Jonathan calmed his father down temporarily, Saul relapsed and once more tried to kill David when he was strumming his instrument in response to YHWH's evil spirit (1 Sam 19:2-10). Saul even attempted to assassinate David when he was in his own home, only to be thwarted this time by Michal, the king's daughter, and David's wife (1 Sam 19:11-17). Were it not for divine help, David's days would have been numbered (1 Sam 19:18-24).

In this light, David could be forgiven for being less than distraught when he heard about Saul's death. Nevertheless, David did not respond in kind when he had the opportunity. As already mentioned, David twice had the chance to take the king's life but refrained out of respect for YHWH's anointed (1 Sam 24:6, 10; 26:9, 11, 16). Still, that may have indicated David's consideration for the office, so to speak, rather than any personal affection *per se*.

Jonathan was another matter, however. Early on Jonathan was fond of David (1 Sam 18:1). Indeed, it is difficult to ignore Jonathan's making a covenant with David as well as the obvious symbolism of giving his own robe, armor, sword, bow, and girdle to David (1 Sam 18:3-4). As time passed, Jonathan's affection for and commitment to David did not wane in the least (1 Sam 20:1-29, 32-42). Clearly, Saul was fully aware of the implications of Jonathan's relationship with David (1 Sam 20:30-31), though this did not deter the scion from helping his dear friend every chance he got. Jonathan's commitment to David was, in fact, so profound that he relinquished any claim he had to succeed his father. Instead, he insisted that David would rule

---

3. Linafelt, "Private Poetry," 497-526.

over Israel—something that he admitted that even Saul knew—and that he himself would have no trouble taking second place (1 Sam 23:17). If David's lament elevated Jonathan over Saul, however subtly, this made perfect sense in light of the relationships David had respectively with the two men. In any case, whether completely evenhanded or not, or entirely sincere or not, David's public display of his personal grief over the loss of Saul and Jonathan was apparently sufficient.

TWO RULING HOUSES

Subsequent to his lament over Saul and Jonathan, David makes a move toward taking political control. He asks YHWH whether he should go up to any city in Judah. God responds affirmatively and then specifies Hebron (2 Sam 2:1). David goes to Hebron, accompanied by two of his wives and his men with their households. Once in Hebron, the men of Judah go there as well to anoint David as king of the House of Judah (2 Sam 2:2–4a).

It had been a while since the prophet Samuel anointed David to be Saul's successor, an action that YHWH had orchestrated and later confirmed (1 Sam 16:13). As the story unfolds, YHWH affirms David in one way or another several times. YHWH answers David when he inquires (1 Sam 23:2, 4), which is in stark contrast to Saul's inability to contact the deity (1 Sam 28:6). The deity even informs David about the intentions Saul had in mind when plotting against David's life, making sure that he remains unharmed (1 Sam 23:6–14). Equally, YHWH takes Nabal's life, which works to David's advantage, and also induces slumber on Saul's men when David is in danger (1 Sam 25:38; 26:12). Jonathan not only revealed that his father knew that David would eventually be king (1 Sam 23:17), but Saul admitted as much himself (1 Sam 24:20). Indeed, when Samuel appeared to Saul in a ghostly form, the prophet confirmed that David was YHWH's choice (1 Sam 28:17). Therefore, when the men of Judah anointed David as king they were simply following, in effect, a well-established precedent.

The first action David takes after having been anointed in Hebron is to commend the inhabitants of Jabesh-Gilead for retrieving Saul's body and giving it a proper burial (1 Sam 31:11–13; 2 Sam 2:4b–7). Given the location of Jabesh-Gilead, north of Judah and across the river in Transjordan, David might have been doing a little politicking. If so, that does not necessarily mean that David was being insincere. We do not know at this point whether David even knew of counter political strategies being implemented elsewhere in Israelite territory.

Regardless of what David may have been thinking at the time, Abner, Saul's commander, lost no time in seeing to it that the House of Saul would not give up political power without a struggle. He brought Ishbosheth, one of Saul's sons, to Mananaim—part of Transjordan—and made him king over Gilead, the Ashurites, Jezreel, Ephraim, Benjamin, and all Israel (*wᵉ'al-Yiśrā'ēl kullō*) (2 Sam 2:8–9). Ishbosheth would rule over this territory for two years while David would reign in Judah for seven and a half years (2 Sam 2:10–11). Israel now had to deal with two kings.

The rivalry between these two ruling houses is illustrated by a bizarre, ritualized military *game* that had dire consequences. On one side was Abner and Ishbosheth's servants and on the other was Joab, Abner's counterpart, and David's servants (2 Sam 2:12–13). These two groups met at a pool in Gibeon, where each group sat on the pool's respective sides (2 Sam 2:13). Abner then suggests to Joab that the men get up and *play* (*wîśaḥăqû*). What this verb means in this context is not clear. What sort of sport would have such deadly consequences? Or, was it a scrimmage of some kind—preliminary to a bigger battle? Whatever it was, it was beyond strange.

Each side had exactly twelve men. As they engaged each other, they each grabbed the other's head—how exactly is hard to visualize—and then proceeded to thrust their swords into each other. That this was done simultaneously and with predictable results is underscored by the cryptic statement: "and they fell together" (*wayyippᵉlû yaḥdāw*). This peculiar encounter was responsible for renaming a section in Gibeon (2 Sam 2:14–16). As though this contest were not outlandish enough, we learn that even though the twelve men grabbed and stabbed their rivals at the same time and collapsed together, David's forces somehow had won (2 Sam 2:17)! How that could be is not explained. One way or the other, however, David improved his political standing in this first confrontation with the remnants of Saul's forces.

The aftermath of this skirmish is equally odd. Abner had fled from this scene, hotly pursued by Joab and his two brothers, Abishai and Asahel. Asahel's ability to run fast is noted, allowing him to easily catch up with Abner (2 Sam 2:18–20). When this happens, Abner attempts to get Asahel to back off by urging him to get spoil from someone else, presumably one of Ishbosheth's soldiers (2 Sam 2:21). Asahel ignores the suggestion. Abner once more tries to get Asahel to desist. This time Abner hopes aloud that bloodshed might be avoided because he does not know how he could look Joab in the eye after having killed his brother. When Asahel persists, Abner reluctantly kills him (2 Sam 2:22–23).

But Abner only took care of one of his pursuers; Joab and Abishai were not as speedy but apparently just as determined as their brother had been

(2 Sam 2:24). The chase took on another dimension when the Benjaminites came to Abner's aid (2 Sam 2:25). Just when it looked as though a battle was brewing, Abner asks Joab how long he is willing to settle matters with the sword, especially since the bitter outcome is so predictable. Abner also plays the fraternity card. He wants to know how much longer Joab is willing to allow his people to run down their *brothers* (2 Sam 2:26). In the light of how Saul and his people, including Abner, had been hunting David in an effort to destroy him, this plea for a cessation of violence rings hollow. Astonishingly, Joab accepts Abner's logic, or, at least it seems so given the ambiguous Hebrew here. Joab basically says that, had not Abner spoken in this manner his troops would have given up the pursuit the next morning (2 Sam 2:27). Now, Joab is willing to call off the pursuit immediately, which he does. Temporarily, at least, a cease fire between the *brothers*—Israelites and Judahites—was in place (2 Sam 2:28).

The two groups therefore disengaged. Abner and those with him returned to Mahanaim in Transjordan (2 Sam 2:29). Joab and his entourage gathered in an undisclosed location and counted their losses, which added up to nineteen men in addition to Asahel (2 Sam 2:30). But these losses were insignificant in comparison to the damage done to Abner's army: three hundred sixty killed in action (2 Sam 2:31). After David's group buried Asahel in Bethlehem, Joab marched back to Hebron as this episode concludes (2 Sam 2:32). The conflict between the two houses ruling in Israel had begun, with David's house slightly ahead, but it was not over yet.

Divine activity in this episode is only implicit. YHWH had instructed David to reside in Hebron, but that was the extent of the deity's involvement (2 Sam 2:1). At the same time, Saul's house had long since been denounced and basically removed from power by YHWH (1 Sam 15:10-11, 17-29). From YHWH's perspective, Saul's rule had been rendered illegitimate. One has to surmise that David's house will eventually supplant Saul's house—now led by Ishbosheth, Saul's son propped up by Abner—but right now this is being played out via raw political actions.

THE CONTINUING WAR BETWEEN THE TWO RULING HOUSES

The ongoing war between the two political factions extends into an indeterminate future. While the conflict remains, however, it is hardly a stalemate. As time goes on, David's position gets stronger while Saul's gets weaker (2 Sam 3:1). That Saul is mentioned at this point lets us know that this is a contest between two dynasties. Even though the House of Saul has not been acknowledged as legitimate since the infamous encounter with the Amalekites (1 Sam 15), Saul and his people acted as though nothing had happened. What would it take for the House of Saul to relinquish control? That remains to be seen.

In the meantime, however, the listing of David's wives and his sons born in Hebron attests to his growing strength. No fewer than six wives are mentioned: Ahinoam (1 Sam 25:43; 27:3; 30:5; 2 Sam 2:2); Abigail (1 Sam 25; 27:3; 30:5; 2 Sam 2:2); Maacah (daughter of a king, Talmai of Geshur); Haggith; Shephatiah; Ithream. Death has most recently plagued Saul's house—the king himself and the heir to the throne both died in the same battle. While there is a pall on Saul's house, birth announcements—of sons, no less—grace David's house. One house laments death, the other celebrates new life. One house is diminishing. The other is increasing. This circumstance bodes well for David's house but bodes ill for Saul's (2 Sam 3:2–5).

ABNER BETRAYS ISHBOSHETH

Because of internal difficulties in Saul's camp, David had an unexpected gift fall into his lap. Abner was gaining strength in Saul's house (2 Sam 3:6). Of course, he had already put forward Ishbosheth as king (2 Sam 2:9), suggesting considerable political influence. Perhaps Abner's ambition exceeded that of being a mere kingmaker, since he apparently was having an affair with Rizpah, one of Saul's former concubines (2 Sam 3:7). Such behavior could be construed as a power play (e.g., 2 Sam 16:20-23; 1 Kgs 2:19-22). Ishbosheth accused Abner of exactly that. Instead of denying the accusation, Abner flew into a rage. He threatened to withdraw support from Ishbosheth and do whatever it took to help David become king over Israel (= the northern territory) *and* Judah (= the southern territory) (2 Sam 3:6-10). Ishbosheth's passive reaction to this threat revealed who truly wielded power in the House of Saul (2 Sam 3:11).

Abner wasted no time in getting word to his erstwhile enemy. He offered to make a pact with David, pledging that he would deliver Israel to him on a silver platter (2 Sam 3:12). It is hardly surprising that David jumped at the chance, but with a condition. He demanded that Michal, Saul's daughter, to whom he had once been married, be returned to him (2 Sam 3:13-14; 1 Sam 18:20-29; 25:44). Possibly, David made this request to test Abner's sincerity, or surmised that it would be beneficial to reestablish his prior relationship with Saul's family, or simply to reunite with a woman for whom he still cared. Maybe all three of these elements were a factor.

Though he struck the deal with Abner, David issues the order instead to Ishbosheth (2 Sam 3:14). Eschewing any attempt at diplomacy, David commands Ishbosheth as if he were a foot soldier, and the hapless son of Saul immediately obeys. This results in a pitiful scene. Ishbosheth took Michal from her current husband, Paltiel of Laish, who followed her while weeping until Abner intervened to tell the poor man to go home (2 Sam 3:15–16).

Michal had once loved David (1 Sam 18:20) and had later thwarted her father's plan to assassinate him (1 Sam 19:11–17). But Saul decided to renege on his agreement (1 Sam 18:21–27) with David by giving Michal to Palti/Paltiel (1 Sam 25:44). This was a crass, cruel, and completely political move on Saul's part. But might not a similar accusation be leveled at David when he demanded Michal back? Neither Michal nor Paltiel were given any choice in the matter. They were simply pawns in a game of *Realpolitik*. In any case, Michal returned to David while Paltiel returned home. One wonders, however, whether Michal's later negative reaction to David's carrying on when the ark was brought into the City of David was a residual effect of this incident (2 Sam 6:16–23).

Abner now puts into motion the actions necessary for the transfer of power. He appeals to the elders of Israel by reminding them that they have for some time been desirous of having David rule over Israel. Whether Abner is fudging the truth, he goes right on to the next point by urging the representatives to make this happen. He even quotes YHWH as expressing his preference for David as the means for rescuing Israel from the Philistines (2 Sam 3:17–18). That Israel is never depicted as wanting David to be king or that YHWH's quote is nowhere to be found in the previous narrative seems not to bother anyone. A transfer of power is underway. Also, Abner confers with Benjamin, Saul's (and Abner's) tribal home, because that group would have cared most about the fate of the House of Saul. Evidently, the negotiations went well because Abner was able to tell David that the arrangements with all the parties had been made (2 Sam 3:19).

In preparation for what was about to take place, David entertained Abner and the twenty men who accompanied him by giving a feast. Abner at that juncture let David know that he would see to any other arrangements necessary for the transfer of power. David gave leave to Abner to make necessary arrangements (2 Sam 3:20–21). We are told that Abner left David *in peace* ($b^e\check{s}\bar{a}l\hat{o}m$).

But that is about to change and change dramatically. Joab and some of David's men had just returned from a raid right after Abner left. That David had sent Abner away *in peace* is repeated (2 Sam 3:22). When Joab is informed that Abner had been in Hebron only a short time earlier and that

David had let him go *in peace*, Joab rushes to David and tries to persuade him that Abner was being traitorous (2 Sam 3:23-26). Before David had a chance to respond to his angry military officer, Joab sent messengers to catch up to Abner so that he could be brought back to Hebron. David knew nothing of this, however (2 Sam 3:26). The fact that Joab sent *messengers* rather than troops to fetch Abner likely meant that Abner thought everyone in David's administration was on the same page about what was transpiring. Abner was even willing to speak privately with Joab in the gate, where business is often conducted. But that was a mistake. Joab avenged Asahel by killing Abner right then and there (2 Sam 3:27).

Joab's action was enormously inconvenient politically for David. As soon as he hears about the assassination, David proclaims his personal innocence and proceeds to curse Joab and his family (2 Sam 3:28-29). It did not matter a whit to David that Joab had done this for personal reasons (2 Sam 3:30). Murdering Abner was not in David's political interests. After all, Abner had orchestrated events that would eventuate in David's ruling all of Israel. Plus, Abner was himself a Benjaminite, a group that would have to be appeased since Saul and his family were positively regarded by that tribe.

David had to do some damage control. To that end, he ordered Joab and his troops to don sack cloth to make at least a pretense of mourning Abner's death during a public funeral (2 Sam 3:31). The king ensured that his mourning was noticeable—he lifted up his voice and wept. The people—*all* of them—joined him in this display (2 Sam 3:32). In David's eulogy, he pointed out that Abner had been a victim of evil forces. That prompted another public display of weeping (2 Sam 3:32-34). David went so far as to fast for the rest of the day and made sure everyone was aware of his gesture. It worked. The people were impressed with the king's reaction to Abner's death and concluded that he had had nothing to do with it (2 Sam 3:35-37). The scene concludes when David laments that a *prince* and *great man* (*śar wᵉgādôl*) had fallen this day and complains once more about the sons of Zeruiah, that is, Joab and his brothers. As a finishing touch, David hopes YHWH will deal with their wickedness (2 Sam 3:38-39).

ISHBOSHETH ASSASSINATED

The news of Abner's death was alarming not only to *Saul's son*—as the Hebrew text has it—but to *all Israel* as well (2 Sam 4:1). Since *all Israel* had responded positively to Abner's previous machinations to elevate David as king over both houses (2 Sam 3:17-21), the group referred to as *all Israel* in this instance must mean those who were still loyal to Ishbosheth. Both had good reason to find it sobering that Abner had died at Hebron, for this meant that he had been at David's headquarters, almost surely for nefarious purposes.

Incongruously, right after we are informed about this reaction in the House of Saul to Abner's death, we have characters introduced whose roles remain mysterious, at least for a while. Two captains of raiding bands are presented: Baanah and Rechab. Both are sons of Rimmon, a Benjaminite. These folk once lived in Beeroth, which was part of Benjaminite territory, before being forced for unexplained reasons to take up residence in Gittaim (2 Sam 4:2–3). We will have to wait to see why these two were introduced in the first place. But it does not take much imagination to speculate that their roles will be anything but positive. In any case, this information retards the drama that was intimated initially.

If we expected the drama to continue apace in the next narrative breath, we are disappointed. Having been told about these two mysterious captains, we are then informed about Jonathan's son Mephibosheth and how it came about that he had been crippled (2 Sam 4:4). How Mephibosheth is subsequently treated will be a feather in David's cap, for it will show how he kept his original pledge to take care of Jonathan's family (1 Sam 20:13–17; 2 Sam 9:10; 19:30 [Eng. 19:29]; 21:7). At present, however, there is no indication that David even knows about the existence of Jonathan's son.

After this pause, the two raiders are back on the scene (2 Sam 4:5). They head straight to Ishbosheth's home to do him harm, though no motivation is indicated. He was napping at the time. That much is clear. Though it is obvious Ishbosheth is killed while in bed, the details are hard to make out because of an extremely difficult Hebrew text. Many translators use the Greek Bible at 2 Sam 4:6. The Hebrew text notes that the two men got to the middle of the house "as though fetching wheat" (JPS). Wheat had not been mentioned (except in the Greek text). Plus, who goes into a house to procure wheat? In any case, the assassins struck Ishbosheth in the stomach—presumably with a sword or dagger—and fled. Curiously, the very next verse repeats the event with added details (2 Sam 4:7). Nothing is said about where Ishbosheth had been stabbed in this iteration, but we do learn that he was not only murdered but decapitated. Again, the particulars are fuzzy except for the fact that the two captains have carried out this *hit*.

It turns out that there was a purpose for the decapitation. Rechab and Baanah brought this grisly trophy to David and announced triumphantly that they had been responsible for taking out "your enemy, who sought your life." They also justified their actions as being against not only Ishbosheth, but on "Saul and his offspring" (2 Sam 4:8). But David would have none of this. Citing the previous example of his ordering the execution of the man who had told him about Saul's death, he saw to it that these two men were summarily executed, too. For good measure, he had their corpses mutilated and hanged. The episode concluded when David arranged for a proper burial for Ishbosheth (2 Sam 4:9-12).

Even if David is being transparently sympathetic to Saul's royal family, these circumstances could not have been more favorable if he had cynically put them in motion himself. Abner was arguably the one in Saul's camp that wielded the most power. He was now gone and no longer a concern. Ishbosheth, though the titular head of Saul's House, had been weak from the start. His days were numbered as soon as Abner defected. Once he was killed, David did not need to worry about a surviving potential king in Saul's house. In terms of public consumption, David was able to curry favor with the people who had supported the House of Saul without his having to lift a finger to orchestrate its removal.

DAVID BECOMES THE SOLE KING OF ISRAEL

With the House of Saul completely diminished, David is poised to be king of all Israel. Consequently, *all the tribes of Israel* (*kol-šibṭê Yiśrā'ēl*) went to Hebron to swear their collective fealty to David (2 Sam 5:1). They declared their kinship with David and, equally, they acknowledged that even when Saul was king in name it was David's actions that demonstrated his leadership qualities. This accorded with YHWH's will, who all along wanted David to be Israel's shepherd and prince (2 Sam 5:2). Israel's elders then made a covenant with David and anointed him as king, completing the plans Abner had in mind before he was assassinated (2 Sam 5:3; 3:17-19). Though he had ruled Judah for a little more than seven years, David was about to rule over *all Israel and Judah* for thirty-three years (2 Sam 5:5). The first divided monarchy was now over.

David then captured Jerusalem and made the city Israel's capitol (2 Sam 5:6-9). Though much had been accomplished through old-fashioned political maneuvering, YHWH was pleased with and had a hand in at least some of the results (2 Sam 5:10). No longer vying for political position, David was free to engage in diplomatic relationships. He therefore procured from Hiram, the king of Tyre, material and workers for David's own palace in Jerusalem (2 Sam 5:11). David was aware that in one way or another YHWH was largely responsible for this favorable outcome (2 Sam 5:12).

Just as earlier the reporting of sons being born to David's wives in Hebron indicated his growing strength vis-à-vis Ishbosheth, so his acquiring more wives and more children in Jerusalem underscores how he continued to increase his power (2 Sam 5:13–16).

The last time Saul faced the Philistine threat, he *inquired* (*wayyiš'al*) of YHWH and received no answer (1 Sam 28:6). But when David was dealing with a threat from the same enemy, he *inquired* (*wayyiš'al*) of YHWH and got an immediate positive answer (2 Sam 5:19). David's success in this battle was never in doubt (2 Sam 5:20–21). The next time David inquired (*wayyiš'al*) YHWH not only replied positively but volunteered battlefield strategy to boot (2 Sam 5:22–25). It had been a very long time, indeed, since Samuel anointed David to be Israel's king (1 Sam 16:13), but now that he was king in fact and not simply theory, and now that the House of Saul was no longer operative, *all Israel* was in good hands.

CONCLUSION

Arguably, this is something of a reversal among the division stories. This is because in this episode, Israel begins divided and ends up being unified. Throughout the narrative in 1 Samuel David has already been anointed at God's behest to replace the failed kingship of Saul. But Saul does not go quietly. He maintains power and does everything possible to get rid of David. But David is still standing when Saul is killed. However, though Jonathan likewise was lost in battle, the House of Saul, though greatly weakened, retained its grip on part of Israel. Still, it was only a matter of time before David's growing strength proved too much for the ebbing strength of the House of Saul. Thus, only for a brief period, Israel had two ruling factions. When the dust had settled, David was in charge and unrivaled by any counter political faction. Israel now enjoyed unity. That was the circumstance during the final years of David's reign. David's son would rule also over a unified Israel, but that unity would come crashing down at the end of that son's kingship. Unity in Israel is at best ephemeral.

Chapter 7

Absalom's Revolt: King David Flees and Israel Divides

DAVID'S IRONIC SELF-CONDEMNATION

It is impossible to deal with the story of Absalom's revolt without paying attention to what led to this disaster. Absalom's actions were triggered by the behavior and the words of his father, King David. David had slept with Bath-Sheba, Uriah the Hittite's wife. When she became pregnant from this liaison David had Uriah murdered (2 Sam 11:1-22). Once Uriah was gone, David married Bath-Sheba. YHWH was angry at this outrage and sent Nathan the prophet to confront the king (2 Sam 12:1).

Nathan called David on the carpet by telling him a simple story. Two men, one rich and one poor, lived in the same city. The rich man's wealth came from his numerous flocks and herds. In contrast, the poor man had a single ewe lamb that he treated as a pet. When a traveler came once to see the rich man, the latter greedily took the poor man's pet and served it as a meal for his visitor (2 Sam 12:1-4).

David blew his stack when he heard this story. The king thought that this offense required a death penalty. If not that ultimate punishment, then David suggested that a man who was capable of such abominable behavior should restore fourfold what he had taken from the poor man. Totally oblivious of his hypocrisy, David could not understand how someone could act without a scintilla of compassion (2 Sam 12:5-6). Of course, David condemned himself with those remarks. At that point, Nathan said pointedly, "You are the man" (2 Sam 12:7).

Then Nathan denounced David (2 Sam 12:7–12). Reminding him how graciously YHWH had treated him, the prophet warned that the sword would never depart from the royal house (2 Sam 12:10). Evil would eventually arise from within David's own family. The punishment would include David's being forced to watch his own wives being taken over by another man. All Israel would witness this spectacle (2 Sam 12:11–12). Though David repented when Nathan was finished, and was even absolved, the consequences of the king's sins nevertheless remained (2 Sam 12:13–14).

The first consequence was the death of the baby Bath-Sheba was carrying (2 Sam 12:14). As it turned out, David's blurting out that the rich man in the story should pay fourfold for his vile deed became an uncannily accurate prophecy. Before David's story is concluded, his family, more specifically, his children, will undergo a series of calamities. As noted, Bath-Sheba's baby died (2 Sam 12:19).[1] Subsequently, in a tragic sequence of events, David's daughter, Tamar, would be raped by her half-brother, Amnon (2 Sam 13:1–14). That half-brother would then be killed by Tamar's full-brother, Absalom (2 Sam 13:23–29). Finally, Absalom would be assassinated after he fomented rebellion against his father's own administration (2 Sam 18:14–15). As David had ironically demanded when he reacted to Nathan's story, he himself would pay at least four times over for his wickedness. This has to be kept in mind as we evaluate Absalom's rebellion.

INTRODUCING ABSALOM

Though Absalom was originally introduced in a genealogical note listing David's sons (2 Sam 3:2–5), 2 Samuel 13 is the first time he has a significant role. The text underscores Absalom's importance by referring to Tamar, another crucial figure in this episode, as *Absalom's sister* rather than *David's daughter* (2 Sam 13:1). Another protagonist, Amnon, is referred to tellingly as *David's son*. Along with this information, we are told that Tamar was pretty. Unfortunately, this seemingly harmless description of the king's family quickly turns dark.

Amnon loved his attractive half-sister, but he could not make any headway with her since she had no sexual experience (2 Sam 13:1). Revealing that his feelings for her were confused, combining emotional attachment and lust, Amnon made himself sick because of this quandary (2 Sam

---

1. David did everything he could to urge Uriah, who had been fighting in David's army, to go home so that friends and neighbors would think that Bath-Sheba's baby belonged to her husband instead of King David. When the king's plan failed, he arranged to have Uriah killed on the battlefield (2 Sam 11:6–25).

13:2). Fortunately for Amnon and unfortunately for Tamar, he had a cousin, Jonadab, who was a manipulative chap (2 Sam 13:3). Upon noticing Amnon's depressed demeanor, he wanted to know what was wrong. Amnon told him the problem was that he loved Tamar. Curiously, he referred to her as *Absalom's sister* rather than *David's daughter*, or his own half-sister for that matter (2 Sam 13:4). Family dynamics are in play here. In any case, the conniving cousin came up with a plan. He encouraged Amnon to lie down, pretend to be ill, and then ask David when he stops by to tell Tamar to take care of her brother (i.e., Amnon) by preparing food and then bringing it to him. Suspecting nothing untoward, Tamar does not mind preparing a meal for her sick half-brother. But when she cooks and brings the food to Amnon, he crudely asks her for sex. She refuses his advances, and even scolds him for violating Israelite behavioral standards. Had she submitted to his blandishments, she maintained, both would be acting shamefully. To be sure, she was not averse to a possible marriage to Amnon—in those times that would have been permissible in spite of the blood relationship—but she wanted Amnon first to ask permission from their father. Amnon had no such intentions, so he overcame her and "laid her" (2 Sam 13:5–14).

Again, reflecting his twisted feelings, right after this rape Amnon suddenly hated Tamar with the same intensity that he had previously loved her (2 Sam 13:15). Once he committed this despicable act, he ordered her to leave, basically discarding her as though she was nothing to him. As contemptible as Amnon had been, in Tamar's mind his sending her away in this manner was even worse (2 Sam 13:16). Amnon was not fazed by her plea and made sure that he would no longer be bothered by having a servant lock her out of his quarters (2 Sam 13:17). Once she was locked out, she ripped the robe that she wore as an indication that she was a virgin daughter of the king, put ashes on her head as a sign of lament, and bewailed her plight (2 Sam 13:18–19).

Afterward, Absalom took Tamar under his wing. Though aware of what Amnon had done, Absalom pretended to downplay the rape by telling his sister not to make too much of what had happened and keep in mind that this was done by her brother. Tamar apparently took the advice to heart and said nothing more. But now she was living in Absalom's house as a desolate woman. When King David heard about Amnon's terrible deed, he was livid. But that was as far as it went, for the king did nothing. He seems to have failed miserably as a father and a king. As for Absalom, he did not let his feelings about what had happened be known. But where Absalom stood is confirmed by the narrator: he hated his half-brother (2 Sam 13:20–22).

Two years elapsed before Absalom found an opportunity for revenge. He set a trap by inviting all of his brothers and their father to a sheepshearing event. But the king thought the gathering would be burdensome for Absalom and therefore said no to the invitation. Even after Absalom insisted, David refused to attend but did give his son a blessing. Absalom then changed gears by asking David's permission to have Amnon accept the invitation. David was adamant and replied in the negative once more, but finally relented when Absalom pressed the matter. David himself would not go to this affair, but all his sons would. This played right into Absalom's hands. He instructed his servants to wait until Amnon had had too much to drink—heavy drinking was common when sheep are sheared—at which time Absalom would give the order to strike. Absalom's servants carried out his instructions at the opportune time. When Amnon fell, the other sons of the king who had been attending the event fled (2 Sam 13:23–29).

While the king's sons were heading home, word reached David that Absalom had killed *all* of his brothers. Obviously, David was shocked and grief stricken. Almost immediately, Jonadab defused the situation by telling David he had been misinformed and that only Amnon had been killed. Jonadab also fingered Absalom as the culprit for Amnon's death, but went on to explain to the king that the murder was hardly capricious in that Absalom acted because of Amnon's behavior. The cousin's appearance at just this moment makes us wonder whether he was responsible for the earlier false report. If so, was he trying to sow dissension in the royal family for ulterior reasons (2 Sam 13:30–33)? No answer to this question is forthcoming.

When the sons returned, Jonadab let David know. He apparently wanted the king to realize that his earlier report had been right about the rest of the princes. Jonadab keeps showing up at crucial points in this developing family drama. It is hard not to be suspicious that he seems to be intruding in the king's affairs to promote his own interests. In any case, when the sons get home, they weep over what had happened. David and his servants join them in this lamentation (2 Sam 13:34–36).

Though there is some ambiguity in Jonadab's inserting himself into these family dynamics, the end result is that Absalom fled and sought refuge with Talmai, Geshur's king. At this juncture, we learn that *he*—presumably, David—mourned over *his son*—presumably, Absalom—continually. Is there purposeful ambiguity here? That is, is David mourning over Absalom or Amnon? Should both sons be considered the reasons for David's lament? Though we cannot say for certain, what is clear is that David did nothing else about this horrible situation. Thus, Absalom spent three whole years in Geshur in a kind of self-imposed exile. Though the text at this point is problematic, it seems that David was sad about Absalom's extended absence. Again, however, he did nothing concrete to address Absalom's being gone for such a long time. All we know is that eventually David got over Amnon's death, though the king remained silent about the circumstance that had brought about these conflicts that were tearing the royal family apart (2 Sam 13:37–39). Sadly, the alienation between Absalom and his father, King David, was growing.

JOAB'S EFFORTS TO HAVE DAVID RECONCILE WITH ABSALOM

Joab, a well-positioned military officer in David's administration (2 Sam 8:16), now decided to enter into this fray. He had noticed the emotional toll that Absalom's absence was taking on David (2 Sam 14:1). To deal with this, he went to another clever person introduced into the narrative, a woman who lived in Tekoa. He persuaded her to act as though she were mourning and therefore needing David's counsel. Joab would coach her about what to say when she got the king's ear (2 Sam 14:2–3).

The woman did as Joab instructed. When she was in David's presence, the king asked her what was wrong. She spun a tale about having two sons, one of whom killed the other in a quarrel. The family consequently demands that the guilty brother die. She complains that were this to happen, her husband would be left without a name or legacy (2 Sam 14:4–7). Because the woman construed the family's response as directed against her, David issued a judgment in her and the remaining son's favor. Neither of them need fear any longer the family's seeking vengeance on her son or otherwise bothering her (2 Sam 14:8–11).

Just as Joab had planned, David took the bait. Once again David is susceptible to a tale (see 2 Sam 12:1–6). Once the woman had heard David's verdict, she deferentially asks permission to say something else. David allows this, at which point she accuses the king of plotting against God's people, in fact, of convicting himself, in that he has done nothing to restore his own son to his rightful place (2 Sam 14:12–13). The woman was saying that David's vision was insightful in the matter affecting her family but completely myopic about the circumstances in his own family.

At this point the clever woman waxes philosophical by remarking that everyone dies eventually—we are all like water poured on the ground that cannot be collected again (2 Sam 14:14). What she says next is difficult Hebrew, but the sense seems to be that God will not punish *you* (i.e., David) for bringing the banished one (i.e., Absalom) home.[2] She insisted that life is too short for David to hold a perpetual grudge against one son, notwithstanding his murdering another son. The woman goes on to flatter David as an angel

---

2. See the comment in the JPS's version, 491.

of God for the decision he made about her predicament (2 Sam 14:15–17). Obviously, in her puffing David for the brilliance of the solution he suggested for the woman's family made it difficult for the king not to conclude that a similar solution should obtain in his family.

David finally sees through the ruse when he asked the woman whether Joab had been behind her coming in the first place. She confesses as much, and then compliments David again. Joab's rationale, according to her, was his wanting to change the course of affairs. She goes on to say that in light of the king's impressive wisdom about the way the world works, David will understand why Joab acted in this way (2 Sam 14:18–20).

In the end, Joab's strategy worked. David ordered Joab to arrange for Absalom to return home. Joab retrieved Absalom from Geshur, but evidently not all was forgiven. Absalom was forced to stay in his own house when he returned. Worse, David refused to see his son (2 Sam 14:21–24).

Though he was unable to see his father, Absalom did have some things going for him. His natural good looks were such that all Israel noticed him. Plus, his family was growing. By now he had four children, three sons and one daughter. His daughter's name, Tamar, revealed how much he thought of his sister with the same name (2 Sam 14:25–27). This daughter was as beautiful as her namesake aunt. Nevertheless, none of this compensated for Absalom's continuing alienation from his father. He had been in Jerusalem for two years without any change in his situation, which amounted to being under house arrest as far as seeing his father was concerned (2 Sam 14:28). Counting the time he had spent in Geshur, it had been five years since Absalom had seen his father.

Absalom eventually took the initiative to break this impasse. Twice he sent word to Joab to come and see him, but Joab did not budge. Apparently, he felt that what he did with the clever woman from Tekoa was as far as he was willing to go to effect reconciliation. Joab's passivity at this juncture prompted Absalom to take desperate measures. He had his servants set Joab's fields on fire. This got Joab's attention! When he confronted Absalom about this outrageous ploy, Absalom complained that he would have been better off staying in Geshur. He demanded that Joab pull whatever strings necessary to get him an audience with the king. Absalom was throwing all caution to the wind. From his perspective, if his father wanted to kill him, then so be it (2 Sam 14:29–32). At long last, David relented and agreed to see his son. Absalom showed proper deference when he finally saw his father, and David kissed his son when they met (2 Sam 14:33). But the damage had already been done.

ABSALOM *STEALS* ISRAEL'S HEART

Given the perfunctory meeting when Absalom after a hiatus of five years met with his father, it is not surprising that the rift between the two men would have foreboding ramifications. Absalom's getting a chariot, having horses at his disposal, and procuring fifty men to *run* with him are actions that reflect a quasi-military operation (2 Sam 15:1). Why would Absalom need to project power at this stage? Almost immediately, we realize that Absalom is making an appeal to ordinary Israelites that calls into question David's administration.

Absalom's methods for undermining his father's government were hardly subtle. He would station himself early in the day at the gate where regular business was conducted. This is a site where the business of government was also done. Absalom set about to cast doubt on the likelihood that an Israelite could expect that judicial or perhaps financial claims could be dealt with justly and promptly. He had no compunction about telling those who had come to the gate seeking redress that, though their claims had merit, they could not get so much as a hearing because King David had not appointed anyone to hear the case (2 Sam 15:2-3).

But this was much more than an effort merely to badmouth his father's administrative ability. When he said to anyone who would listen that things would be greatly improved were he in charge, that Israelites could count on being judged fairly with him at the helm, his complaints transformed from being standard citizen disgruntlement with perceived governmental incompetence to borderline sedition. In time, this daily campaign for Israelite support became more and more successful. Either because of Absalom's rhetorical skills or the fact that there was an element of truth to his criticisms, or both, a critical mass of Israelites came to believe the king's son. Because Absalom's target was "all Israel who came to the king for judgment," and given how successful his efforts were, it is scarcely startling that eventually Absalom "stole the hearts of the men of Israel" (2 Sam 15:4-6). This was not yet a *coup d'état*, but it certainly set the table for one.

ABSALOM'S REBELLION

After an indeterminate period—the Hebrew text specifies forty years (!), surely a textual error—Absalom put a plan in motion. He asked King David for permission to travel to Hebron to pay a vow made when he was holed up in Geshur. While there, Absalom had promised YHWH to worship the deity at that site on the condition that he was brought back safely to Jerusalem.

Obviously, Absalom had been living in Jerusalem for some time now, so that it was appropriate for him to worship YHWH in Hebron, just as he vowed. Of course, no such vow was mentioned when the text recounts Absalom's sojourn in Geshur. Thus, it is a fair inference that Absalom had concocted this story. Regardless, Absalom was granted leave (2 Sam 15:7-9).

Then Absalom via spies spread the word throughout Israel that he was headed for Hebron and that his presence there would be signaled by the blowing of the trumpet. Also, Absalom gathered two hundred men from Jerusalem as guests of the religious ceremony that was to take place in Hebron. According to the text, these people were unaware of any plotting on Absalom's part. Were these people random guests that had been invited? Or, were they functionaries in David's administration, such that their absence would weaken David's bureaucracy a little? Were they perhaps prominent people, whose influence in Jerusalem Absalom wanted to neutralize? These are all possibilities, though the text does not satisfy our curiosity at this point (2 Sam 15:10-11).

One more thing that Absalom wanted to do as he made plans for a takeover was to enlist the support of Ahithophel, a counselor to David (2 Sam 15:12). Absalom sent for the man while he was performing a religious ritual in Hebron. At this point, it is unclear what role Absalom has in mind for Ahithophel. Apparently, though, it was surely ominous since the sentence immediately after the one describing Absalom's summoning of Ahithophel to Hebron states without ambiguity that the conspiracy put into motion by David's son had become strong and the number of Israelites behind him was growing. Ahithophel's defection to Absalom was especially concerning in that David did not even enjoy the loyalty of those closest to him. Absalom's having an insider from David's inner circle surely did not bode well for the king. Whatever unity in the body politic David once counted on was beginning to disintegrate.

KING DAVID'S FLIGHT

An unidentified messenger had the dubious duty to let David know that Absalom had captured the support of a critical mass in Israel (2 Sam 15:13). Seeing no other recourse, David spoke to his servants and urged a swift retreat from the city. David seemed to think that Absalom had the ability to match the king's forces and even take over Jerusalem (2 Sam 15:14). David still enjoyed the loyalty of the people closest to him, all of whom are ready to flee with the king. Except for ten concubines left to manage house affairs, everyone else took off with David (2 Sam 15:16). While the size of the contingent fleeing with David was impressive, the fact that such a large group saw no alternative reveals how formidable they must have considered Absalom to be (2 Sam 15:17–18). In any case, David and many in his administration abandoned Jerusalem because of the threat that Absalom posed. A rebellion was under way. It looked for all the world that it would succeed.

As he was departing Jerusalem, David spoke to Ittai the Gittite—at least six hundred Gittites were fleeing with the king (2 Sam 15:19)—and wanted to know why he was following the royal party. David pointed out that Ittai, and the other Gittites, for that matter, were foreigners. Therefore, the Gittites should go back home, meaning Philistia. The king noted that this contingent in his army had been with him only for a short time and currently he did not know what would transpire. However, Ittai, apparently speaking for the other Gittites, expressed fealty to David and offered to stay with the king throughout this crisis. Ittai won the argument, so the Gittites marched with David (2 Sam 15:19–22). The response in the countryside to this chaotic situation accents how much trouble Israel was in with this impending revolt (2 Sam 15:23).

It comes as no surprise that David had some backing in the religious sector. Abiathar and Zadok, who were priests, and other Levites as well decided to transport the ark of the covenant for those leaving with the king (2 Sam 15:24). But David decided against this. The king saw this move as presumptuous, in that having the ark with him suggested that he thought YHWH favored him. Instead, he ordered that the ark be returned to Jerusalem. David figured that if YHWH wanted him ultimately to go back to Jerusalem, so that he could see the ark, the deity would make that happen. Otherwise, the king would simply be in YHWH's hands, come what may (2 Sam 15:26). David at this point seems resigned or even fatalistic.

At the same time, David was not completely passive. He asked Zadok and Abiathar, along with their sons, to go back to Jerusalem and keep alert for any news that would be helpful. The king thought that the priests could do more for him in Jerusalem rather than tagging along. David would await any word from these moles (2 Sam 15:27–29). With these actions, David displays a curious combination of resignation and clever counter strategy. In any case, the priests left the king's entourage and returned to Jerusalem.

The combination of David's fatalism and simultaneously formulating a plan for regaining power is manifested as the story unfolds. Indicating the level of David's despair, as he approaches the Mount of Olives during his escape, he is barefooted, his head is covered (a sign of distress), and he is weeping. Others are imitating the king as they collectively weep with their heads covered as well (2 Sam 15:30). This is a sorry sight. Still, in the next narrative breath, we are told that David has not yet thrown in the towel. When the king is informed that Ahithophel had cast his lot with the conspirators, he prays immediately that YHWH confound the man's advice by making it seem foolish (2 Sam 15:12, 31). This prayer shows that David still has hope. Nonetheless, David needs for YHWH to intervene. There is no way at this point to determine whether this prayer was a function of the king's confidence in God's intervention or a function of desperation.

Regardless, as the king arrives at a summit where God is worshipped, he is met by Hushai the Archite. The fact that Hushai's clothes are torn, and he has dirt on his head (both indicating lamentation) certainly does not inspire confidence that things are going well (2 Sam 15:32). Maybe sensing that Hushai is in no position to render help at this point, David discourages him from coming along. Still, David believes that Hushai might be helpful if he returns to Jerusalem and promises to serve Absalom. That would put Hushai in a position to undermine Ahithophel's counsel at an opportune time. After all, David has already seen to it that Zadok, Abiathar, and their sons are situated for a little espionage. With people on the inside, David has a chance of getting some invaluable intelligence about what Absalom's plans are (2 Sam 15:34–36). Hushai readily complies with David's suggestion and returns to Jerusalem just as Absalom was entering the city himself (2 Sam 15:37). David may be down, but he is by no means out.

THE HOUSE OF SAUL REEMERGES

When David reaches a place the text calls "beyond the summit," he runs into a man named Ziba, who happened to be a servant of Mephibosheth. Mephibosheth was a son of Jonathan, Saul's son. Of course, Saul had been David's predecessor. Ziba was carrying some provisions on a couple of asses (2 Sam 16:1). When David inquired about the provisions, Ziba answered that the asses were at the disposal of the king's house and that the goods were for general use (2 Sam 16:2). Not quite satisfied with this answer, the king asks where Ziba's master was. David was apparently curious about Mephibosheth. Ziba reports that his master is in Jerusalem hoping to recover the kingship for the House of Saul (2 Sam 16:3). This is astonishing. Somehow, Mephibosheth thought he would benefit by Absalom's revolt by assuming rule as a member of Saul's family. Did he think that Absalom would simply relinquish power? Or, did he believe that Absalom would not have sufficient strength to maintain the kingship himself? What made him assume that Israel would restore Saul's family to the pinnacle of power when Absalom had done all the heavy lifting in this coup? No answers are forthcoming.

But David's reaction is unambiguous. The king told Ziba that he could now take possession of everything that once belonged to Mephibosheth, meaning evidently not only property but any other claims (2 Sam 16:4). This offer was calculated to urge Ziba to defect from Mephibosheth. Upon hearing David's proposal, Ziba proclaimed that he would have no objection to coming over to David's side.

David's effort to neutralize any complications arising from the reemergence of Saul's family into this messy situation was successful, but that is not the last we hear about the House of Saul. As David continues his escape, he arrives at Bahurim, where he is confronted by another member of the House of Saul, one Shimei ben Gera. "Confronted" is the appropriate word to describe this encounter since Shimei approached David not only cursing the king but throwing stones at him, even though David was surrounded by his people and "mighty men" (2 Sam 16:5–6). Shimei continues his rant by calling the king a man of blood and worthless to boot. He goes on to declare that David is being avenged by YHWH for what he did to the House of Saul. Part of that vengeance, according to Shimei, is that YHWH has given David's kingdom to Absalom (2 Sam 16:8). It is difficult to ascertain whether the narrator at this point is speaking through Shimei. That is a possibility in that, as we noted at the outset of this chapter, that David's adultery with Bath-Sheba and his murder of her husband, Uriah, set into motion a narrative in which David would pay "fourfold" what the rich man in Nathan's parable should pay. Shimei may have been wrong that David is being punished for his treatment of the House of Saul but may be closer to the truth that what is transpiring in David's life is because of YHWH.

Nevertheless, as one would expect, people standing with David would consider this affront on Shimei's part as outrageous. A man in David's entourage, Abishai ben Zeruiah, asks David rhetorically why he should not take off this "dead dog's" head (2 Sam 16:9). David's response to the attempt to deal with Shimei violently is quite revealing. The king upbraids Abishai! It may be the case that Shimei is cursing David at YHWH's behest (2 Sam 16:10). If that is so, Shimei is in effect speaking in God's behalf. David then explains further to Abishai and the rest of his servants. Since the king is fleeing for his life from his own son, what is so remarkable that someone from the House of Saul has a grudge against him? David orders that Shimei be left alone, because the man is surely doing this at YHWH's bidding (2 Sam 16:11). Then David plaintively hopes that as YHWH looks at his iniquity the deity will eventually repay him with good as a result of this cursing (2 Sam 16:12). That sounds like another confession, of sorts. Regardless, David and those with him continued their journey even as Shimei did not stop cursing and throwing stones at the king (2 Sam 16:13). Finally, the king and his group came to an undisclosed place—the Greek version of the story has the place as the Jordan River—exhausted. At long last, they managed to take a little break.

AHITHOPHEL (THE ADVISOR) AND ABSALOM

The scene shifts back to Jerusalem, where Absalom and the general populace have gathered. Ahithophel, the famed advisor, was among this company (2 Sam 16:15, 23). Hushai, David's friend and plant, was also there (2 Sam 16:16). By twice uttering the famous words, "Long live the king," he announced his loyalty to Absalom. But Absalom was leery, wanting to know why he had not stayed with David, to whom Hushai had most recently been loyal. Hushai explains by insisting that his loyalty was to the one now chosen to rule by the people, indeed, *all Israel*, not to mention YHWH. Indeed, just as he had served David, why should not Hushai serve David's son (2 Sam 16:17–19)? Satisfied with this explanation, Absalom did not press the matter further.

At this juncture Absalom seeks advice from Ahithophel. Even though Absalom was in Jerusalem and David had departed, there was much to do to solidify the situation. Obviously, Absalom had enough popular support to oust David for the time being, but surely his father still would have enjoyed the support of a percentage of the people. Absalom's work was not done if he wanted to keep the throne. His question to Ahithophel was simple: "What shall we do?" (2 Sam 16:20).

Ahithophel minced no words. Though it was extreme, he had a strategy in mind that he knew would establish Absalom's position. He told Absalom to take over David's concubines who had been left in Jerusalem (2 Sam 15:16) and make certain that the public was aware that he had done this. There is no doubt about what this meant. "To go into" is one of the most common ways to describe sex in the Bible. That is exactly the term that is used here. Such a brazen act would make any future reconciliation with David impossible and in addition would strengthen everyone supporting Absalom. There would be no going back from such public display (2 Sam 16:21). Obviously, too, this would humiliate David. Absalom jumped at the chance to implement Ahithophel's plan. A tent was pitched on the roof and Absalom had sex with his father's concubines. Also, he was sufficiently brazen as to make certain the public knew about this (2 Sam 16:22), just as Ahithophel had suggested. It should not be lost on us that, as depraved as

Absalom's behavior was in this instance, it fulfilled the prophecy delivered by Nathan the prophet to King David in the aftermath of his adultery and murder (2 Sam 12:12). What David tried mightily to keep secretive, YHWH exposed to the whole Israelite population.

But Ahithophel was not done giving advice. He had another plan he wanted Absalom to implement. He offered to select 12,000 men who subsequently would pursue David, catching the king off guard while he was exhausted and discouraged. In this way, his troops would abandon him, leaving the king completely exposed (2 Sam 17:1–2). Once David is dealt with, meaning being assassinated, Ahithophel will be able to return to Jerusalem with the rest of the king's troops in tow, "as a bride comes home to her husband" (2 Sam 17:3). This would have the added benefit of not subjecting the general populace to bloodshed. This strategy required the death of only one man—David—and would allow the people to remain at peace (2 Sam 17:4). Absalom and the Israelite elders liked what Ahithophel had proposed.

Inexplicably, however, Absalom sought a second opinion. He wanted to know what Hushai had to say (2 Sam 17:5). Indeed, Absalom wanted Hushai to weigh in on Ahithophel's specific advice. If he had any problems with what Ahithophel wanted to put in motion, then Hushai should suggest an alternate strategy. At this point, we see how brilliant David had been in encouraging Hushai to stay near Absalom where, when the time came, he could confute anything Ahithophel had contrived to further the coup (2 Sam 15:34). Making no bones about his willingness to contradict the legendary advisor's scheme, Hushai says flat out that in this instance Ahithophel has given bad advice (2 Sam 17:7).

Hushai's counterproposal to Ahithophel's proposal was diametrically opposite. Basing his contrary idea on the premise that David and his mighty men had stellar military reputations, not to mention that they were as angry as a mother bear robbed of her cubs, Hushai pointed out that it was folly to believe that the king would be easy to find. Surely, David is far too wily to spend the night with the troops. Almost certainly, David is hiding out right now. Further, Hushai warns of the possible rumors that David's forces might spread the news that Absalom has suffered a serious reversal. A rumor like that would prompt even experienced soldiers now on Absalom's side to let their fear of David get the best of them (2 Sam 17:8–10). To prevent such a circumstance, Hushai recommends that Absalom personally lead an enormous army gathered from all Israel against David. That would ensure finding David, and at the same time, neutralize his forces. Should David flee to a city, Absalom's soldiers would have no trouble in destroying that city (2 Sam 17:11–13).

Anything close to an objective analysis would hardly judge Hushai's plans as obviously superior. For one thing, Hushai's strategy risks Absalom personally. If Absalom goes into battle, he will be vulnerable. As well, what Hushai was proposing would require conscripting troops throughout Israel. That would take time and considerable effort. Plus, how would two large armies squaring off be an improvement on a surgical strike targeting only one person, namely, David? Regardless of how dubious Hushai's plan of action was, incredibly Absalom and his supporters thought this was the preferred option (2 Sam 17:14). Before we remark on the apparent naïveté if not stupidity of Absalom and those closest to him, we need to take note of the narrator's affirmation that YHWH was responsible for this outcome. The deity wanted to undercut Ahithophel's smarter strategy and replace it with Hushai's suspect version. YHWH did this to bring Absalom under judgment, which means that his days are numbered.

THE DECISIVE BATTLE

The first thing Hushai did to put his plan into operation was to let Zadok and Abiathar, the priests, know what Ahithophel had counseled Absalom and what he, Hushai, had said to counter that counsel (2 Sam 17:15). Hushai wanted Zadok and Abiathar to inform David that he had to act quickly. By no means should he stay "tonight" by the wilderness fords. Instead, the king needed to move his forces to "pass over," otherwise the king and the troops with him risked being "swallowed up" (2 Sam 17:16). Apparently, the method of getting the word to David involved a young woman communicating with a couple of David's men, Jonathan and Ahimaaz, who were waiting at Enrogel. Under no circumstances were they to enter Jerusalem, where they might be spotted (2 Sam 17:17). Still, a lad happened to notice these couriers. At once he informed Absalom, which meant it was necessary for the two men to hide quickly. They went to a man's house in Bahurim, which was close to Enrogel. Evidently, the residents were sympathizers of David. Jonathan and Ahimaaz hid in a well that the owner of the house had. *The woman*, presumably the man's wife, spread a covering over the well's mouth and then scattered grain on the covering (2 Sam 17:18–19). Absalom's men went out searching for David's men and soon were at the very house where they were hiding. It is unclear how Absalom's men had an inkling that David's men would be holing up somewhere on this property. Were the residents somehow known to sympathize with David? In any case, Absalom's servants ask the residents whether these men—using their names—were nearby (2 Sam 17:20). The woman lied by telling Absalom's servants that the men had already gone, where is difficult to ascertain because the Hebrew is uncertain at this point. The fabrication, however, worked. Not discovering the men, Absalom's frustrated servants returned to Jerusalem.

As soon as they are able, the men hiding in the well emerge and run to David with their pertinent information regarding Ahithophel's advice (2 Sam 17:21). Immediately, David crosses the Jordan with all his troops (2 Sam 17:22). Meanwhile, once Ahithophel realized that his advice had been rejected for Hushai's, he went home, took care of his affairs, and committed suicide (2 Sam 17:23).

Once David and those supporting him were in Mahanaim, across the Jordan, Absalom and his troops—*all the men of Israel*—were not far behind (2 Sam 17:24). Then we learn that Absalom had replaced his military strategist, Joab, with Amasa (2 Sam 17:25). These forces following Absalom and Amasa encamped in Gilead (2 Sam 17:26). Though Absalom was probably not counting on this, David was able to rely on considerable logistical support in the form of beds, basins, and earthen vessels, not to mention a variety of foodstuffs (2 Sam 17:27-28). David's hungry, thirsty, and tired forces had their needs taken care of through the largess of three men, Shobi, Machir, and Barzillai. These three seem to be related to non-Israelite groups. Nevertheless, they were willing to supply David's troops. Nothing is said about Absalom's army enjoying similar support. That speaks well for David but is concerning for Absalom.

ABSALOM FALLS—THE COUP FAILS

David reverts to full military command mode as he musters his soldiers, then sets over them officers in charge of thousand-men and hundred-men units. The king also deployed a third of his army under each of three field marshals: Joab, Abishai, and Ittai (2 Sam 18:1-2). David was all set to march with his army, but he ran into an obstacle. These three men cautioned David about his desire to go into battle. They made clear that David was far too important to risk himself. If he wanted to help, it would be better for the king to send in reinforcements from the city (2 Sam 18:3). David relents. He remained at the gate while his army went forth. David's final order to the three men entrusted with this battle was to go easy on Absalom. His troops heard what he had said when he gave this order about his son (2 Sam 18:5).

The two forces met in the forest of Ephraim, resulting in David's army defeating Absalom's army. Twenty thousand Israelites lost their lives in that battle (2 Sam 18:6-7). Curiously, given the nature of the terrain, the narrator emphasizes that the forest devoured more soldiers than the sword did on that fateful day (2 Sam 18:8).

As the battle was raging, Absalom came across men on David's side. Absalom had been riding on a mule. When the mule went under the thick branches of a tree Absalom somehow got his head stuck; in fact, he was left hanging from the tree as the mule went out from under him (2 Sam 18:9). Almost immediately, Joab was told by a soldier that he had seen Absalom dangling from a tree. Joab was flabbergasted that the man did not kill Absalom on the spot, something for which a good sum of money could have been earned (2 Sam 18:11). The man defended his actions. No matter what reward was offered, he was not about to kill David's son, not after hearing what the king said about how he wanted Absalom not to be harmed (2 Sam 18:12–14). Plus, the man added, if he had gone ahead and killed Absalom, Joab would not have defended him in public (2 Sam 18:13). Joab was in no mood to argue. He took three darts and thrust them into Absalom's heart, after which point the king's son was finished off by Joab's ten armor-bearers (2 Sam 18:14–15). With his death, Absalom's revolt was quashed.

Meanwhile, David was watching events unfold. Watchmen with David noticed someone running toward them from the battlefield. David thought that if the runner were alone, he must have urgent news. Next, another runner appears. David is anxious to hear what this man has to report as well. One of the watchmen thinks he recognizes one of the runners, a man by the name of Ahimaaz ben Zadok. David is sure that the man is bringing good news (2 Sam 18:24–27). Ahimaaz reaches David and, indeed, brings good tidings: "All is well." He elaborates by informing the king that those who revolted against him were vanquished by "YHWH your God" (2 Sam 18:28). David does not respond to this news at all. Instead, he asks about Absalom. Though the Hebrew is difficult at this point, the gist of what the man said is that there was a commotion of some kind, but he knew nothing about Absalom's fate. The king told Ahimaaz to stand aside (2 Sam 18:29–30). Clearly, David seemed more interested about what had happened to Absalom than how the battle had gone.

Then the second runner, a Cushite, arrived. He, too, arrived with good news. His report matched the previous one, namely, YHWH has delivered David from those who had rebelled against him (2 Sam 18:31). Once again, David brushed aside this exceedingly good news to ask whether Absalom had survived. The messenger could not bring himself to state explicitly that Absalom had been killed, or by whose hand. But the implications of what he did say were unmistakable: "May the enemies of my lord the king, and all who rise up against you for evil, be like that young man" (2 Sam 18:32). Though the man studiously did not offer the "young man's" name, there was no getting around the fact that Absalom had succumbed. David knew this immediately. In his poignant lament, David wails Absalom's name three times (2 Sam 19:1 [Eng. 18:33]). David had won the battle of his life. But he had lost another son. He did not respond at all to the former. He reserved all his emotions to express his anguish about the latter.

In light of David's reaction, there would be no victory celebration. Where there should have been victory songs ringing out, the king's grieving dampened everyone's mood. When the troops returned, instead of marching triumphantly, they slunk into the city as though they had been routed. As they arrived, David was still carrying on, refusing to be consoled (2 Sam 19:2–5 [Eng. 19:1–4]).

By then, Joab could not take David's antics any longer. He lit into the king for treating those who fought on his behalf as though they did not count. Joab accuses David of taking the absurd position that he would have been happier had Absalom survived and those fighting in David's behalf had perished (2 Sam 19:6–7 [Eng. 19:5–6]). Joab demanded that David speak to his servants and explain himself. If he did not do this, he risked losing all his support. David accepted Joab's counsel, got up, and took his seat in the gate. Once the people realized that David was there, they all went before the king. We are never told whether David spoke to his grief, or said he was sorry for the disrespect he had displayed or explained that he was now ready to move forward. One way or another, however, after he made this appearance at the gate, David was ready to resume command as king (2 Sam 19:8–9 [Eng. 19:7–8]).

DAVID'S RETURN TO JERUSALEM

For a while Israel remained politically chaotic. The people characterized the situation by noting that David had previously delivered Israel from their enemies, particularly the Philistines, but subsequently fled from the usurper Absalom (2 Sam 19:10 [Eng. 19:9]). Now that Absalom was dead people wondered why no one was making a move to bring David back to Jerusalem (2 Sam 19:11 [Eng. 19:10]).

While the people were collectively considering what course of action to take, David took the initiative. He sent a message to Zadok and Abiathar. David wanted these priests to confront Judah's elders by asking them why they were not preparing for David's return to the throne. After all, the word on the street would have made David's restoration to power not only feasible but requisite. That was especially the case when it came to Judah, for David enjoyed especially close kinship with these Israelites (2 Sam 19:12–13 [Eng.

19:11–12]). It makes no sense, according to David, for the elders of Judah not to insert themselves into this situation. David simultaneously made an executive decision to replace his military commander Joab with Amasa, doubtlessly the king's reaction to Joab's outburst at David's response to Absalom's death (2 Sam 19:14 [Eng. 19:13]). With this effort, just as Absalom once stole Israel's hearts (2 Sam 15:6) so David now swayed the hearts of the men of Judah, fostering a new sense of unity (2 Sam 19:15 [Eng. 19:14]). Almost immediately, David and his men were invited to go to the Jordan, where Judah came to Gilgal to meet the king and help him cross the river (2 Sam 19:16 [Eng. 19:15]). David is not quite yet back on the throne, but he is much closer than he had been for some time.

As David was getting ready to return to Jerusalem Shimei ben Gera came with the men of Judah to meet the king, as did Ziba, the servant of the House of Saul, with his fifteen sons and twenty servants (2 Sam 19:17 [Eng. 19:16]). They were trying to facilitate David's return. Both Shimei and Ziba had had very different encounters with David previously.

Ziba had supplied David and those accompanying him with provisions for their escape from Absalom (2 Sam 16:1–4). There is no question that he was an ally. Conversely, Shimei was the man who had cursed David when he was trying to escape Absalom (2 Sam 16:5–8). Since David was fleeing his own son, the king thought that was a greater humiliation than some Israelite hurling invectives. David, therefore, did not allow any in his entourage to deal harshly with Shimei. The king let the man rant and rave as much as he wanted. Of course, circumstances had now dramatically changed. The man whom Shimei had cursed so lustily was about to assume power once again. This time around Shimei assumes a totally different posture; indeed, he begs for forgiveness (2 Sam 19:20 [Eng. 19:19]). He admits that he sinned against the king and further hopes that he might get a little credit as the first one in the House of Joseph to greet David as he was about to assume the throne anew (2 Sam 19:21 [Eng. 19:20]). That seemed an odd compensation for his prior cursing, but that was apparently the best Shimei could offer.

As Shimei is pleading his case, Abishai ben Zeruiah demands that anyone who cursed the king deserves death (2 Sam 19:22 [Eng. 19:21]). This was the same man who wanted Shimei to be decapitated when he first imprecated David (2 Sam 16:9). Abishai had a zero-tolerance policy when it came to disrespecting the king. David, on the other hand, was as gracious in this instance as he had been in the previous one. Inquiring as to whether Abishai was his foe or friend, he made abundantly clear that now that he was about to be back on the throne in Jerusalem no such vengeance should be exacted (2 Sam 19:23 [Eng. 19:22]). After this reprimand, David made a solemn oath to Shimei that he would not die because of what he had done (2 Sam 19:24 [Eng. 19:23]). He was off the hook.

After dealing with this matter, David comes face-to-face with Mephibosheth, Saul's grandson (2 Sam 19:25 [Eng. 19:24]).[3] He was quite disheveled in that he had forsaken any personal grooming since this whole political mess had begun. Right off the bat, David demanded to know why Mephibosheth had not accompanied him while he was a fugitive from Absalom (2 Sam 19:26 [Eng. 19:25]). Recall that before David had been extremely generous to Mephibosheth, since he was his dearest friend's son (2 Sam 9:1–8). The king had basically cared for Jonathan's son as though he was part of his own family. Given David's earlier treatment, why would not the king expect Mephibosheth to remain with him through thick and thin? Mephibosheth's answer was that he had been undercut by one of his servants. Though he had planned on saddling his ass to compensate for his lameness and indeed follow David, his servant's slandering him in front of the king somehow prevented Mephibosheth from following along (2 Sam 19:27–28 [Eng. 19:26–27]). Mephibosheth even recalls that Saul's house was denounced and all but dead when David became king, but that did not deter David from inviting members of the Saul family, in this instance Mephibosheth, Jonathan's son, to eat at the king's table (2 Sam 19:29 [Eng. 19:28]). In that light, Mephibosheth has no standing to ask David to disregard the slight involved in his failure to stay with the king throughout the ordeal. Once again, though, David remains gracious. He wants Mephibosheth to drop the subject. Instead of being upset, David rewarded not only Mephibosheth but also Ziba by ordering that they both inherit a field (2 Sam 19:30 [Eng. 19:29]). Presumably, this refers to some parcel that both men can use to bolster their economic holdings. In any case, that part of Saul's family is now safely aligned with David.

The last man that David encountered before he finally got to Jerusalem was Barzillai the Gileadite (2 Sam 19:32 [Eng. 19:31]). He had come down from Rogelim to escort David to the Jordan. Barzillai was old and wealthy. He had seen to it that David had had provisions in Transjordan (2 Sam 19:33 [Eng. 19:32]). David was keen to return the favor by having Barzillai accompany him to Jerusalem where the king could take care of him. However, given his advanced age—eighty years old—Barzillai thought he was no longer able to enjoy the benefits that being in court would offer. So, he declined to go with David. He would just as soon stay put, die in his own city, and be buried close to his father's and mother's grave. Though he refused to

---

3. There is a problem with Mephibosheth's identity. Though he is identified as Jonathan's son in 2 Sam 4:4, in the note in 2 Sam 21:5 he is Saul's son by Rizpah. In that same context, Mephibosheth is referred to as Jonathan's son (2 Sam 21:7). In 2 Sam 19:24 Mephibosheth is Saul's *grandson* rather than son, despite the Hebrew text's having the word *son*.

take advantage of David's largess, he suggested that "your servant," Chimham, go with David instead. Chimham may be Barzillai's son, though the text does not say so explicitly (1 Kgs 2:7). Regardless, David is more than glad to extend the same offer to this man (2 Sam 19:34-39 [Eng. 19:33-38]). Having said their goodbyes, David, with Chimham in tow, continued on his journey while Barzillai returned home (2 Sam 19:40 [Eng. 19:39]).

Then the story quickly shifts from dealing with these individual encounters to the people as a whole. Subsequent to Barzillai's going back to his own territory we learn that *all the people of Judah* and *half the people of Israel* brought the king the rest of the way (2 Sam 19:41 [Eng. 19:40]). This created serious conflict at the communal level. *All the men of Israel* complained to the king that the *men of Judah* had stolen you (i.e., David) away, only to bring back the king's household and all of his men back over the Jordan (2 Sam 19:42 [Eng. 19:41]). Not one word is said about Absalom in this altercation. It is as though David's being forced to leave Jerusalem was explicable primarily in terms of rival factions within Israel. The men of Judah had a ready answer to this charge. Without denying it outright, they appeal to the fact that David is a closer relative to them than the other Israelites (2 Sam 19:43 [Eng. 19:42]). Furthermore, the Judeans argue that David has not favored them with either provisions or gifts. Israel's rebuttal has to do with their claim of having ten shares in King David, likely a reference to the ten tribal segments other than Judah and Benjamin (2 Sam 19:44 [Eng. 19:43]). As well, the Israelites did not understand why their expressed interest in bringing David back to Jerusalem first was not appreciated. Indeed, they thought those in Judah had despised them. Without supplying any details, this episode concludes by noting that what Judah said was harsher than what Israel said. In other words, Judah had won, in some sense, the acrimonious debate.

CONCLUSION

There is an ironical touch to the division in Israel we just treated. The irony is that though YHWH sanctifies a *unified Israel*, quite often God punishes the elect people by being complicit in fostering a *divided Israel*. The Absalom episode fits this pattern. Since David reacted to Nathan's parable by demanding that the only appropriate judgment for the rich man was to pay *fourfold* for his heartless theft of the poor man's lone ewe lamb (2 Sam 12:1-6), the king paid at least that much for his sins. Every feature of that fourfold punishment involved David's children. David's first child by Bath-Sheba died; Tamar was raped by her half-brother Amnon; he was in turn killed by Absalom, Amnon's half-brother and Tamar's full brother; and finally, Absalom was killed after staging a *coup d'état* against his father David.

Though from a personal perspective, David's loss was incalculable, in the end he was able to sit once more on the throne in Jerusalem over a unified Israel. At the same time, that unity was extremely tenuous as the final argument between the people of Judah and the people of Israel illustrates (2 Sam 19:42–44 [Eng. 19:41–43]). Unfortunately, the unity which Israel achieved at the end of this episode was fragile at best. This is why we should not be surprised to encounter subsequent stories in which division of the community is prominent. Israel's disunity was hardly rare.

Chapter 8

Sheba's Revolt: Quickly Generated, Immediately Quashed

SHEBA FOMENTS REBELLION

At the end of the last chapter, it was difficult to shake the impression that, although David had finally quelled Absalom's rebellion and once again unified Israel, that unification was fragile. This is suggested by the last paragraph of 2 Samuel 19. Given this, it comes as no surprise that we encounter yet another revolt in 2 Samuel 20. This time it is a *worthless fellow* (*'îš b*ᵉ*liyya'al*) by the name of Sheba ben Bichri who was behind the foment. Curiously, though it was the northern part of Israel who followed his lead, he was himself a Benjaminite, typically considered part of the southern part of Israel (2 Sam 20:1). Just as Absalom had sounded the horn to indicate that the rebellion was on, Sheba used a similar tactic. This revolt's song or slogan, so to speak, was expressly directed against David:

> We have no portion in David,
> and we have no inheritance in the son of Jesse;
> every man to his tents, O Israel.

The result of this summons was nothing short of spectacular, for "all the men of Israel" withdrew from David and marched in lock step with Sheba (2 Sam 20:2). However, there were no defections from the southern regions, where the "men of Judah" followed David steadfastly. While that speaks well for David and his administration, this was hardly a minor setback. A very large part of Israel no longer recognized David as king.

In a flashback, we learn that when David returned to Jerusalem after Absalom's revolt he dealt right away with the issue of his royal harem.

He took back the ten concubines he had left behind when he fled, the very women that Absalom had taken over as his own wives, quite visibly, so that the rest of Israel could not help but notice (2 Sam 16:22). Once David regained power, he treated these women as royal wives should be treated, but he no longer slept with them. Apparently, what Absalom had done had permanent implications. From now on, though they were still David's wives, it was as if they had been widowed (2 Sam 20:3).

DAVID'S COUNTER STRATEGY

Having sequestered his formerly abducted wives, David confronts head on the difficulties that had been precipitated by Sheba. To do this, he wanted Amasa, currently head of his armed forces (2 Sam 20:4; 19:14 [Eng. 19:13]), to summon Judah. For unexplained reasons, however, Amasa did not act promptly (2 Sam 20:5). Because of this delay, David next turned to Abishai, the brother of Joab, the military leader that the king had recently sacked. David was worried that Sheba would do more damage even than Absalom had inflicted were he not immediately stopped. The king had ordered Amasa to go after Sheba before the latter was able to build his power base with fortified cities (2 Sam 20:6). Yet, amazingly it was not Amasa who went after Sheba but Joab, along with his men as well as Cherethites, Pelethites, and all the *mighty men*—a description of David's elite military guard (2 Sam 20:7). Though Joab had been relieved of duty, he was nevertheless acting as a military officer. When this group arrived at the great stone in Gibeon, Amasa also finally appeared (2 Sam 20:8). Joab was outfitted in typical military garb, which included a sword tucked in a garment. The Hebrew text is difficult at this point in that it indicates that the sword fell to the ground on its own. That would have prevented Joab from concealing his weapon. Whatever we are to think of this odd description, the sword eventually ends up being concealed without Amasa's noticing it. When Joab grabbed Amasa's beard and was about to kiss him, the unobservant man suspected nothing. After all, Joab's gestures appeared to be completely nonthreatening. Joab even referred to Amasa as "my brother" (2 Sam 20:9). Suddenly, with a single blow, Joab eviscerated the man, obviously killing him on the spot (2 Sam 20:10). With Amasa out of the way, Joab had reinserted himself into a leading role in David's army. Subsequently, he and Abishai, his brother, resumed the pursuit of Sheba.

At this juncture, one of Joab's men demands that folk make their political loyalties known. He made sure that folk knew that following Joab was the same as supporting David (2 Sam 20:11). Not only had Joab reclaimed his previous military position, he also was bolstering his political standing as well. In the meantime, Amasa was lying on the ground, his corpse covered with blood. Naturally, this attracted onlookers as people passed by. Apparently, thinking this ghastly sight was a distraction, the man who had demanded people to make their loyalties known decided to get rid of the body. Thus, he took it from the main road, deposited it in a field, and covered it with a garment (2 Sam 20:12–13). Afterward, there was no obstacle in the way of the people rejoining Joab in his pursuit of Sheba.

SHEBA ESCAPES TO ABEL

In his desperation to get away, Sheba passed through all the tribes of Israel trying to find a hiding place.[1] He thought he had found a safe haven in Abel of Beth-Maacah. Members of his extended family evidently followed him there.[2] It is not clear why that particular city was chosen. As it turned out, it was a terrible choice.

They—implying Joab's armed forces—were soon at the door of the city. Immediately they employed siege-ramps, erecting them against the rampart (2 Sam 20:15). Though these soldiers were not interested in demolishing or plundering the city, their intentions would have meant little to Abel's inhabitants. All Joab's men wanted to do was to seize Sheba. At the same time, they were willing to do what was necessary to accomplish that task. The city's only crime was harboring the rebellious Sheba. We have no way of knowing whether people in the city realized who Sheba was or what he had done. Presumably, all the city dwellers knew was that Sheba was an outsider.

It turns out that Abel had a spokeswoman, who happened to be a sage (2 Sam 20:16). Assessing what was going on, she summoned Joab. Somehow, she was aware that he was in charge of the assaulting troops. When he appeared, she asked whether he was, in fact, Joab. He answered that he was. Then, the wise woman informed Joab about the reputation of the city as a place where one could inquire into a matter and results would be forthcoming. In other words, the city was famous as a source for wisdom and the advantages that accrue from that tradition (2 Sam 20:17–18). "Inquiring at Abel" was a slogan of sorts. Having pointed out why Abel was prominent in Israel, she identified herself as a peaceful and faithful woman in Israel. Further, she went on, the city was nothing short of a "mother in Israel" such that Joab and his forces were about to "swallow up YHWH's heritage"

---

1. Sheba is implied. The Hebrew text simply has "he" in 2 Sam 20:14.

2. The Hebrew is problematic in that it says the Berites followed him there. Presumably, the members of Sheba's family as indicated in 2 Sam 20:1, 6, 10, 13 are meant.

(2 Sam 20:19). This sage is doing everything in her power to protect her city. In doing so, she has pulled out all the stops to describe an Israelite city in glowing terms.

Joab retorts that he has no designs on Abel. The only reason he and his men are here at all is to capture Sheba. After all, this man from the hill country of Ephraim had lifted up his hand against King David; indeed, he had instigated a civil war (2 Sam 20:21). Should Abel give up Sheba, then Joab and his army would leave the city. The situation was that simple. Incredibly, the sage had a ready answer for Joab. Her city was in a precarious position. Saving it in exchange for a single life, especially someone who was not even a resident, seemed the right thing to do. The woman then promised Joab that Sheba's head would soon be thrown over the wall. Though extreme, to say the least, that action should solve everyone's problem except, of course, Sheba's! Joab would get his man, the rebellion would almost surely dissipate, and Abel would remain unscathed. All the sage had to do is make this happen.

Joab was willing to give the woman time to get the townspeople to go along with what she had proposed. The woman went immediately to *all the people* with her *clever plan* (2 Sam 20:22). Though the Hebrew word here is the ordinary word for "wise plan," I am translating "clever" on the analogy of the use of wisdom vocabulary found in 1 Kings 2. That chapter describes David's deathbed instructions to his son, Solomon, to use his *wisdom* to avenge his father. In that scene, David admonishes Solomon to apply his *wisdom* to see to it that Joab does not die an old man (2 Kgs 2:6). Also, after reminding Solomon again that he was a *wise man*, David wanted his son to deal appropriately with another enemy (2 Kgs 2:9). In a context where such malicious plans are being set, a word such as *clever* seems to capture the nuance better. Wisdom is not always a positive characteristic in the biblical tradition. Keep in mind, in the famous temptation account in Genesis 3, as the woman contemplates eating from the tree of the knowledge of good and evil, an aspect of the temptation is that her eating the forbidden fruit had the capacity of making her *wise* (*lᵉhaśkîl*; Gen 3:6), that is, sovereign.[3] This is the sort of wisdom that should be understood in this context.

In any case, the woman was sufficiently clever that she convinced Abel's citizens that Sheba was dispensable. Therefore, instead of harboring him as a fugitive, which plausibly might have been expected given the hospitality protocols typically operative in the ancient Near Eastern and biblical worlds, Sheba was decapitated, and his head was unceremoniously thrown over the wall (2 Sam 20:22). Once more in this episode the trumpet was sounded,

---

3. See Mendenhall, "Shady Side of Wisdom," 319–34.

except that this time it did not announce a rebellion but indicated the ignominious end of the person responsible for that rebellion (2 Sam 20:1, 22). Once Sheba had been dispatched, the troops no longer threatened Abel and instead went home, while at the same time Joab returned to Jerusalem and its king, David. This revolt ended almost as quickly as it had begun.

ADMINISTRATIVE NOTES

After this episode comes to an end, the chapter concludes with a listing of current posts in David's administration. Most significantly, perhaps, is noting that Joab was now in charge of Israel's armed forces (2 Sam 20:23). Joab had had a colorful career with David. Early on we were informed of Joab's role in David's army (2 Sam 8:16). Later on, he secured strategic victories in David's behalf, but was also politically sensitive by making sure that he did not upstage the king (2 Sam 12:26–31). The seasoned military man even was involved in David's relationship with Absalom, whose interactions with the king were strained due his murdering Amnon (2 Sam 13:23–29). Joab orchestrated events to reconcile Absalom and David (2 Sam 14:1–24). Though Joab managed to pull this off, unfortunately son and father remained at odds. Eventually, Absalom led a coup against his father, which in turn led to Joab finally assassinating the king's son and criticizing David for caring more about his son than his role as Israel's king (2 Sam 15:1–6; 18:9–15). At that point, it was hardly surprising that David fired Joab (2 Sam 19:14 [Eng. 19:13]). Somehow, though, Joab reversed his fortunes in dealing with Sheba's revolt and Sheba himself. Thus, he is once more in charge of David's military. The text is silent about whether David approved of Joab's reinstatement. Maybe Joab's reasserting himself intimated some political diminishing of David's power.

The other officers in this list have important roles. Benaiah was over the Cherethites and Pelethites (2 Sam 20:23). Adoram oversaw forced labor. Jehoshaphat ben Shilud was the recorder (2 Sam 20:24). Sheva was David's secretary. Finally, Zadok, Abiathar, and Ira served as priests under David (2 Sam 20:25–26).

Perhaps this list underscored David's monarchy achieving a degree of stability after the disastrous events that Absalom's and Sheba's revolts engendered. Are we to conclude that David's rule had reached a stage in which smooth sailing, or at least smoother sailing, would be normal? If so, we will soon be disabused. Not only were the circumstances revolving around the rise of David's successor (1 Kgs 1–3) enormously destabilizing, but even Solomon's impressive reign showed signs of disunity from the very beginning. We should not be surprised that the *great schism* followed Solomon's kingship.

CONCLUSION

From one perspective, the story featuring Sheba hardly seems momentous. Mostly, this is because of the cryptic nature of the narrative. Sheba comes out of nowhere, declares that a rebellion is afoot, and is immediately successful in splitting the kingdom. But there are virtually no other details to provide context. Even recounting the part of the story in which Sheba is sought, found holing up in Abel, and eventually being killed by residents at the instigation of a female sage, appears to emphasize Joab's managing to regain authority over David's army as much as accenting Sheba's ultimate demise. All in all, it comes off as a secondary story.

From another perspective, however, the story could not be more crucial. This is due to the fact that *all the people of Israel* defected from David while Judah remained loyal to the king. In short, this minor event adumbrates the great schism that is narrated at the end of Solomon's reign. Indeed, though Sheba did not last long after announcing the revolt, the text never states that the two sides—the north (Israel) and the south (Judah)—were ever reconciled. It is as though the divisions evident in Israel were left to simmer until everything boiled over at the conclusion of Solomon's tenure. That is suggested by the similarity between the song/slogan that precipitated the two rebellions as reflected in 2 Sam 20:1 and 1 Kgs 12:16, respectively. On the surface, the episode dealing with Sheba may seem minor, but a closer look at the narrative prepares us for the most divisive event that Israel will ever experience. To that story we now turn.

Chapter 9

The Great Schism

INTRODUCTION TO SOLOMON: SUPERLATIVES AND AREAS OF CONCERN

Because there are so many superlatives used to describe Solomon, it seems unfair to charge him with precipitating the *great schism* that is recounted in 1 Kings 12. After all, Solomon is variously presented as the wisest (1 Kgs 3; 4:29–34; 10:4), richest, (1 Kgs 3:13; 4:7), most powerful (1 Kgs 4:20; 5:1 [Eng. 4:20–21]), and arguably the greatest of Israel's kings (1 Kgs 10:4–5). Besides, Solomon built the Jerusalem temple, as expensive as it was grand (1 Kgs 6:1–10, 14–36). In spite of all these accomplishments and accolades, however, there are indications from the beginning not only that the king was not as good as advertised but that Israel was on a destructive path under Solomon's leadership.[1]

Even before Solomon sat on the throne the manner in which he assumed power was dubious at best and nefarious at worst (1 Kgs 1–2). He gained control through the machinations of Zadok the priest, Benaiah, Nathan the prophet, Bath-Sheba, Shimei, Rei, and David's elite forces (1 Kgs 1:8). YHWH was conspicuously absent when Solomon via palace intrigue wrested control from Adonijah, David's *oldest* son. Solomon even killed his (half-)brother to eliminate a potential rival to the throne (1 Kgs 2:13–25).

Though Solomon eventually consolidated his power (1 Kgs 2:46c), the narrator describes the king in contradictory terms. Solomon is depicted simultaneously as the best and worst monarch. The first thing we are told is that Solomon married the pharaoh's daughter (1 Kgs 3:1). In light of

---

1. See Spina, "*In* but Not *Of* the World," 17–30.

Joshua's strictures in his final speeches (Josh 23-24; esp. 23:12) about being involved with, not to mention marrying, people who have no commitment to YHWH, taking an Egyptian wife is a serious lapse.² Given the king's penchant for acquiring foreign women for his harem, Solomon's marrying Pharaoh's daughter is merely the first step in multiplying wives, which is warned against in the strongest of terms in the *law of the king* in Deut 17:14-20.

Solomon's sacrificing in the high places (1 Kgs 3:2, 4) should not be viewed definitely as a negative datum since the Jerusalem temple had not yet been constructed. Still, often *high places* are pejoratively portrayed as places where non-Israelite, pagan practices are often conducted (e.g., 1 Kgs 12:31-32; 13:2; 15:14; 10:8; Mic 1:5). Regardless, Solomon's later tendency of promoting non-Israelite forms of worship renders this activity as playing with fire, religiously speaking. In fact, the narrator intimates that Solomon's sacrificing in the high places as well as Gibeon, which was the *great high place* (*habbāmāh hagg^{e}dôlāh*), was the one exception to Solomon's loving YHWH and following in the steps of David, his father (1 Kgs 3:3-4).

Granted, once YHWH bestows wisdom on Solomon his reputation soars, at least for a while. Having been endowed with wisdom as a gift from God and provided with riches as a bonus (1 Kgs 3:5-13), the king demonstrated how sage he was by arbitrating a dispute between two prostitutes, each claiming that they were the mother of the same baby (1 Kgs 3:16-28). Of course, this wisdom was also tied to obeying torah, something at which Solomon mostly excelled (1 Kgs 3:14). After the episode involving the prostitutes, superlatives abound. Solomon had an impressive administrative staff (1 Kgs 4:1-6), an extensive table at which the elite ate regularly (1 Kgs 4:7-19), and ruled over a numerous, happy people, in line with the promises YHWH long ago made to the ancestors. Even other countries paid tribute to Solomon (1 Kgs 4:20—5:1 [Eng. 4:20-21]). The narrator pulls out all the stops to praise Solomon for what it took to feed the royal household, the size of the territory over which he ruled, how many horses he owned, and how many men rode those horses for the realm's benefit (1 Kgs 5:2-8 [Eng. 4:22-28]). Solomon's accrual of the wisdom bestowed on him by YHWH also led to his belonging in a veritable hall of fame for the wise (1 Kgs 5:9-11 [Eng. 4:29-31]), not to mention legendary prowess in the production of proverbs and songs, and his acumen about trees, plants, animals, birds, reptiles, and fish (1 Kgs 5:12-13 [Eng. 4:32-33]). It is hardly surprising that he enjoyed the world's adulation (1 Kgs 5:14 [Eng. 4:34]).

---

2. For a study that emphasizes Joshua's role as Moses' successor, see Spina, "Moses and Joshua," 65-92.

Add to this resumé Solomon's erection of two magnificent buildings, the temple and his own palace, both in Jerusalem (1 Kgs 5:15—7:51 [Eng. 5:1—7:51]). By all accounts, Solomon was a royal figure whose abilities and accomplishments were incomparable.

At the same time, the text intimates growing concerns about Solomon and his policies. His marriage to the pharaoh's daughter and his using the *high places* for worship have already been cited. But there were other worrisome signs. For example, though Solomon may have not violated Israelite tradition in using forced labor (1 Kgs 4:6), he was clearly wrong to subject *Israel* to forced labor (1 Kgs 5:27 [Eng. 5:13]).³ While only suggestive, it is difficult not to raise one's eyebrows when we learn that it took Solomon seven years to construct the temple but thirteen years to finish his own palace (1 Kgs 6:38; 7:1). Even Solomon's counting on Hiram, the king of Tyre, for materials and other assistance in building the temple is a little suspect (1 Kgs 5:20-25 [Eng. 5:6-11]). Compare the lengths to which Israel goes, at YHWH's behest, to ensure that Israelite craftsmen were available for the tabernacle (Exod 31:1-11). To be sure, all these matters need to be understood in the context of YHWH's granting Solomon wisdom and the king's ability in using that gift properly (1 Kgs 5:26 [Eng. 5:12]). Nevertheless, these concerns seem to be mounting as time passes.

Perhaps Solomon reached his highest point, religiously speaking, in the episode when he dedicated the temple with a remarkable prayer (1 Kgs 8:22-53). After this impressive prayer, Solomon went on to bless Israel (1 Kgs 8:56-61). This blessing also doubles as a call to Israel to devote themselves unreservedly to God (1 Kgs 8:61). Even YHWH in a second appearance confirms the validity of Solomon's remarks after the temple was completed (1 Kgs 9:1-9). At the same time, YHWH reiterates the requirements of Israel's maintaining their covenant with the deity, and the implicit responsibility Solomon has as Israel's king. Whether Solomon will use his vaunted wisdom appropriately and make torah a priority remains a question, however.

It is difficult to evaluate whether Solomon was wise when he built a house for his Egyptian wife (1 Kgs 9:24), but mentioning her at this point in

3. It is important to pay attention to the contradictory statement in 1 Kgs 9:22, which states that Solomon did not conscript Israelites as slaves. Such contradictions are likely the result of fusing disparate sources, each with its own perspective on Solomon. The tradition that asserts that Solomon, in fact, did enslave some Israelites is later confirmed when Rehoboam, Solomon's son, sent Adoram, who had been in charge of forced labor, to negotiate with those Israelites who had rebelled. Before any negotiations took place, the disaffected Israelites stoned Adoram to death. That would be a strange reaction had the man only presided over forced labor that consisted of non-Israelites exclusively (1 Kgs 12:18).

the story seems a little odd. When the Queen of Sheba visited Solomon and gushed about not only his massive wealth but his amazing ability to answer any questions she posed, the focus is so much on Solomon that Israel, as God's elect people and the purpose God had in mind when electing them, recedes into the background (1 Kgs 10:1–5). Curiously, the theological assessment that all of Solomon's greatness should be attributed to God (1 Kgs 10:9) comes from the queen's mouth rather than the narrator's statements. Not only does the queen praise Solomon as simply incomparable she contributes substantially to his wealth (1 Kgs 10:10).

In the remainder of this same chapter, the text puts into bold relief Solomon's incredible wealth (1 Kgs 10:11–12, 14–22). It is so massive that Solomon could send the Queen of Sheba away with everything she desired and whatever she requested (1 Kgs 10:13), presumably without making so much as a dent in the unbelievable amount of wealth he retained. No other king had been so rich or wise (1 Kgs 10:23). Indeed, not only did the *whole earth* seek out Solomon to benefit from his wisdom, but these other monarchs, who paled in comparison to the Israelite king, only made Solomon more opulent with their own presents (1 Kgs 10:24–25). As though this adulation was insufficient, the chapter ends with a summary of the number of chariots and horsemen Solomon could boast about, the fact that silver was as common as stone, that expensive cedar was more plentiful than an ordinary bush, that horses were imported from Egypt and Kue, and how favorable his trading policies were (1 Kgs 10:26–29). It was no wonder that the Queen of Sheba was exhausted from hearing about the king's unprecedented wealth (1 Kgs 10:5)!

Before we go on to the next section, it is significant also to note something that the Queen of Sheba said to and about Solomon. Acknowledging that his fame, wealth, and wisdom all derived from YHWH, she pointed out that this same deity made Solomon king so that he would execute justice and righteousness (*mišpāṭ ûṣᵉdāqāh*) (1 Kgs 10:9). Almost surely, she was right about what YHWH had in mind for Solomon, since wisdom and obedience were both supposed to be prominently displayed in everything Solomon did as Israel's king. We will soon see whether that played out in Solomon's case.

SOLOMON'S TRAGIC FAILURE

The beginning of 1 Kings 11 creates a whiplash effect. After almost ten chapters of virtually unrestrained praise accompanied by intimations of areas of concern, Solomon is roundly condemned. So far, the narration has noted the king's marriage to Pharaoh's daughter (1 Kgs 3:1) and the fact that Solomon had built a house for her (1 Kgs 9:24). After the notation of that single marriage, we learn that the king loved many foreign women (*nāšîm nokriyyôt rabbôt*), all belonging to populations that ordinary Israelites were expressly forbidden to marry (1 Kgs 11:1–2). If average Israelites were not allowed to marry Egyptians, Moabites, Ammonites, Edomites, Sidonians, and Hittites, how much more did that admonition apply to the Israelite king? The answer is obvious. Nevertheless, Solomon indeed loved these very women. One need not guess the number of women involved, for the text supplies specifics: seven hundred wives or princesses, and three hundred concubines (1 Kgs 11:3). Apparently, these were not merely marriages of convenience. Twice the narrator mentions Solomon's love for them, even accenting in the second reference that the king *clung* to these wives in *love* (*dābaq . . . lᵉ'ahăbāh*) (1 Kgs 11:2).

Keep in mind that these marriages were not forbidden for ethnic reasons, but for religious reasons. These women represented people who recognized and worshipped other gods. Even if part of their pantheon, YHWH demanded exclusive commitment. In this case, religious influence unfortunately went in only one direction. Instead of convincing his wives to adopt and serve YHWH, they turned the table. Indeed, they turned Solomon's heart away from the God who supported him, gave him wisdom and riches, and admonished him to walk in David's footsteps, excepting only the matter of David's affair with Bath-Sheba and murder of Uriah.

Solomon's attitude toward the deities whom his vast harem worshipped was hardly casual. It was instead decidedly proactive. For example, the king *walked after* (*wayyēlek . . . 'aḥărê*) Ashtoreth, the goddess of the Sidonians, and Milcom, the god of the Ammonites (1 Kgs 11:5).[4] Obviously, Solomon is denounced for this (1 Kgs 11:4, 6). Still, the king was resolute about demonstrating his religious stance. He built a *high place* for Chemosh, Moab's god, and for Molech, the Ammonite deity, in Jerusalem of all places (1 Kgs 11:7). In perhaps the most damning statement of all, we learn that the king erected shrines to honor the gods of *all his foreign wives*, the number of which, as we have seen, was staggering (1 Kgs 11:8). In sum, Solomon had made Jerusalem into a center of polytheism. Describing Solomon's sins also required superlatives!

---

4. *Walking after* is one of the most prominent metaphors in Hebrew to indicate religious commitment (e.g., Deut 6:14; 8:19; Judg 2:12, 19; Jer 2:23).

DIVINE REACTION TO SOLOMON

As one might expect, YHWH reacted angrily to Solomon (1 Kgs 11:9). Solomon had had every advantage, religiously speaking, in that God had appeared to him twice (1 Kgs 3; 9) and communicated directly to him on at least one other occasion as well (1 Kgs 6:11–12). The text explicitly mentions these two divine appearances and YHWH's warnings about idolatry (1 Kgs 11:9–10). Solomon's sin was not an inadvertent or impulsive slip, but a premeditated and calculated violation of one of the most central tenets of torah.

After the denunciation, YHWH went immediately to the punishment stage. It would not be a slap on the wrist. Solomon's egregious behavior would eventuate in dividing Israel into two different entities. Due to YHWH's deference to David, part of Israel would be retained for his sake (1 Kgs 11:12). Not only does YHWH want to honor David in this manner, but for the sake of Jerusalem, which God had specifically chosen (1 Kgs 11:13). The remainder of the kingdom, however, YHWH would *tear away* (*qārōaʿ ʾeqraʿ*) "from you and your son" (1 Kgs 11:11–12). Only one tribal unit would be preserved for the Davidic dynasty. The rest of Israel would be ruled by other people not connected to David.

Given God's desire for Israel's unity elsewhere in the biblical tradition, this particular form of punishment underscores the degree of YHWH's wrath. The deity was so disgusted with this blatant disregard for such a fundamental belief that only the severest penalty would drive the lesson home. YHWH struck at the very heart of Israel. God's elect people would never be the same. The one and only deity, who had elected one people, would henceforth be a God presiding over a divided people. The *great schism* was on the horizon!

There was no doubt about the source of Solomon's troubles. YHWH instigated them. The deity *raised up an adversary* (*wayyāqem YHWH śāṭān*) against Solomon, Hadad the Edomite (1 Kgs 11:14). A flashback explains why Hadad was the perfect candidate to cause difficulty for Solomon, should the opportunity ever arise. During David's reign, when the king and his military officer, Joab, were in charge, they had once encroached on Edom. The result of that campaign was wholesale slaughter of the male population, with one exception. Somehow, Hadad, along with a few other Edomites, managed to flee to Egypt and find sanctuary there (1 Kgs 11:15–17). At the time Hadad was a child. Eventually, Hadad was treated well by Egypt's king; in fact, he eventually married the sister of Pharaoh's own wife (1 Kgs 11:19). Thus, Hadad had the luxury of being part of Egypt's royal family, which included the advantages provided by the Egyptian court (1 Kgs 11:20). From this stance of privilege and, presumably, power, Hadad became interested in Israelite political affairs when he learned that both David and Joab had died (1 Kgs 11:21). Undoubtedly, Hadad had plenty of incentive in light of Edom's previous devastating defeat at the hands of these two Israelite leaders. Though the pharaoh tried to dissuade Hadad from leaving the security of Egypt, Hadad pled for permission to go (1 Kgs 11:22). That made Hadad a perfect foil for God to use against the wayward Solomon.

Then God put another obstacle in Solomon's way, when the deity raised up a second adversary against him (*wayyāqem 'ĕlōhîm lô śāṭān*) (1 Kgs 11:23). This time it was Rezon, who had fled from Hadadezer, king of Zobah. King Hadadezer had suffered badly also when David attacked. As well, when Aram/Syria allied with Zobah, they did not fare any better (2 Sam 8:3-6; 10:15-19). Both had dreadful losses. In the aftermath of this defeat, Rezon managed to surround himself with sufficient muscle to end up in Damascus, the capitol of Aram/Syria, where he became king (1 Kgs 11:24). From that position, Rezon did what he could to be a thorn in Solomon's side, since he naturally detested Israel (1 Kgs 11:25). Even though this seems to reflect the *Realpolitik* of competing countries when David and Solomon reigned, the biblical text does not shrink from attributing these upheavals ultimately to divine activity.

The last person to become a nemesis to Solomon was Jeroboam, an Israelite, and a previous servant of the king (1 Kgs 11:26). When introduced, we learn that he had lifted up his hand against the king. In the following explanation that underlies Jerobaom's reasons, briefly we are led to believe that an ordinary conflict is being narrated rather than the deity's orchestrating what is about to take place. First, we are informed about a building project that Solomon undertook, the specifics of which are difficult to ascertain. This involved constructing a section of the city called the Millo and closing up the breach of the city of David, perhaps another section of Jerusalem (1 Kgs 11:27). Second, during this activity, Jeroboam demonstrated his talent, perhaps in the area of administration, something that the king noticed. Because of this capability, Solomon put Jeroboam in charge of the forced labor in Israel (1 Kgs 11:28). While Jeroboam was executing these new duties, he was confronted by Ahijah the Shilonite, a prophet. That changed everything.

It turned out that YHWH used prophetic mediation via Ahijah to communicate the divine intentions regarding Solomon. The first two adversaries, Hadad and Rezon, God had induced directly to move against Solomon. In this instance, prophetic mediation was in play. When the prophet found Jeroboam, Ahijah was clad in a new garment (1 Kgs 11:29). Being told this was not merely to let us know that the prophet had donned new clothes for the occasion. Since prophets often used props to enhance an oracle, one expects that this garment will itself become a prop. That indeed is the case here.[5] Before Ahijah uttered a single word, he tore his new robe into twelve pieces (1 Kgs 11:30). He offered ten pieces to Jeroboam and then started his oracle. The symbolism of Ahijah's doing this is quite obvious—Solomon's kingdom is about to be torn apart. In the oracle itself, speaking for YHWH, Ahijah points out that ten tribal units will be designated for Jeroboam. Only one tribal unit will be retained for the sake of David and for the sake of Jerusalem (1 Kgs 11:31–32). Ahijah then specifies Solomon's violations, even though the prophet uses a grammatical construction intimating that Solomon was not the sole offender: "because *they* have forsaken me and bowed down to Ashtoreth, Sidon's deity, and bowed down to Chemosh, Moab's deity, and to Milcom, the Ammonite deity; and *they* have not walked in my ways by doing right in my eyes, or by keeping my statutes or ordinances like *his* father did" (1 Kgs 11:33). The Greek version corrects this anomaly, but the Hebrew may subtly convey that Solomon *and* Israel were equally guilty of idolatry. Regardless, not only the monarchy but the people will bear the brunt of this severe punishment.

Jeroboam is about to become the king of Israel, that is, the northern portion of Israelite territory (1 Kgs 11:37). The southern kingdom will be called Judah. Because this is divinely mandated, there are still requirements about obedience to the covenant (1 Kgs 11:38). Nevertheless, Israel's disunity is about to become a reality. Though this punishment will not last forever, when it will be over is not specified (1 Kgs 11:39).

Somehow, Solomon got wind of the exchange between Ahijah and Jeroboam, prompting the king to try to kill Jeroboam (1 Kgs 11:40). In response, the marked man sought sanctuary in Egypt. How ironic it was that Jeroboam, a man high in the administration of an Israelite king, felt safer in Egypt than in Israel. YHWH's rescuing Israel from Egyptian slavery was a basis for the Mosaic covenant and an act of divine grace to which later prophets would consistently and persistently call attention. With Solomon, though, Israel had traded places with Egypt. Solomon had become an Israelite pharaoh! In any case, Jeroboam stayed in Egypt until Solomon died. Thus, Solomon did not live to witness the great schism, but he had prepared all the ingredients necessary for that ultimate rift in Israel. Rehoboam, Solomon's son, and successor, acted in a manner that guaranteed that Israel would undergo the *great schism*.

---

5. For example, note the use of iron horns by Zedekiah, a prophet in Ahab's court, to underscore the prophetic prediction that the king would be victorious in the next battle (1 Kgs 22:11–12).

REHOBOAM AND THE STRAW THAT BROKE THE CAMEL'S BACK

Israel was still unified when Rehoboam went to Shechem to be crowned as king. That is why *all Israel* had gone there (1 Kgs 12:1). It did not take long for Jeroboam to realize that this ceremony was taking place. He returned from Egypt, where he had been hiding (1 Kgs 12:2). Indicating how fragile Israel's unity was at this juncture, *they*—meaning *all the assembly of Israel* (w^ekol-q^ehal $Yiśrā'ēl$)—summoned Jeroboam. In the span of two verses, *all Israel* stood on opposite sides. The language of *all Israel* accents the people as a unified body acting in concert with their mission as a divinely elected body rather than being literally true. It reflects *mythic veracity* by underscoring the unity that is essential to Israel's elect status as the people of YHWH. Seeing *all Israel* juxtaposed on two different sides of Israel, representing differing factions, demonstrates rhetorically that Israel was teetering as a potential hopelessly divided body. Jeroboam and this part of *all Israel* was about to present its demands to Rehoboam, who was standing with a counterpart of *all Israel* (1 Kgs 12:3). This is an ominous situation.

The appeal from one side was quite simple. Not only that, it offered the possibility of maintaining unity and avoiding division, depending on the other side's response. At the same time, given God's raising up adversaries against Solomon and the grim prophecy of Ahijah, we should not hold our breath thinking that the community would maintain a semblance of unity after this confrontation. In any case, Jeroboam and his segment of *all Israel* complained about Solomon's heavy yoke and asked that Rehoboam make things easier when he assumed power (1 Kgs 12:4). Should the new king agree to these terms, the unity of the kingdom might have a chance of being preserved. Indeed, if Rehoboam reverses his father's policies, Jeroboam and his deputation promises that "we will serve you." Perhaps there is a glimmer of hope in that Rehoboam made no decision on the spot. Instead, he asked for three days before he would issue a verdict. The people left, presumably hoping for the best (1 Kgs 12:5).

To his credit, Rehoboam sought advice. The first group he consulted was comprised of *the elders* ($hazz^eqēnîm$) who had stood before Solomon (1 Kgs 12:6). In light of the wisdom motif found throughout the Solomon story, being an *elder* possibly reflected something more than age, but prudence, insight, and common sense. Regardless, Rehoboam asks them to advise him about answering the ultimatum that the Jeroboam deputation had put forward.

The elders' response was the essence of reason. Basically, they argued that the new king could expect Israel to serve him as he in turn served the people. Indeed, when the elders responded they twice used both the noun *servant* and the verb *serve* to put in bold relief the posture they were encouraging the new king to assume (1 Kgs 12:7). Should the king adopt this strategy, and also speak *good words* ($d^e b\bar{a}r\hat{i}m\ \underline{t}\hat{o}b\hat{i}m$) when the king answers, almost certainly the population would happily become servants *all the days*. Essentially, the elders concede that Solomon's policies had been intolerable, and a change would not only be welcome but perhaps smart politics as well.

But Rehoboam was unimpressed with this advice and rejected it outright. Having spurned the elders' suggestion, Rehoboam turned to another group. Despite the conventional translations of most English versions, the people with whom Rehoboam consulted were designated *children* ($y^e l\bar{a}d\hat{i}m$) (1 Kgs 12:8). The customary word in Hebrew for *young men* is $n^{e\prime}\bar{a}r\hat{i}m$. Why use the term *children* in this context? Given the advice they give to Rehoboam, with whom they had grown up and beside whom they had stood (1 Kgs 12:8), it is difficult to avoid the impression that the narrator's calling them *children* had little to do with their age. Instead, the word put the accent squarely on their immaturity, impulsiveness, selfishness, and even stupidity. These advisors may have been young men chronologically, but otherwise they were indeed children. The advice they offered to Rehoboam was virtually guaranteed to backfire.

Rehoboam asked this second group directly; indeed, more directly than the question he had posed to the elders. In fact, with this second question Rehoboam incorporated the advice proffered by the elders. They had recommended that the new king serve and speak more positively to the people in return for their loyalty (1 Kgs 12:7). That, obviously, would have amounted to *lightening up* Solomon's policies, which is what the deputation led by Jeroboam had requested (1 Kgs 12:4). Without mentioning the elders' advice, Rehoboam focuses on what the citizens had demanded: "What do you advise that *we* answer this people who have said to *me*, 'Lighten the yoke that your father put on us' (1 Kgs 12:9)?" Is Rehoboam using the royal *we* when he asks about how *we* should respond? Or, is this a subtle signal that the advisors themselves might have a role in implementing the policies about which they are presently being questioned?

Regardless of how that question is answered, there is no subtlety whatsoever about what the *children* with whom Rehoboam consults are advising. Instead of Rehoboam's making things easier for the Israelite population, the new king should double down on Solomon's policies. If Israel thought Solomon was unfair or unduly harsh, they had better get used to it. Using a crude metaphor, the *children* urge Rehoboam to tell the people that "my little finger is thicker than my father's loins" (1 Kgs 12:10). Quite obviously, *loins* in this instance are a euphemism for another part of the male body!

Just in case the people do not quite comprehend this metaphor, Rehoboam is encouraged to remove all doubt by telling the people that, while Solomon used whips on them, Rehoboam will use scorpions (1 Kgs 12:11). In effect, Solomon's reign would seem like a picnic when compared to what Rehoboam had in mind. The yoke is about to become heavier. At least that will be the case should Rehoboam listen to this second set of advisors.

Defying common sense, Rehoboam decides to opt for what the *children* had advised. When Jeroboam and *all the people* returned to Rehoboam to see whether their demands were taken seriously, they discovered that their situation was about to take a turn for the worse. Rehoboam answered harshly (1 Kgs 12:13). The narrator repeats what we had just witnessed, namely, that the new king had no interest in what the elders suggested and every intention to follow the *children's* advice (1 Kgs 12:13–14). Even on the surface, what the *children* urged could not have been more stupid. This was not only bad advice, but tone-deaf politically. A skilled, howbeit devious, politician would have assured the people of policies that would have improved their lives, regardless of the fact that he was not in the least interested in that outcome. But informing the people at the outset that the king was about to make their lives more difficult, rubs salt into the wound. If this advice was stupid, the man who followed it without thinking about its consequences took stupidity to another level.

As it turns out, though, as tempting it is to attribute the advice the *children* gave and Rehoboam followed to old-fashioned stupidity, that explanation is not sufficient. Divine sovereignty has to be factored into this equation. This is not the first time in the biblical tradition that God works through human predilections and evil propensities. These events have unfolded with a combination of divine orchestration and human perfidy. Though Rehoboam and those who gave him such colossal bad advice did what they did for their own selfish motives, which included exercising power over hapless subjects, God used their behavior as a means of bringing judgment on Solomon's kingship (1 Kgs 12:15). This is precisely what YHWH had in mind when the deity spoke through Ahijah the prophet. At this juncture, what was transpiring in Israel was a function of human behavior and the inevitability of divine providence.

ISRAEL (JEROBOAM) AND JUDAH (REHOBOAM) DIVIDED

The way the people responded to Rehoboam's ill-advised announcement that he would have no difficulty in outdoing his father's exploitation of Israel was all but predictable. Rehoboam had left no room for further negotiation. In essence he had said, "This is what I am going to do, for I am king. Take it or leave it." It is impossible to know what Rehoboam thought the people would do with this dictatorial stance. Still, he demonstrated incomprehensible arrogance by apparently thinking that they would merely accept his intransigence and go home with their tails between their legs. If that is what he thought, Rehoboam was in for a rude awakening.

Using an eerie imitation of the slogan/song that David had once heard when Sheba rebelled, once more a member of the House of David heard the strains of a rebellious cry. On the previous occasion, *he* blew the trumpet and declared (2 Sam 20:1):

> In David we have no portion,
>> nor in the son of Jesse an inheritance.
> Everyone to his own tent, O Israel.

This time it was not a single man, but *all Israel* (*kol-Yiśrāʾēl*) who declaimed the same sentiment, and for good measure added this ominous line:

> Look to your own House, O David (1 Kgs 12:16).

After this defiant response, Israel indeed went home. But it would not take long to realize that the people did this not to attend to normal chores or any other quotidian matters. A full-scale rebellion was taking shape.

Rehoboam evidently suspected this. As a monarch who presided over Israelites living in the cities of Judah (1 Kgs 12:17), he decided to take decisive counter measures. The king *sent* Adoram, who was head of forced labor (1 Kgs 12:18). But where did Rehoboam send him? Presumably, inferring from what happened, the king had sent Adoram either to negotiate further or perhaps to talk the rebels out of the course on which they were embarking. Regardless, whatever results Rehoboam was hoping for by sending Adoram, it ended up being a disaster. Adoram was assassinated before he was able to utter a word. Upon seeing this, Rehoboam got in his chariot and fled from Shechem back to Jerusalem. The narrator summed up what had taken place by noting that Israel since that time has been in rebellion against the House of David (1 Kgs 12:19). The ensuing schism was destined to be more permanent than any previous rift. Right after Rehoboam made it to Jerusalem, we learn that the rest of Israel immediately made Jeroboam their new king. Just as Ahijah had proclaimed, only Judah remained loyal to the Davidic dynasty (1 Kgs 12:20). From now on, Israel would be divided into two kingdoms.

Still, that was a circumstance that Rehoboam wanted to prevent. To do that, he mustered troops from Judah and Benjamin, even though strictly speaking only one tribe was supposed to stay in the Davidic camp (1 Kgs 12:21). Rehoboam's army was massive, consisting of 180,000 troops. Sending Adoram had been ineffective. From Rehoboam's perspective, a sizeable show of force might yield more positive results. Once more, however, God intervened with a prophetic word. Shemaiah was the prophet who spoke in God's behalf. The divine word was simple. Rehoboam was to do nothing about this schism. Under no circumstances were Judah or Benjamin to wage war in order to force the rebellious north back into the fold. This is the outcome that God had orchestrated as a judgment against Solomon. The judgment had to stand. God's advice via the *man of God* was that the troops were to go home. And, that is precisely what happened (1 Kgs 12:24).

When the war that Rehoboam had planned to wage was in effect canceled by prophetic interference, Jeroboam was able to fortify the new northern kingdom. First, he rebuilt or enlarged Shechem in the hill country of Ephraim and resided there (1 Kgs 12:25).[6] He also built Penuel. Then, we are given an insight into Jeroboam's long-term strategy. Worrying that Israelites from the north might in time compromise their loyalty when offering sacrifices in the Jerusalem temple, he decided to nip that practice in the bud. Jeroboam wanted to make sure that Israelites in the northern sections had no need to go to Jerusalem to offer sacrifices (1 Kgs 12:26–27). Being in Jerusalem might make Israelites nostalgic for the Davidic dynasty which they once revered.

Jeroboam sought advice—from whom is not mentioned—and as a result constructed two golden calves (1 Kgs 12:28). Then he proclaimed, "For long enough you have gone up to Jerusalem. Look now: 'Your God, O Israel, who brought you up out of the land of Egypt.'"[7] In doing this, Jeroboam is mirroring what Israel did in the infamous incident of the golden calf that Aaron had fashioned when his brother, Moses, had been on the mountain for too long (Exod 32:1–6). Of all the Israelite traditions that Jeroboam might have imitated, he could not have chosen a worse example. The golden calf was emblematic of a day that lived in infamy in Israelite lore. Making this bogus worship as easy as possible, Jeroboam erected shrines in Dan and Bethel, basically northernmost and southernmost sites that would accommodate Israelite worship. How ironic that the new northern kingdom came

---

6. Depending on context, Hebrew *bānāh* has the nuance of *rebuilding* or *enlarging*. Since the city was already in existence (1 Kgs 12:1), that seems to be the meaning in this verse.

7. The word *'ĕlōhîm* can also be translated *gods*, as it is a masculine plural noun. However, because in this context the name being invoked is the same as the deity who brought Israel out of Egypt, almost certainly Jeroboam is equating the two calves with the Israelite deity, YHWH, and not merely generic gods.

about because YHWH was judging Solomon for his idolatrous practices when this new kingdom was no improvement over the idolatry that was rampant in Solomon's time. Jeroboam's making these two golden calves constituted a paradigmatic example of sin for the new kingdom (1 Kgs 12:30).

As bad as that was, though, Jeroboam did not confine his offenses to the two golden calves. He violated other Israelite religious traditions as well. He also made houses on *high places*, presumably to accommodate the personnel who conducted worship on these sites. In addition, he appointed non-Levitical priests to preside over various rites (1 Kgs 12:31). Demonstrating that Jeroboam fostered regular rather than desultory religious practices, he held a feast on an appointed day (1 Kgs 12:32). He also sacrificed on the altar, at least at the site in Bethel. Leaving no doubt, the text underscores that these sacrifices were offered to the golden calves. As well, Jeroboam saw to it that priests who were in charge of worship at the high places also served at the Bethel sanctuary. The narration makes sure that we know that all of these plans came from Jeroboam himself (1 Kgs 12:33). As bad as the southern kingdom became under Solomon, the new northern kingdom was equally bad.

ANOTHER PROPHET ON THE SCENE

Just as Ahijah once denounced Solomon's administration and detailed the judgment that the Davidic dynasty would face, the new northern kingdom did not get a pass either. Because this new group committed sins of the same sort, it also provoked divine disfavor. This time, though, the judgment was announced by an unnamed prophet, called here a *man of God*. Interestingly, he was from Judah (1 Kgs 13:1). When he appeared, Jeroboam happened to be standing by the altar in Bethel about to burn incense, an activity that typically was indicative of non-Israelite ritual. In a curious form of prophetic speech, the *man of God* addressed the altar as though it were pulsating with life (1 Kgs 13:2). Of course, those standing by the altar would have no trouble hearing what the prophet had to say.

The prophet informs the altar (!) that the time would come when a future member of the House of David, namely Josiah (see 2 Kgs 22:1ff.), would take the throne. This king would sacrifice on *you*—meaning the altar—the very priests who had been sacrificing on this site; moreover, on *you*—again, meaning this altar—human bones will be burned (1 Kgs 13:2). By all means, these prophetic words predict serious judgment. As the *man of God* was uttering these dire words, he also gave a sign to back up the oracle. The sign would be the altar's being broken down, with ashes being poured out from the residue (1 Kgs 13:3). Before the prophet could say another thing, however, King Jeroboam interrupted by stretching out his hand toward the *man of God* and ordered that he be seized. At once, the king's hand dried up so that he could no longer use it properly (1 Kgs 13:4). Simultaneously, just as the prophet had predicted, the altar was mysteriously torn down and the ashes scattered. All of this was to fulfill the sign given by YHWH's prophet (1 Kgs 13:5).

Upon seeing what had happened, Jeroboam became contrite. He desperately asked the *man of God* to plead with YHWH to restore his hand (1 Kgs 13:6). The *man of God* immediately did as Jeroboam had requested, with the result that the king's hand was restored. Then, Jeroboam invites the *man of God* to his home to refresh himself and receive a reward (1 Kgs 13:7). Apparently, Jeroboam was trying to curry favor after he had incurred the prophet's wrath. But that ploy did not work. Under no circumstances, regardless of how large the reward might be, would the prophet go to the king's house for so much as a piece of bread or drink of water (1 Kgs 13:8). The reason was simple: God had specifically commanded that the *man of God* neither eat nor drink after his oracle; as well, he was to return home taking a different route than the one he took when he came initially (1 Kgs 13:9). The *man of God* had no further dealings with Jeroboam (1 Kgs 13:10).

THE AFTERMATH OF THE SCHISM

Unfortunately, this schism was not temporary. From the time of this terrible division, disunity in Israel was the norm; unity was both sporadic and ephemeral. Furthermore, though Solomon's idolatry was the main reason that Israel had been condemned, now that there was a southern and northern version neither entity avoided idolatrous behavior. Worshipping many gods became the new normal. As with disunity, keeping the covenant that YHWH had made with Israel was also sporadic and ephemeral.

Ironically, the same prophet who had announced to Jeroboam that he would be the new king of all Israel except for the part reserved in deference to David (1 Kgs 11:29-37), now condemned Jeroboam for his idolatrous practices. Jeroboam was no improvement. Part of the judgment on Jeroboam involved his son's death. Another aspect of the judgment would implicate all the people (1 Kgs 14:1-20). Ahijah had denounced Israel because Solomon had catered to the foreign deities worshiped by his many wives, which led to Israel being divided into two opposing peoples, both of which in turn ended up being equally polytheistic. Taking these paths did not bode well for the future of God's elect people.

As noted, the hostility that eventuated in schism in the first place, divinely induced, to be sure, continued between the northern and southern nations. Rehoboam and Jeroboam battled one another constantly even after the original events that led to the establishment of the two new kingdoms (1 Kgs 14:30). As well, Asa and Baasha, kings of Judah and Israel, respectively, warred against each other *all their days* (1 Kgs 15:16). On occasion, one of the Israelite *nations* forged an alliance with a foreign power against their counterpart. This happened when Asa, king of Judah, sought the help of Benhadad, king of Aram/Syria, to confront Baasha, king of Israel (1 Kgs 15:16-24). Granted, sometimes the south and north allied with each other against a common enemy. That was the case when Ahab of Israel asked Jehoshaphat of Judah to join him in recapturing a city from Aram/Syria (1 Kgs 22:1ff.), a period when there was peace between the two Israelite communities (1 Kgs 22:44). A similar situation obtained when Jehoshaphat of Judah came to the aid of Jehoram of Israel (Joram ben Ahab) as he made a move against Moab (2 Kgs 3:6-8). Mostly, however, Judah and Israel remained at each other's throats, as when Amaziah of Judah sought to smooth relationships with Jehoash of Israel by meeting face-to-face. Jehoash flatly rejected the offer, which ended up in a bloody confrontation when Amaziah pressed the issue (2 Kgs 14:8-14).

The disunity that plagued God's people after the schism was manifested not only *between* Israel and Judah, but also *within* them. This was especially true when it came to Israel. The Davidic dynasty remained intact throughout Judah's existence. In Israel, however, political instability was the rule. It was commonplace for one brand-new dynasty to replace another. Sometimes this was a function of old-fashioned political maneuvering and sometimes it involved God's continuing judgment. Either way, though, conspiracy against sitting kings and assassinations were regular occurrences from the time that Israel was founded until their defeat at the hand of the Assyrians. The following Israelite kings were removed and replaced by conspiracy and assassination: Nadab ben Jeroboam (1 Kgs 15:27-28); Elah ben Baasha (1 Kgs 16:8-10); Joram ben Ahab (2 Kgs 9:14, 24; aka "King Jehoram" of Israel); Zechariah ben Jeroboam (= Jeroboam II; 2 Kgs 15:10-11); Pekahiah ben Menahem (2 Kgs 15:23-25); Pekah ben Remaliah (2 Kgs 15:30). In each of these cases, another dynasty came to power. Conspiracy and assassination were not unknown in Judah either. However, in those instances, which involved Joash/Jehoash ben Ahaziah (2 Kgs 12:20-21), Amaziah ben Joash/Jehoash (2 Kgs 14:18-20), and Amon ben Manasseh (2 Kgs 21:19-23), the Davidic dynasty was not replaced by another *house*.

As though these instances of conspiracy and assassination were not bad enough, from time to time the violence was excessive. For instance, the whole house of Jeroboam was exterminated (1 Kgs 15:29). Equally, after Elah had been killed, Zimri, the man who assassinated the king, proceeded to eliminate every male in the house of Baasha (1 Kgs 16:11-12). Zimri had managed to rule for only seven days after this atrocity (1 Kgs 16:15)! Zimri avoided assassination himself only by committing suicide (1 Kgs 16:18). Right after this, two factions were in charge of differing parts of Israel; one group being led by Tibni ben Ginath and the other following Omri (1 Kgs 16:21). Then again, when Jehu was in the process of purging the House of Ahab, at God's instigation (2 Kgs 9:6-10), he not only took the life of the current Israelite king, Joram ben Ahab, but the life of Azariah, king of Judah, too (2 Kgs 9:27-28). Later Jehu had Jezebel, Ahab's infamous wife, thrown out of a window (2 Kgs 9:30-33). Most egregious, however, was Jehu's diabolical plot which eventuated in decapitating Ahab's seventy sons (2 Kgs 10:1-10). Anyone else who had a role in Ahab's administration was slaughtered with these scions (2 Kgs 10:11). Similarly, when Amnon's servants conspired against and murdered him, these conspirators were themselves killed by *the people of the land* (2 Kgs 21:24). In both Israel and Judah after the *Great Schism*, violent actions triggered even more savage reactions.

Also, both Judah and Israel offended equally as far as obeying torah was concerned. Some kings were unmitigated disasters when it came to taking the covenant YHWH had made with Israel seriously. But even so-called good kings were often said to be only partially obedient to an Israelite way of life. The narrator's denunciation of Jeroboam and thus Israel (1 Kgs 14:7-11) is paralleled by a denunciation of Rehoboam and thus Judah (1 Kgs 14:21-24). Morally speaking, neither kingdom came off as moral exemplars. Even when the narration praises a king for being obedient to God's ways, often there is a disclaimer. Asa of Judah, for example, is portrayed as eliminating certain abominable practices (1 Kgs 15:11-13, 14b-15), but still leaving other non-Israelite rituals in place (1 Kgs 15:14a). Likewise, Jehoshaphat, Asa's son, earns high marks (1 Kgs 22:43, 46), but was not as thorough as he should have been (1 Kgs 22:43cd). Then again, Jeroboam II of Israel was a slight improvement over his notorious father (2 Kgs 3:2), but the improvement was marginal (2 Kgs 3:3). Another Israelite king, Jehu, got rid of Baal worship (2 Kgs 10:28) and yet managed to earn as much approbation as Jeroboam, the original king of the northern kingdom (2 Kgs 10:29, 31). This same pattern obtained with Joash/Jehoash of Judah (2 Kgs 12:2-3), Amaziah (2 Kgs 14:3-4), Azariah (2 Kgs 15:3-4), and Jotham (2 Kgs 15:34-35). One king of Judah, Ahaz, went so far as to sacrifice his own son (2 Kgs 16:1-4).

Even when Hezekiah and Josiah became model kings of Judah—after Israel had suffered defeat at the hand of the Assyrians—their example was too little and too late to reverse divine judgment. Hezekiah was a veritable exemplar (2 Kgs 18:1-8). YHWH had responded very positively to his heartfelt prayer when Sennacherib, the Assyrian king, threatened (2 Kgs 19:15-19, 20-34). Yet, that did not keep his son, Manasseh, from being the epitome of an evil king in Judah (2 Kgs 21:1-9). Indeed, Manasseh's reputation was so vile that even a king who was incomparably good, namely, Josiah, was not able to do enough religious reform to induce YHWH to forego exile (2 Kgs 23:21-23, 26-27). The *Great Schism* concluded when Israel and Judah were exiled by foreign powers, which was orchestrated by Israel's God.

CONCLUSION

The Great Schism is the quintessential example of division in Israel. Yet, well before that time, Israel had experienced disunity in varying circumstances, as we have tried to demonstrate. This time around, however, the division was deeper, more sustained, and longer lasting. Circumstances this dire naturally would lead to prophetic reflection. How would Israel's prophetic tradition react to a hopelessly divided Israel? To that topic we now turn.

Chapter 10

Israel's Division in Prophetic Perspective

INTRODUCTION

It is hardly surprising that in the biblical prophetic materials Israel's division is an important subject. After all, virtually every prophet either denounces Israel and predicts eventual exile orchestrated by God or promises that, after enduring exile for a time, YHWH will forgive, and then eventually restore Israel. However, none of the prophetic oracles are addressed to Israel *as a whole*. The prophets directed their words either to the southern kingdom, Judah, or the northern kingdom, Israel. That is, the prophets spoke to a divided Israel. This means that prophets geared their messages primarily to Israel or Judah, only rarely to both. At the same time, an aspect of the forgiveness and restoration they envisioned was that in time divided Israel would become once again a single, unified community.

From a historical perspective, it is difficult to know precisely what Israelite experiences or traditions prompted these prophetic perspectives. But from a canonical perspective we are on much firmer ground. Since a basic source for the prophetic material derives from the Latter Prophets, part of the second section of the Bible in its Hebrew format, it is hardly a stretch to read this material as well in light of the Former Prophets, from which all of the stories of Israel's division derive.[1] The nomenclature of calling this biblical section Prophets ($N^eb\hat{i}$'$\hat{i}m$), divided into Former and Latter elements,

---

1. The Former Prophets consist of Joshua, Judges, 1–2 Samuel, and 1–2 Kings. The Latter Prophets include Isaiah, Jeremiah, Ezekiel, and the Book of the Twelve (sometimes called Minor Prophets because of their shorter length). Because Christian Bibles follow the order of the Greek version, they have a different order than the three-part form of the Jewish Bible: Torah/Law; Prophets (Former and Latter); Writings.

suggests that those responsible for ordering the canon in this manner had precisely this in mind. These two sections mutually inform each other.

In this chapter, I will take into account those prophetic passages that acknowledge the sins of Israel and Judah, respectively, but concentrate on features in the text that speak to the issue of the community's eventual restoration as a unified community. To do this, I will follow the canonical ordering of the Latter Prophets.

ISAIAH

For the most part, oracles in the book of Isaiah are specific to Judah, the southern kingdom, just as one would expect based on the introduction (Isa 1:1).[2] Indeed, throughout the book even the name *Israel* is used more or less generically to indicate primarily Judah (e.g., Isa 27:6; 43:1). On occasion, though, the text alludes to both kingdoms, as seems to be the case for instance in Isa 9:20 (Eng. 9:21) and Isa 10:11. In the former reference, places in the northern kingdom are depicted as arrayed against Judah. In the latter reference, Jerusalem, here a cipher for the whole southern kingdom, needs to brace for a punishment such as God had formerly administered to Samaria, a common name for the northern kingdom. For all practical purposes, though, the book of Isaiah is oriented to Judah, the southern kingdom.

But that is not the case when it comes to texts that emphasize restoration. For example, in a passage that clearly concentrates on restoration *in that day* (*bayyôm hahû'*) (Isa 11:10), YHWH will recover the remnants of the chosen people from various places, including Assyria (Isa 11:11), the very place where some from the northern kingdom had been deported. The people God has in mind are called *the outcasts of Israel* (*nidḥê Yiśrā'ēl*) and *the dispersed of Judah* (*nepuṣôt yehûdāh*) (Isa 11:12). The very next verse demonstrates that both kingdoms are in view in that Ephraim will not be envious of Judah, and vice versa (Isa 11:13). This restoration will eventuate in an Israel as it was when coming out of Egypt, as a unified people (Isa 11:16).

---

2. It has long been a scholarly consensus that the present book of Isaiah consists of sections which were originally written in different eras. With only a few exceptions due to final editing, the first thirty-nine chapters reflect a time around the middle of the eighth century. Chapters 40–55 belong to a period when return from Babylonian exile was possible in the late sixth century, whereas chapters 56–66 derive from a time later still. For our purposes, these genetic issues are subordinated. We will concentrate on the text in its final canonical form.

One of the features of the future restoration the prophet has in mind for God's people is that non-Israelites will be included. This emphasis occurs, for example, in Isa 44:5. People will say, "I belong to YHWH," or refer to themselves as Jacob or Israel. Even though all of the book of Isaiah is oriented to Judah, surely in those passages that underscore foreign participation in Israel's being made whole the northern kingdom would participate in this glorious restoration and reunification. When YHWH refers to Jacob as "my servant" and Israel "whom I have chosen" (Isa 44:1), a unified Israel is in view. This community will be blessed with water or streams that refresh dry ground and with an outpouring of God's spirit (Isa 44:3). It seems inconceivable that foreigners would be part of this incredible divine action while the northern kingdom might be excluded.

Isaiah 56 has a similar emphasis. The first line of Isa 56:8 reads: "Utterance of the lord YHWH, who gathers Israel's outcasts" (*nidḥê Yiśrā'ēl*). These *outcasts* are Israelites primed to be rescued from their previous exile. But they are not the only ones about to be gathered. Anyone who is inclined to conduct himself or herself in a manner reflective of Israelite moral and religious behavior will participate in this divine gathering (Isa 56:1–7). This gathering is something operative *for all peoples* (*lᵉkol-hā'ammîm*) (Isa 56:7). Once again, such an inclusive gathering in which YHWH is the *gatherer* would not neglect the northern kingdom of Israel. Under what circumstance would the northern part of God's chosen people not be part of *all peoples*?

Equally, when Isaiah alludes to the traditions reflective of the exodus and subsequent covenant that YHWH made with Israel, *all Israel*—and not the southern kingdom only—is without question to be regarded as an essential part of God's reconstituted unified people. Allusions to Moses, the exodus from Egypt, the wilderness wanderings, all indicative of divine power, are used to appeal to YHWH to employ similar divine power, return to the chosen people, and act once again in their behalf (Isa 63:10–19). That appeal continues in Isaiah 64, made all the more poignant in light of Judah's destruction (Isa 64:10–11). After YHWH's response in chapter 65, in which the deity rehearses the divine efforts to induce faithfulness and obedience, and is finally resigned to point out that the persistently sinful will undergo judgment while those seeking God will fare better, the deity finally announces the creation of a new heavens and a new earth (Isa 65:17; cf. 65:1–16). This will require a new Israel in which blessings of every sort abound (Isa 65:18–25). There is no question that this new Israel includes Judah and Jerusalem, its capitol (e.g., Isa 65:18–19). Just as certainly, it obviously also includes the rest of Israel, especially in light of the fact that *all flesh* (Isa 66:23) will experience this glorious restoration. Not only will Israel become unified, but they will also be a catalyst for a newly unified humanity.

JEREMIAH

In the book of Jeremiah, the distinctions between Israel as the northern kingdom and Judah as the southern kingdom are more pronounced than they were in Isaiah. As early as chapter 3 Israel, representing the north, is held up as a negative example to induce Judah, representing the south, not to follow in the footsteps of *that backsliding one, Israel* (*mᵉšubāh Yiśrāʾēl . . . hîʾ*), who engaged in reprehensible behavior (Jer 3:6–10). In the same context, the prophet notes that Israel is less guilty than Judah (Jer 3:11). At this point, the prophet is urged to proclaim a word to the northern kingdom in which it is invited to return to YHWH and acknowledge its own guilt (Jer 3:12–13). In time, presumably after both communities repent, mend their ways, return to covenant obedience, and the like, then the *House of Judah* will come back together with the *House of Israel* to the promised land (Jer 3:18).

Sometimes in Jeremiah language that conceivably denotes the northern kingdom, like *Israel* or the *House of Israel* (e.g., Jer 4:1; 5:11), refers primarily to Judah/Jerusalem in the south. It is difficult to know how often *all Israel* is reflected in a particular passage. When YHWH, for instance, is quoted, so to speak, as referring to "my people," a cipher common to the exodus tradition, should we regard that as specifying only Judah? Granted, the northern kingdom had already been defeated and many of its prominent members exiled to Assyria when Jeremiah enters the scene. Still, because the restoration of both sections of Israel is so strategic to the overall prophetic message in this book such language may have a double purpose. That is, to be sure, Judah is being specifically addressed in Jeremiah, but the prospects of its northern siblings one day rejoining the family may also be in view.

This may especially be the case whenever language designating God's people, whether it is designated as Israel or Judah, is combined with allusions to the exodus from Egypt, the wilderness trek, and the Mosaic covenant. This occurs, for example, in Jeremiah 11, where the initial addressees are the *men of Judah* and the *inhabitants of Jerusalem* (Jer 11:2). Immediately following this identification are references to the covenant God made with the people whom the deity had rescued from Egypt—the *iron furnace*—an agreement that was predicated on YHWH's being "your God" and Israel being "my people." Even the promise of land made to the ancestors is mentioned (Jer 11:3–5). Clearly, this quintessential Israelite tradition involved Israel as a whole. Even though Jeremiah 11 has Judah/Jerusalem in mind, Israel as an entire community cannot be far from the prophetic imagination. Indeed, the rehearsal of Israel's infamous breaking of the covenant implicates *all* Israel, not merely Judah/Jerusalem (Jer 11:10). In light of Israel's collective past, one should not automatically construe the *House of Israel* and the *House of Judah* as mutually exclusive terms (Jer 11:17). As well, when the return from Babylonian exile is equated with the exodus from Egypt (e.g., Jer 16:14-15), once again that suggests Israel is more extensive than simply the southern segment.

Jeremiah 23 appears to configure Judah and Israel as part of a unified community. In the context of denouncing *shepherds*, probably meaning kings or religious leaders, or both, who have scattered the *sheep*, a reference to the chosen people, not only will YHWH deal appropriately with these bad shepherds but the deity also will gather the *remnant of my flock* ($š^{e}$'*ērît ṣō'nî*) and bring them back to the fold. This divine action will in addition entail installing caring shepherds, and raising up a righteous *Branch* in the Davidic line who will rule wisely and justly. This will eventuate in Judah being saved and Israel dwelling securely (Jer 23:1-6). The argument that this is inclusive of all Israel is as follows: (1) the gathering of the people who had been deported to foreign countries is equated to the rescue from Egyptian bondage, when Israel was unified (Jer 23:7-8); (2) prophets from the northern kingdom (= Samaria) and the southern kingdom are simultaneously excoriated (e.g., Jer 23:13-15).

Both Israel and Judah are surely included in the restoration passage in Jeremiah 30. The fortunes of *my people*, typical exodus language, will be restored when God brings them to the land that the deity had once promised and then later given to the ancestors (Jer 30:3). The release from the punishment that God had condemned the people to and is about to reverse is offered to *Israel and Judah* (Jer 30:4-9). Once again, in this context allusions to the exodus are significant (Jer 30:22), for the exodus evokes a period when Israel was unified.

This emphasis continues, much more explicitly, in Jeremiah 31. This oracle is directed to *all the families of Israel* (*l^{e}kōl mišp^{e}ḥôt Yiśrā'ēl*), who are further designated as *my people*, with YHWH as the speaker (Jer 31:1). Twice in the first part of this oracle the people are referred to as people planting vineyards on Samaria's mountains and hearing a summons in the hill country of Ephraim (Jer 31:5-6). Both these sites commonly denote the northern section of Israel. Granted, the people are called to go to Zion/Jerusalem, but that is always the ultimate destination for a restored Israel. In this case, Zion/Jerusalem is more than a location. It encompasses a comprehensive religious reality. The extent of this restoration is also indicated in Jer 31:8, when Israel finally becomes *a great community* (*qāhāl gādôl*). Once again, Ephraim is specifically mentioned three times (Jer 31:9, 18, 20). Toward the conclusion of this oracle, the people whom YHWH will make fertile and with whom a new covenant will be made are called the *House of*

Israel and the *House of Judah* (Jer 31:27, 31). This promise of a new covenant is as certain as the natural order of things which YHWH has orchestrated, including the light that comes by day, the regularity of the moon, the stars fixed in the heavens, and the roaring sea (Jer 31:35). This divine activity ensures the continuity of the descendants of Israel (Jer 31:36), indeed, *all* the descendants of Israel (Jer 31:37).

For the most part, a literal reading of Jeremiah 32 seems oriented exclusively to Judah. But there are a couple of exceptions to this exclusive take. One exception comes in the form of the use of phrases evoking the old Mosaic covenant tradition found in Exodus. Specifically, the repetition of God's saying that a restored Israel will be (once again) *my people* and I will be (once again) *their God*, obviously alludes to a time when Israel was a unified entity (Jer 32:38). Also, when the places are listed in which Israel's fortunes will be realized in the future the cities of the *hill country* are mentioned (Jer 32:44). Often, this hilly territory designates the northern kingdom.

However, one need not cast about looking for vague allusions to the ultimate reunification of Israel and Judah in the future. The concluding section of Jeremiah leaves no doubt on that score. The exile of Israel, referring to the northern kingdom, at the hands of the Assyrians is specifically mentioned (Jer 50:17). God promises to punish Babylon just like God punished Assyria, notwithstanding that the exile was ultimately engineered by YHWH (Jer 50:18). Israel will not only be avenged, though, they will also return to the land. Standard northern sites are mentioned in this prophecy: Carmel, Bashan, hills of Ephraim, and Gilead (Jer 50:19). In both communities, the north and the south, no iniquity will be discovered (Jer 50:20). Granted, only a remnant will experience this benefaction, but it will be a remnant of Israel *and* Judah. Finally, the *people of Israel* and the *people of Judah* are mentioned in tandem in an oracle that outlines the features of divine punishment on their oppressors (Jer 50:33). In sum, regardless of Jeremiah's orientation to the southern kingdom, Judah, the restoration material includes *all* of Israel, north and south.

EZEKIEL

Ezekiel is also oriented to Judah, just as we saw in Isaiah and Jeremiah. And, like those latter two books, there is in Ezekiel a handful of passages in which the northern kingdom is presented as a separate entity but also destined to be eventually reunified with Judah, thus making God's elect people whole once more.

Ezekiel 16 depicts the northern kingdom, here referred to as Samaria, as Judah's *sister*. But this designation comes with a twist. According to this passage, a third *sister* is Sodom, an infamously wicked place (see Gen 18:16—19:29). According to Ezekiel, both Samaria and Sodom were notoriously evil. As bad as they were, though, they were not as bad as Judah (Ezek 16:49–51)! Eventually, Judah will suffer as did the other two *sisters*, whose wickedness Judah exceeded (Ezek 16:53–58). This is an odd text in that it equates the northern kingdom with Sodom. Fortunately, though, it is not Ezekiel's final word about the ultimate relationship between Samaria/Israel and Judah.

Ezekiel 20 lists Israel's sins during the Egyptian sojourn, the wilderness wanderings, and their time in Canaan (Ezek 20:1–44). At the conclusion of this denunciation, YHWH finally acts toward the people not according to their deeds, which were deplorable, but according to divine grace (Ezek 20:44). In this context, God's people are called primarily the *house of Israel* (Ezek 20:13, 27, 30, 31, 39, 40, 44). Despite this nomenclature, the prophet surely has Judah in mind. However, as was the case in Isaiah and Jeremiah, the grace—almost certainly entailing rescue from exile—that God extends to Judah should be seen as applying to Israel too. That is, just as the sins enumerated were committed when Israel was unified, then any potential reversal involves Israel as a whole.

Elsewhere, however, more explicit differentiations of Israel obtain. That is, there are passages in Ezekiel that demonstrate an awareness that Judah *and* Israel, though separate entities, remain constitutive of God's elect people. One of these passages is Ezekiel 23, where one encounters an allegory featuring two daughters. The names of these two women were Oholah and Oholibah, unusual names to say the least. Both involve *tents*. Though names using the Hebrew root for tent (*'hl*) are attested in the Bible (e.g., Gen 36:2, 5, 41; Exod 31:6, 1 Chr 1:52; 3:20), the exact significance of the names is difficult to determine. The first name seems to mean *A Tent, Toward the Tent*, or *Her Tent*; the second name appears to mean *My Tent Is In Her*, depending on vocalization.[3] Regardless, what these two sisters signify is as obvious as the meaning of the names is obscure. Oholah stands for Samaria; Oholibah stands for Jerusalem. Oholah, therefore, represents the northern kingdom, Israel, whereas Oholibah represents the southern kingdom, Judah (Ezek 23:1–4).

---

3. Zimmerli rehearses the options, but finally decides that the names are meant to evoke a nomadic background during Israel's time in the wilderness (cf. Hos 12:10 [Eng. 12:9]). The tent-names may be also relatable to the *tent of meeting* (*'ōhel mō'ēd*), a very important site for religious activities (e.g., Exod 27:21; 28:43). See Zimmerli, *Ezekiel 1*, 483–84.

The allegory focuses initially on the first sister: Oholah. She is pictured as a lustful woman who throws herself at equally lustful men. The latter represent the Assyrians (Ezek 23:5-7). This behavior has been a constant for Oholah/Samaria, something of which she was guilty since the time spent in Egypt (Ezek 23:8). As might be expected, her punishment came in the form of abuse at the hand of her ostensible lovers: the Assyrians (Ezek 23:9-10). In this context, sexual immorality is a metaphor for ill-advised diplomacy, dubious alliances, and eventual military defeat.[4] As well, the abuse the Assyrians inflict is a thinly-veiled reference to the exile in the eighth century.

By the prophet's lights, Oholibah is worse than her sister (Ezek 23:11). Not only was she flirtatious with the Assyrians but behaved similarly with the Babylonians (Ezek 23:12-16). Like her sister, she displayed the same behavior while in Egypt (Ezek 23:19-21). Because of this, God will consign this sister also to a terrible fate (Ezek 23:22-35). The whole chapter continues this diatribe using language that can only be described as lurid (Ezek 23:36-49). But the point to be emphasized is that Ezekiel condemns *both* sisters, the north and the south, Samaria/Israel, and Jerusalem/Judah, as woefully sinful and subject not only to military defeat but exile. The question then presents itself is: Will both communities enjoy a similar future of forgiveness and restoration after being punished so severely?

The answer is yes. One passage suggesting Israel's future unity is Ezekiel 34, which emphasizes that in time they will be a single flock that is led by one shepherd, namely a new David (Ezek 34:23-24). Granted, this oracle is critical of past shepherds, that is, kings (Ezek 34:1-6). Instead of tending the sheep, they have exploited them. This has eventuated in scattered sheep, who have in addition become prey (Ezek 34:7-10). YHWH will replace these hopelessly deficient past shepherds and rescue the flock from wherever it has been scattered (Ezek 34:11-16). Though this divine activity does not preclude judgment, as mentioned, in time *one* flock will be presided over by *one* Davidic shepherd. This glorious future will involve not only another covenant but *showers of blessings* (Ezek 34:26), such as no longer being prey to other nations, enjoying agricultural bounty, being secure in the land, and the like (Ezek 34:25-31). At this time the people will realize that YHWH is their deity and that they are YHWH's people. In YHWH's own words: "You are my sheep . . . and I am your God" (Ezek 34:31).

---

4. Unfortunately, the patriarchal slant of the Bible comes through loudly and clearly in this metaphor. Contrary to human experience, often the Bible portrays women as primary instigators of promiscuous behavior, either as opting for prostitution or being sexually provocative and completely undisciplined. Nevertheless, female promiscuity is a common metaphor in the Bible. See Bird, "'To Play the Harlot,'" 75-94.

To be fair, this restoration passage probably has Judah primarily in mind. At the same time, the language itself intimates a more inclusive understanding of Israel. For one thing, though Judah may be uppermost in the prophetic imagination at this point, the people nevertheless are referred to as the *House of Israel* (Ezek 34:30). For another thing, when the deity says "I will be your God" while you will be "my people," such language is replete in narratives about the original covenant that YHWH made with Israel when their unity was not in question (e.g., Exod 3:7, 10; 5:1; 7:4, 16, 26 [Eng. 8:1]; 29:45–46; 32:11–12).

However, Ezekiel 37 removes all doubt about the prophetic vision of an ultimately restored and reunified Israel. Famously, this chapter contains the vision of the *dry bones*. God commands the prophet to prophesy to this valley of dry bones (Ezek 37:4). These desiccated remains will, at the prophet's word and by means of God's power, don sinews, flesh, and skin, thus becoming animated (Ezek 37:5–6). Ezekiel's prophecy was efficacious (Ezek 37:7–10). The resurrection of these bones was symbolic of the resurrection of the *whole house of Israel* (Ezek 37:11). For Israel, exile was indistinguishable from death itself. Being rescued from exile could only be explained with this stunning image of resurrection (Ezek 37:13). When YHWH refreshes these bones with the divine Spirit, the task is accomplished (Ezek 37:14). Israel will live and breathe again.

But the prophet was not quite finished. Another word from YHWH commanded Ezekiel to take a piece of wood and write something on it (Ezek 37:16). What was the prophet to write? The answer to this question would be decisive for Israel's future. On this piece of wood, the prophet was to write the words: "For Judah and the children of Israel united with him." On a second piece of wood these words were to be written: "For Joseph (the 'stick of Ephraim') and all the house of Israel united with him." Then, the two pieces of wood should themselves be joined together, thus making them a single piece (Ezek 37:17).

Of course, this prophetic demonstration will engender curiosity on the part of the people who witness it. People will want to know the significance of this symbolic action. The prophet's explanation is straightforward. This is YHWH's assertion that Israel will become one, singular people. In sum, the north and the south are to be transformed into a single piece of wood (Ezek 37:19). This divine action will include gathering the *people of Israel* from the lands into which they were dispersed during the two exiles and bringing them back to their own land (Ezek 37:21). God had every intention of making Israel *one nation* (*gôy 'eḥād*), having them live on the mountains of Israel, and be ruled by *one* king. The concluding statement is decisive: Israel will no longer be two nations or divided into two kingdoms (Ezek 37:22).

Once more, in this glorious future YHWH will be able to declare that Israel is *my people*, and *I am their God* (Ezek 37:23). The last paragraph of this incredible prophecy enunciates the particulars that the prophet envisioned, including Israel's having one shepherd, a new David, their being obedient as they live in the land originally given to their ancestors, as they live under a covenant of peace. YHWH's temple will manifest the divine presence, something of which everyone else will be aware (Ezek 37:24-28).

Ezekiel ends with a veritable flourish relative to its perspective on Israel's ultimate unity. In the penultimate chapter, the boundaries of Israel's twelve tribal units are delineated. Though Joseph is to have two portions of land, the rest is to be divided equally (Ezek 47:13-14). The remainder of the chapter describes down to the last detail the boundaries according to the four compass points (Ezek 47:15-23). The final chapter is dedicated to describing the territory each tribal or priestly unit, which is listed by name, will occupy. The names are found throughout the chapter (Ezek 48:1 [Dan]; 48:2 [Asher]; 48:3 [Naphtali]; 48:4 [Manasseh]; 48:5 [Ephraim]; 48:6 [Reuben]; 48:7 [Judah]; 48:8-14 [Zadokites and Levites]; 48:23 [Benjamin]; 48:24 [Simeon]; 48:25 [Issachar]; 48:26 [Zebulun]; 48:27 [Gad]. The artificial geographical locations and idealization of these final allotments notwithstanding, Ezekiel's vision concludes with an Israel that has been unified as a community.

HOSEA

Hosea is the first book of what is commonly referred to as the Minor Prophets or the Book of the Twelve.[5] Though much shorter than Isaiah, Jeremiah, and Ezekiel, a number of these prophetic books speak to the issue of Israel as a divided community and its ultimate restoration as a unified community.

Hosea acknowledges the existence of both the north and the south, that is, Israel and Judah, at the very beginning of the book. In an extended metaphor featuring a dysfunctional marriage, Israel is compared to an unfaithful spouse (Hos 1:2-5). In the same breath, the prophet asserts that though Israel will not be regarded compassionately by YHWH, Judah will not only be regarded compassionately but delivered as well (Hos 1:6-7).[6] However,

---

5. Over the last forty years or so there has been scholarly debate about whether the twelve smaller prophetic books should be read individually or collectively as a single edited unit. See the voluminous bibliographies in Nogalski and Sweeney, *Reading and Hearing the Book of the Twelve*; Redditt and Schart, *Thematic Threads in the Book of the Twelve*. The resolution of this debate is immaterial to the present study.

6. Some scholars regard the reference to Judah as a later addition to Hosea. Regardless, a canonical reading requires even a later interpolation to be taken seriously as part of the final received text.

Israel will not remain in perpetuity in this state beyond YHWH's mercy. Eventually the ancestral promise to them will also be fulfilled. Moreover, Judah *and* Israel will ultimately be reunited and have only one leader (Hos 2:1–2 [Eng. 1:10–11]).

In chapter 4, once more Israel is distinguished from its counterpart, when the prophet accuses the former of whoring around—again, a metaphor for idolatry—and at the same time exonerates Judah (Hos 4:15). The remainder of the chapter continues its diatribe against Israel (Hos 4:16–19). Yet, in the very next chapter both communities are denounced; Judah will stumble along with Israel/Ephraim (Hos 5:5). While the judgments against the northern kingdom are clearly articulated, the southern kingdom will not be exempt from the pending disaster (Hos 5:8–14).

YHWH laments equally about the two communities:

> What shall I do with you, O Ephraim?
> What shall I do with you, O Judah? (Hos 6:4)

Because their love for YHWH is as fleeting as morning mist or early dew (Hos 6:4), they are subjected to prophetic denunciation (Hos 6:5). Most of the vitriol in this material is reserved for Israel, but Judah is never far from the prophet's attention (Hos 8:14). Even when Judah is favorably compared to Israel (Hos 12:1 [Eng. 11:12]), the southern kingdom cannot escape entirely prophetic censure (Hos 12:3 [Eng. 12:2]).[7]

There is no final proclamation of ultimate reunification of Israel and Judah in Hosea. At the same time, judgment will not be YHWH's last word in regard to the northern kingdom. It also will be finally forgiven and eventually restored to God's good graces (Hos 14:4–7). Indirectly, then, this is Hosea's way of saying that a forgiven Israel and a slightly less guilty Judah will have no recourse but to become one again.

AMOS

Though Amos almost exclusively targets Israel, the northern kingdom, he also has something to say about foreign nations and even Judah in his first oracle (Amos 1:1—2:5). He makes no bones about the source of YHWH's prophetic word: Zion/Jerusalem, that is, the capitol of the southern kingdom (Amos 1:2). The prophet is so identified with Judah that Amaziah the priest accuses him of conspiring against Jeroboam II, further demanding that Amos confine his oracles to the southern kingdom (Amos 7:10–13).

---

7. The mention of Judah in this verse is problematic in that the rest of Hosea seems so focused on Israel. Nevertheless, *Judah* is in the Hebrew text.

Amos' comeback is that he is speaking on the basis of YHWH's unmistakable instruction to prophesy to Israel (Amos 7:15). From Amaziah's perspective, however, prophets from Judah should refrain from preaching in the north because Bethel is the king's sanctuary and the kingdom's temple (Amos 7:13). Of course, Amos was unimpressed with Amaziah's argument, applying choice words of judgment on Amaziah and his own family (Amos 7:16–17).

Amos is considered the ultimate *doom and gloom* prophet. This is one of the reasons why the optimistic ending of Amos (Amos 9:11–15) seems out of place when compared to the negative tenor of the rest of the book. Scholars have regarded the ending of Amos to be a later addition, presumably designed to moderate the effects of its overly pessimistic outlook. The scholarly assessment of the ending of Amos, in my opinion, is probable. At the same time, reading the text from a canonical perspective requires taking the final form seriously, whether it was part of the original composition or not.

We need to keep in mind that the ending of Amos seems out of place for two reasons. One is, as stated, that after nine chapters of castigating (mostly) Israel for a variety of sinful behaviors and outlining the consequential punishments, Amos does a veritable U-turn by announcing complete restoration in the conclusion. The second reason is perhaps more decisive, namely, that the restoration has to do with the *booth of David* (Amos 9:11), surely an allusion to Jerusalem and the southern kingdom, Judah. Why would Amos denounce Israel, the northern kingdom, for nine chapters only to predict the ultimate restoration of the southern kingdom? That was the incongruity that led to the scholarly consensus about Amos' final couple of paragraphs.

But considering the text from the perspective of the final form, another conclusion is plausible or even warranted. The text calls for not a simple rebuilding of Jerusalem after return from exile, but something much more radical. Granted, Jerusalem will be rebuilt, but this will involve more than brick and mortar. The newly reconstituted kingdom will in the future include not only the *remnant of Edom* but also *all the nations* who are called by the name of Israel's deity. This is something that YHWH plans to do (Amos 9:11–12). When this happens, unimaginable prosperity will be a reality. This will be a time when the *plowman overtakes the one who harvests* (Amos 9:12). *In that day* (Amos 9:13) YHWH will set about "to restore the fortunes of my people Israel" (Amos 9:14). Combining the Mosaic covenant (*my people*) and the promise of the land (Amos 9:15), this text does not pertain only to Judah the southern kingdom, but to Israel, the entire people whom God had originally elected. Amos proclaims that judgment on the north is inevitable. But even that judgment will not prevent YHWH from reconstituting God's people in the eschatological future. In Amos, both the south (Amos 2:4-5) and the north will undergo certain judgment. Equally, they will both be not only restored, but unified as well (Amos 9:11-15).

MICAH

Micah has no difficulty in denouncing both Israel and Judah. Asking rhetorically what Jacob's transgression is, the answer is: Samaria. A similar rhetorical question asking about Judah's sin yields a comparable answer: Jerusalem (Mic 1:5). Though divided, both kingdoms are equally culpable.

The emphasis on Israel's eventual forgiveness, restoration, and unification is unmistakable in Micah, although not explicit as in other prophetic texts. As noted, both the southern and northern kingdoms are guilty in God's eyes. The emphasis on restoration focuses on Judah, Jerusalem, and David, but not in a manner that would suggest that the northern kingdom is excluded from this divine action. For example, the *peoples* and *many nations* that will ultimately benefit from God's reversing Israel's fortunes would certainly include all Israel, not merely the south (Mic 4:1-2). Could one imagine the prophet not envisioning Israel as a whole participating in this idyllic future (Mic 4:3-4)? Granted, this prophecy remains centered on Zion (Mic 4:7, 8, 10, 11, 13) but the gathering that God is effecting will include those who had been expelled from the land, a remnant, and what once was a strong nation (Mic 4:6). Eventually, the rest of the kin will return to the *people of Israel* (Mic 5:2 [Eng. 5:3]). Among the enemies that will be defeated are the Assyrians, the very people who attacked the south but exiled the north (Mic 5:4-5 [Eng. 5:5-6]).

When the prophet rehearses what YHWH has done for Israel, he mentions the mighty divine acts accomplished when Israel was a unified community. These include the exodus from Egypt, the ministries of Moses, Aaron, and Miriam, and what YHWH did through Balaam when Balak had it in for Israel (Mic 6:4-5). Even in the prophet's insistence that Judah's sins are not distinguishable from Israel's (Mic 6:16), the logic obtains that if Judah can survive the consequent divine judgment, then so can Israel.

A personified Israel speaks in the first person in the final chapter of Micah. No enemy should rejoice, because "though I fall, I will get up; when I sit in darkness, YHWH is my light" (Mic 7:8). Israel can endure God's anger because deliverance is on the way (Mic 7:8). God will be Israel's new shepherd, feeding the sheep in Bashan and Gilead, like before (Mic 7:14). Bashan and Gilead both once belonged to the northern kingdom. God will soon be in the business of forgiving iniquity and overlooking transgressions for the *remnant* of the elect people (Mic 7:18). Ultimately, the deity will remain faithful to Jacob and display covenant love to Abraham (Mic 7:20). These ancestors are the ancestors of Israel, whether they once belonged to the southern or northern kingdom. Israel will thereby experience unity in its future.

ZEPHANIAH

Since this prophetic text is set in the time of Josiah, famous reformer king of Judah, its orientation is obviously on the southern kingdom (Zeph 1:1). King Josiah concluded his rule just a handful of years before the Babylonian exile. Given this orientation, it is difficult to know whether the restoration envisioned includes the north (e.g., Zeph 1:7). One does encounter language reminiscent of the exodus tradition (*my people*) (Zeph 2:9), which alludes to Israel when it was unified. Still, it is not clear whether the northern kingdom is included in the future restoration. In the most extensive passage that features Judah's being forgiven and restored (Zeph 3:8–29), there are a couple of references that plausibly allude to Israel as a unity (e.g., Zeph 3:13, 14, 15), but none of them are sufficiently explicit. Read from a canonical perspective, Zephaniah does nothing to justify the belief that Israel's reconstitution will be confined to only the southern kingdom. It is simply the case that the text is not as explicit as others in the prophetic corpus about Israel's ultimate reunification.

ZECHARIAH

Given its setting in the sixth century, one would expect compelling visions from Zechariah of Israel's future as a holistic community. The prophecy does not disappoint. Right off the bat, the text intimates that this prophetic material will involve Judah, Israel, and Jerusalem (Zech 2:2 [Eng. 1:19]). Though weighted to Judah (e.g., Zech 2:14 [Eng. 2:10]), surely the northern kingdom is to be included in the group YHWH refers to as *my people* in Zech 2:15 [Eng. 2:11]. If *many nations* are to be part of this renewed group of God's people, the north would scarcely be excluded. The use of exodus language—Israel being *my people* (with YHWH as speaker) and YHWH *their God* (with YHWH as speaker)—again suggests a future unified community (Zech 8:8). Indeed, both the *house of Judah* and the *house of Israel* are mentioned in the same context (Zech 8:13). At the same time, this restoration extends to others—*many peoples* and *strong nations* (Zech 8:22)—who will eventually seek YHWH and the people with whom this deity dwells. *In those days*[8] ten representatives from the nations of every tongue will take hold of the robe of a Jew and say, "Let us walk with you because we heard that God is with you" (Zech 8:23).[9] The conversion of non-Israelites is also reflected (Zech 9:7). This glorious age will be a time when military action is no longer needed, so that neither Ephraim (the northern kingdom) nor Jerusalem (the southern kingdom) will require chariots or war horses (Zech 9:10).

During this period when a new king will arise (Zech 9:9), God plans to strengthen the *house of Judah* and the *house of Joseph* (Zech 10:6). Clearly, this designates both the southern and northern kingdoms. Regardless of whether the Israelites had been dispersed to Egypt or Assyria, God will retrieve them (Zech 10:10). YHWH will ultimately forgive and restore a community that becomes once more a single people.[10] Presumably (though this is less than explicit), this unified Israel will obtain also when YHWH enjoys kingship not only over all Israel but over all others as well (Zech 14:1-21). After all, one of the effects that bad shepherds (= kings) had on Israel was destroying the fraternal relationship between Judah and Israel (Zech 11:4-14; especially v. 14).

CONCLUSION

As we have seen, several prophetic passages envision a coming era when Israel will no longer be divided. Indeed, their reunification is part of Israel's glorious future. In numerous prophetic texts this reunification is stated in explicit terms. Sometimes, however, the reunification is intimated by evoking the particular language that had become symbolic of God's mighty acts in Israel's behalf, such as the exodus from Egypt, the wilderness wanderings,

---

8. The phrases *in those days*, *in that day*, or *days are coming*, and the like are common indicators of Israel's eschatological future in prophetic literature.

9. The term *Jew* or *Jewish* is derived from, of course, the name *Judah*. Only in exilic and postexilic eras did this nomenclature as descriptive of Israelites become widespread. This is why the term is found only in later written portions of the Hebrew Bible / Old Testament.

10. Anthony R. Peterson also cites a similar motif in Ps 78, which accents YHWH's judgment on the tent of Joseph and the tribe of Ephraim (Ps 78:67) only to reverse course by envisaging a time when a new David would shepherd not only the south but the north (Ps 78:71). Peterson argues that the references to the house of Judah and the house of Joseph in Zech 10-11 should be understood similarly. See *Behold Your King*, 159-60.

the covenant, the occupation of the promised land, and the like. Those divine actions involved an Israel that had not yet been divided.

Added to this prophetic vision is the strong belief that eventually all peoples will acknowledge Israel's deity. Speaking from a canonical perspective, this divine activity will fulfill the promise made to Abraham and Sarah that a time would come when all the families of the good earth would be blessed through this exclusive election (Gen 12:1–3). Obviously, if all the nations are destined to participate in this great reversal, it is impossible not to include every segment of Israel as well. The emphasis on Zion/Jerusalem theology and a new David arising notwithstanding, the Israel who would be part of this grand divine plan would be a unified community. Israel would no longer be divided into north and south. God's people would finally be only Israel, God's elect people.

Chapter 11

Israel as a Figure for the Church: Conclusions and Reflections

THREE PERSPECTIVES

As I conclude this study and reflect on its implications for the church, three perspectives, in my judgment, should be considered. One is the conviction that Israel, as it is depicted in the Christian canonical text, namely, the Old Testament, should be understood as a *figure* for the Christian church. This means that when Christians read about Israel in Scripture, it is not about *them* (meaning Israel, an ancient historical people) but *us* as the church (meaning a religious community to which Christians belong by virtue of their belief in and commitment to Jesus of Nazareth, Israel's Messiah or Christ). A second perspective is related to what the New Testament has to say about the unity and disunity of those who were convinced that Jesus of Nazareth was indeed Israel's Christ or Messiah. This addresses the question: How unified was the *earliest* church as reflected in the New Testament? Finally, on the basis of the first two perspectives, what does this study have to offer *the one, holy, catholic, and apostolic church* which has been characterized by divisions throughout its history? What, indeed, does this study have to say to a church that continues to multiply divisions?

ISRAEL AS A FIGURE OF THE CHURCH

To the extent that Christians think at all of the church's relationship to Israel, their first impulse is likely to associate Israel with the synagogue (a place where Jews worship) or Judaism (a religion that Jews practice) and therefore as differentiated from themselves. Even though Israel's story is narrated in the *Old Testament*, which of course is a distinctively Christian term for the longest section of the Christian Bible, that story is nevertheless construed to be about *them* or the *other*. In a word, Israel's story features *someone else*. To be sure, some material in the Old Testament may be thought of as applicable to Christians indirectly, but that does not obviate the fact that the Old Testament is not viewed primarily as a Christian document despite its formal canonical status. The Old Testament is viewed as primarily about Israel, not the later Christian church. As for Jesus, the Old Testament is largely seen either as background to his story or a prophetic prediction of it. At the popular level at least, that is what a majority of Christians think.

As well, to the extent that Christians think about Israel as reflected in the New Testament, they tend to view it as a failed nation—in terms of religious purchase—that is now being represented by *the Jews*, also a religious failure and therefore differentiated from Christians. It does not seem to matter that Jesus' ministry was not geared to *Christians*—a completely anachronistic term during Jesus' era—or that Jesus did not intend to establish the Christian church. In fact, only after Jesus was no longer on the scene did Christian nomenclature emerge (Acts 11:26; 26:28; 1 Pet 4:16). The word *Christian* occurs only three times in the New Testament, and never in the Gospels. This is why in Matt 10:6 Jesus is depicted as instructing his disciples to confine their ministry to "the lost sheep of the House of Israel."

Though Christians acknowledge that Israel or their later representatives, the Jews, were indeed once the elect people of God, most of these same Christians assume that *they*, that is, those who follow Jesus and believe that he is the Christ, have ultimately replaced the Jews/Israel as God's true people. The argument is that *they*, namely those who would be later be called Christians, believed in Jesus and what he stood for and what he accomplished by his death and resurrection, whereas the Jews, namely, Israel, not only did not believe in him but were also responsible, at least in part, for his death. Granted, most Christians are willing to be reminded that almost all people who first believed in Jesus as Israel's Christ or Messiah were themselves Jews, but that is basically an intellectual concession lacking religious conviction. In short, though that datum may be accepted, Christians religiously, theologically, emotionally, and even sociologically, no longer think of Christian origins in Jewish terms. The historical memory of robust Jewish origins has long since faded.

Once the church became a majority *gentile* community, a belief arose that Christians, now identified almost exclusively as gentiles, belonged to the *church* whereas Jews, who were seen as ethnically homogenous for the most part, belonged to the *synagogue*. It was as though Christians had been separate from Jews from the beginning. In time, Christians had no qualms about maintaining that Israel or the Jews represented a completely different religious tradition from their own, a tradition that was eventually seen in primarily pejorative terms. Christians went so far as to contend that they, the gentiles, had replaced Israel or the Jews as God's elect people. For all practical purposes, that is the prevailing viewpoint among Christians today. Perhaps Israel and later the Jews were once God's people, but after Jesus the Christ came, died, and was resurrected, those who believed in and followed him took Israel's place. Simply put, Christianity (= the church) displaced Judaism (= the synagogue) as God's people.

It may be conceded that this assumption that Christianity displaced Judaism is belied somewhat by a more positive outlook on Jews and Judaism that obtains presently on the part of many Christians. But there are very different rationales for this more congenial stance. For example, Christians who identify as Fundamentalists or Evangelicals have been supportive of the State of Israel since its inception in 1948. But that is primarily related to a particular—and highly contested—interpretation of biblical prophecy that was thought to be fulfilled when Israel became a modern state. This support for Israel, however, has not changed the fact that Jews are still a primary objective for Christian evangelistic efforts. Most Christians in this camp believe that Jews *should* become Christians.

As for Christians who identify as Mainline Protestants and therefore adopt a more liberal or progressive outlook, the State of Israel is not the reason for a more sanguine assessment of Judaism. Rather, as a function of a commitment to tolerance or inclusion that is extended theoretically to virtually everyone, Mainline Protestants have no difficulty whatsoever with Judaism. At the same time, this stance has little to do with a self-conscious theological position relating to the relationship between Judaism and Christianity. This position derives mostly from liberalizing attitudes that are extended to any religious tradition. Interestingly, unlike the Fundamentalists and Evangelicals, these Mainline Christians tend to be highly critical of the modern State of Israel for its perceived mistreatment of the Palestinian population.

It may also be conceded that at a formal level many Christian communities—including Protestant denominations and the Roman Catholic Church—have not only repented of anti-Semitic attitudes, postures, and policies, but at the same time have fostered, sponsored, and engaged in numerous Jewish-Christian dialogues of one sort or another. All of these efforts are, in my judgment, to be lauded (and continued!). At the same time, it is fair to say that the vast majority of Christians, whether lay or ordained, are either unaware of such efforts or have not used the results of such dialogues for serious and sustained self-reflection that addresses personal spirituality and general Christian growth. In sum, these efforts have not seeped into a communal Christian self-consciousness.

Though already intimated, I need to emphasize the point that using *Christianity* and *Judaism* as appropriate terminology for describing religious groupings in Jesus' day is completely anachronistic. That is because both Judaism and Christianity forged their distinct identities in the decades following the destruction of the Second Temple at Rome's hands in 70 CE. Before that epochal event, the arguments between a *minority* group of Jews who believed that Jesus was the Christ or Messiah and a *majority* of Jews who did not believe that the messianic age had arrived with Jesus may be fairly characterized as an intramural *Jewish* debate. This meant that Jews were debating with other Jews. This was the case for decades before either an apostolic Christian church or rabbinical Pharisaic Judaism were on the way of becoming discernible entities. Still, for the purposes of this chapter synagogue and church as signifying Judaism and Christianity respectively remain convenient and helpful terms.

The belief that the church had replaced the synagogue as emblematic of Israel, God's elect people, is commonly referred to as *supersessionism*. Some have contended not only that the fathers of the church in the earliest centuries CE believed that the church had superseded the synagogue but that the New Testament itself from front to back, from top to bottom, promoted this teaching as well.[1] To be sure, some theologians have argued that the church's relationship to Israel is an immensely complex issue requiring serious reflection.[2] Mostly, though, throughout the church's history very few Christian laity and only a handful of Christian theologians have concluded that the New Testament presented Israel as a viable and perpetual religious entity. As a corollary to this negative perspective, Israel as it is presented in the Old Testament was seen primarily in unflattering ways, mostly as a failed religious community. Israel, therefore, became the antithesis of the church. The historical consequences of Christians construing their relationship with

---

1. To my knowledge, no one has been more persistent on the matter of supersessionism than Ruether, *Faith and Fratricide*. Of course, she argues not to support this position, but to criticize it vehemently. Nevertheless, she is unrelenting in her criticism of the New Testament position as she sees it on this score.

2. Famously, Barth in *Church Dogmatics*, 671. See more extensive references to Barth's treatment of the relationship between Israel and the church in Sonderegger, *That Jesus Christ Was Born a Jew*. See also Rendtorff, "Christliche Identität in Israels Gegenwart," 3–12. As well, R. Kendall Soulen has written extensively from a number of perspectives on the theological problems that the church encounters by adopting a supersessionist stance. See *The God of Israel and Christian Theology*; *The Divine Names and the Holy Trinity*; *Irrevocable*.

Israel, the Jews, and later Judaism in this manner has not only precipitated inexcusable immoral behavior but has had horrific social and political consequences for Jews in general.

However, instead of giving in to the belief that the church replaced the synagogue as representing God's elect people, in my judgment Israel as it appears in the Old Testament (for Christians), or in the Hebrew Scriptures (for Jews), should be understood as a *figure* for both the synagogue (= Judaism) *and* the church (= Christianity).[3] My justification for advocating this for both Judaism and Christianity is as follows: (1) Neither community is adequately explained as a replication of the religious beliefs and practices that are endemic to their respective canonical traditions. (2) Both Judaism and Christianity have legitimate claims that they are an extension, historically and theologically, of Israel as that elect people is portrayed in the Hebrew Bible / Old Testament. (3) Both Judaism and Christianity use methods for interpreting the Hebrew Bible / Old Testament that cannot be adjudicated by some alleged objective standard outside of the religious tradition itself. Judaism, for instance, reads its Scripture according to the canons of the Oral Torah whereas Christianity follows Christological readings like those that are reflected in the New Testament. For this reason, David Novak has contended that both communities are in effect a product of two *novi testamenti*.[4] The Oral Torah is not familiar to most Christians. The Oral Torah is predicated on the belief that God revealed—initially orally, of course—to Moses how the Torah was to be interpreted. Moses communicated that tradition to Joshua, who in turn communicated it to other worthies over the years. Eventually, that material was written down in various Mishnaic or Talmudic documents.[5] It functions for Judaism the way the New Testament functions for Christianity, which explains Novak's remark. (4) Though it seems obvious to concede that Judaism, for historical, religious, and ethnic reasons, has an absolute claim to view itself as a continuation of Israel, that same claim should not arbitrarily be denied to that small group of Jews who believed fervently that Jesus of Nazareth was Israel's Messiah/Christ. Despite the later gentile character of Christianity that soon developed, the thoroughly Jewish origins of Christianity cannot and should not be denied. Neither the church's amnesia nor the sordid history of Christianity's anti-Judaic and anti-Semitic postures should be allowed to obscure these uncontested Jewish origins.

---

3. See Spina, "Israel as a Figure for the Church," 3–23.
4. See Novak, "From Supersessionism to Parallelism," 108–10.
5. See Avery-Peck, "Oral Tradition (Judaism)," 34–35.

Given my argument, it is incumbent on me to demonstrate that the New Testament, taken as a whole, is amenable to this interpretation. To be sure, as noted, some believe that the New Testament is without remainder not only anti-Judaic but supersessionist to the core.[6] However, I believe a case may be made from the New Testament itself that not only allows for the viability of the Jesus movement but also insists that God's original promises to Israel are to be fulfilled. To the New Testament, therefore, we now turn.

The Nativity Stories

The Gospels of Matthew and Luke obviously have nativity stories. In both these narratives, Jesus' relationship to Israel is unmistakable. Not only is Jesus related to Israel from birth, having been born to Israelite/Jewish parents, but the role he is to have throughout his life *in* Israel and *for* Israel is pronounced.

In Matthew's Gospel, the stylized genealogy of Jesus places him squarely in Israel's epic story (Matt 1:1-17). After this genealogical introduction, when the angel of the Lord appeared to Joseph, who was contemplating what to do with a pregnant woman to whom he was engaged, the divine agent said not only that her conception was "of the Holy Spirit" but that the son who was soon to be born to her was to be called *Jesus*. This child would eventually save *his people* from their sins (Matt 1:20-21). *His people* without question refers to the Israelite community, or Jews, as they were called in that era. Jews may have been Pharisees, Sadducees, Zealots, and the like, but the common denominator was being Jewish or Israelite. These constituted Jesus' *people*.

As well, upon Jesus' birth sages from the east came to seek this baby, whom they believed was destined to be *king of the Jews*, that is, *Israel*, because of celestial evidence (Matt 2:1-2). The present (puppet) king of the Jews and other Jewish officials were concerned, even alarmed, by what the sages had said (Matt 2:3-8, 12-18). After determining that Bethlehem was the site for this epochal birth, King Herod asked the sages to let him know of the precise location so that he, too, could worship this child (Matt 2:3-8). The sages were warned in a dream that the king's request had been disingenuous, and so they went home another way (Matt 2:12-18). King Herod's reaction underscored the claims of kingship being attached to the birth of this baby.

Similar emphases are to be found in the nativity account in Luke's gospel. First, an unnamed angel appears to Zechariah to reveal to him the

---

6. See Reuther's *Faith and Fratricide*.

vocation of the child about to be born to his wife, Elizabeth. This child will be a son, whom they are to name John. Among other things, this son will be filled with the Holy Spirit and further he will be a new Elijah-type prophetic figure. When grown, he will carry out a mission designed to turn many Israelites to the LORD. Primarily, John would prepare the people for the LORD, a potential double reference not only to the Israelite deity but eventually to another child soon to be born, namely, Jesus (Luke 1:11–17). Leading Israel to the LORD for repentance and amendment of life is a familiar trope in the prophetic material found in Jewish Scripture/the Old Testament.

A second appearance of an angel follows, only this time the angel is named: Gabriel. In this instance, the recipient of the revelation is a woman, Mary, who was engaged to Joseph. This couple is from the House of David, a supposed requisite for Israel's messiah. When Gabriel tells Mary not to be afraid of his announcement that "the LORD is with you," he went on to inform her that she will soon bear a son whom she is to name Jesus. This child's role is decisive. Notably, he will be *great* and referred to as *the Son of the Most High*. Perhaps more importantly, the LORD God will give him the *throne* of his father, David, so that he will reign over *the House of Jacob* forever (Luke 1:26–33). Clearly, Jesus' mission will be carried out with God's chosen people, Israel. Mary acknowledges this in her famous response when she points out that what God is doing through her involves God's servant Israel, just as God had promised Abraham and the other ancestors (Luke 1:54–55). Jesus is not to inaugurate a new religion, so to speak, but rather fulfill what God had been planning all along for Israel, the elect people of God. Jesus cannot be understood apart from that strategic role. Jesus' efforts to fulfill what God had in mind for Israel is also accented in Matthew's Gospel when Jesus becomes an adult (Matt 5:17–20).

After these two angelic revelations in Luke, Zechariah prophesied as he was filled with the Holy Spirit (Luke 1:67). In the prophecy, he asserted that God has visited and redeemed *Israel*. As well, the Israelite deity raised up a horn of salvation from *David's house*, just as the prophets of old had proclaimed (Luke 1:68–69). All this divine activity is related to God's keeping the covenant made with Abraham (Luke 1:72). John, Zechariah's son, will have a decisive role in this divine action (Luke 1:76–79). *Israel* remains central to what God will do as proclaimed by John, who will pave the way for Jesus.

Luke leaves no doubt about Jesus' Jewish roots, noting both his circumcision and his purification according to the torah (Luke 2:21–24; see, also Matt 5:17–20). But this does not merely emphasize Jesus as an individual Jew (or *Israelite*). The narrative leaves no stone unturned to put into bold relief Jesus' role relative to *Israel*. Thus, Simeon, a righteous and devout man who had been looking for the *consolation of Israel*, was privileged by a special revelation to see the LORD's Christ, or Messiah, before he, Simeon, died (Luke 2:25-26). The *consolation of Israel* does not occur in exactly this form in the Hebrew Bible / Old Testament (whether in Hebrew or Greek), but is implied in the prophetic corpus, especially in Isaiah. When the word (*paraklēsis*) occurs in Isa 57:18 (LXX), the *comfort* or *consolation* being promised is for *my people* (Isa 57:14). Since the speaker in this instance is the Israelite deity, the people being referred to are obviously Israel. When Simeon also praises God for seeing to it that salvation is offered to gentiles (Luke 2:31) as well, this too accords with a prophetic outlook (e.g., Isa 42:6; 49:6).

After Simeon's confirmation of the significance Jesus' birth would have for Israel, next in line is the word of the elderly prophetess Anna (Luke 2:36). She was at least as devout as Simeon, in light of her spiritual disciplines of prayer and fasting continually in the temple (Luke 2:37). When she realized that Jesus was being presented to the temple, she gave thanks to God and spoke of him (i.e., Jesus) to anyone who was looking for the *redemption of Jerusalem* (Luke 2:38). In this context, the *redemption of Jerusalem* is a virtual synonym for the *consolation of Israel*.

Equally, the version of Jesus' genealogy in Luke presents him as an integral part of the Israelite, that is, Jewish story (Luke 3:23-38). That this version does not replicate Matthew's genealogy is immaterial, primarily because ancient and consequently biblical genealogies supply something more than merely biological information. According to Luke's Gospel, Jesus' origins obviously go back to the Israelite ancestors, just as was the case with Matthew's genealogy.[7] However, in Luke Jesus is traced back even to Adam (Luke 3:38). Among other things, this is the way the evangelist draws implications for Israel's relationship to all of humanity. What God is doing with and through Jesus has implications for the entire human family. Nevertheless, Jesus is squarely in the Israelite orbit.

The Conclusions of the Four Gospels

The epochal events that dominate the conclusions of the four canonical Gospels, including Jesus' arrest and trial, his death by crucifixion, and his resurrection, return to themes that are found in the two nativity accounts.

---

7. It is popularly, but erroneously, thought that the differences between Matthew's and Luke's genealogy relates to which parent is being featured. One genealogy is said to emphasize Joseph's family whereas the other genealogy is said to emphasize Mary's family. However, both genealogies are related to Joseph (Matt 1:16; Luke 3:23).

In Matthew, for example, when Jesus enters Jerusalem in his final week the crowd addresses him as *the son of David* (Matt 21:9), thus echoing the genealogy found in this Gospel. The children later address Jesus similarly (Matt 21:15). Then again, after Jesus had been arrested, the first question that Pilate put to him was whether he was *king of the Jews*. Jesus' indirect answer suggests an affirmative response (Matt 27:11). Likewise, when Pilate eventually condemned Jesus, the soldiers mocked him by kneeling before him and saying, "Hail, king of the Jews" (Matt 27:29). Even the charge affixed over Jesus' head read, "This is Jesus the King of the Jews" (Matt 27:37). As well, the chief priests, scribes, and elders joined in the mocking by declaring, "He is the king of Israel; let him come down now from the cross, and we will believe in him" (Matt 27:42). Jesus' alleged kingship over the Jews, that is, Israel, is still prominent toward the end of Matthew's gospel, just as this was emphasized in the Nativity section.

In Mark's gospel, Pilate asks Jesus if he is *king of the Jews* (Mark 15:2). Again, Jesus' answer is cryptic, but indirectly affirmative. Later, when the governor wants to know whether he should release Barabbas, an insurrectionist, rather than Jesus, Pilate refers to Jesus as "the king of the Jews" (Mark 15:9). Pilate insists on calling Jesus the king of the Jews once more in the deliberations (Mark 15:12), only this time he mentions that Jesus is the one "you call the king of the Jews." Also, in this gospel account the soldiers preparing Jesus for execution mock him by putting a purple robe on him—purple was a royal color—and plaiting a crown of thorns that they thrust on his head. Clearly, they were making fun of what they thought were absurd claims of kingship. As in Matthew, the soldiers knelt down, pretending to pay homage to the condemned man (Mark 15:17–19). The soldiers took off the purple robe only when they led him out to be hanged (Mark 15:20). All their ridiculing had to do with claims about Jesus' status as king of the Jews. Likewise, in Mark the sign listing the charges for which Jesus was being executed read simply, "The king of the Jews" (Mark 15:26). People in the crowd kept up the mocking by inviting Jesus to come down from the cross. After all, if he had been the Christ, or messiah, as well as the king of Israel, the condemned man should have no difficulty doing just that. In any case, the mockers insisted that only such an astounding act of self rescue would induce their belief (Mark 15:32).

In the final Synoptic Gospel, Luke, kingship is also central to the narration of Jesus' last week.[8] Luke's emphasis on kingship is a little different,

---

8. Scholars refer to the first three canonical gospels as *synoptic* because they share so much textual material. About 80 percent of Mark, for example, appears in Matthew and Luke. The others add to Mark, rearrange texts, and the like to enhance their own perspective on the Jesus story. The Gospel of John does not share the synoptic material.

but is nevertheless pronounced. When Jesus is brought before Pilate, the accusers charge that Jesus saw himself as "Christ, a king" (Luke 23:2). This prompted Pilate's question: "Are you the king of the Jews" (Luke 23:3). Later, once Pilate had sent Jesus to Herod, the soldiers treated Jesus with contempt, mocked him, and clothed him with fine clothes, probably to make the kingship claims seem ridiculous, though nothing specific about royal clothing is mentioned (Luke 23:11). At the cross, only the soldiers refer to the claim that Jesus was king of the Jews (Luke 23:37). As well, the inscription over Jesus' head read, "This is the king of the Jews" (Luke 23:38).

Though not specific to kingship *per se*, the unique story of the two people on the road to Emmaus is instructive regarding Jesus' relationship to Israel. While discussing the events they had just experienced—contextually, those having to do with Jesus' death—Jesus appeared and walked along with them. Curiously, they did not recognize him. He asked them what they were talking about. One of them, Cleopas, wanted to know if this stranger was oblivious to what had just taken place. When the stranger pressed for more details, they gave this answer: "Concerning Jesus of Nazareth, who was a prophet mighty in deed and word before God and all the people, and how our chief priests and rulers delivered him up to be condemned to death and crucified him" (Luke 24:19-20). By mentioning *our priests and rulers*, they indicated that they were Jews, people who identified as Israelites. They continued their remarks by saying that they had hoped he was the one to *redeem Israel* (Luke 24:21). The point they made was that Jesus could not be understood apart from his relationship to Israel and their future as the elect people of God. Presumably, *redeeming Israel* would require either a king or a messianic figure. In any case, they were counting on Jesus *redeeming Israel*, which they believed was precluded by his death.

In John's version of the final events in Jesus' life, Pilate is the first one to ask about Jesus' claim to being king of the Jews (John 18:33). In response, Jesus elaborates on the nature of his kingship, noting that it was unconventional (John 18:36). When Pilate pressed Jesus on this subject, Jesus implied that he was actually born to be Israel's king (John 18:37). In this gospel, Pilate asks Jesus' accusers whether he should release *the king of the Jews* in order to satisfy the custom of freeing a prisoner during Passover (John 18:39). Also in this gospel, Jesus was mocked for the kingship claim. The soldiers plaited a crown of thorns and dressed him in a purple robe (John 19:2, 5). As well, they reviled him by saying, "Hail, king of the Jews" (John 19:3). After several failed attempts on Pilate's part to release Jesus, the governor finally relented

---

Much of the material in the fourth gospel is unique (e.g., Jesus changing water into wine, the interview with Nicodemus and the woman at the well, the raising of Lazarus).

and gave in to the crowd, at which point he presented Jesus with the words: "Behold your king" (John 19:14). In a final effort to change minds, Pilate asked whether he should "crucify your king" (John 19:15).

In this version of the story, when Pilate had a sign made for the occasion, it read in Hebrew, Latin, and Greek, "Jesus of Nazareth, the king of the Jews" (John 19:19). The chief priest protested, insisting that the sign be revised to indicate only that Jesus *claimed* this, not that it was a fact (John 19:21). Famously, Pilate refused to alter the sign and ended the discussion by saying, "What I have written I have written" (John 19:22).

Clearly, though the stories make their points according to the unique purposes of the respective gospels, all four of them accent Jesus' kingship over the Jews, or Israel. This fits with the emphases we saw in the two nativity accounts in Matthew and Luke.

Other Features in the Four-Gospel Tradition

Having dealt with the two Nativity stories in Matthew and Luke, as well as the description of Jesus' last week in all four Gospels, we now turn to other features in these Gospels that underscore Jesus' enduring relationship to Israel. Again, keep in mind that Jesus was not introducing a new religion, but claimed that he was fulfilling the mission that God had assigned to Israel from the beginning. Jesus' life, work, and teaching are inexplicable when divorced from his integral connection to Israel, the elect people of God. It is immaterial that *Jews* had become the way Israel was referred to in Jesus' era. Israel remained central to Jewish religious life, notwithstanding the variety of Jewish religious expression or Jewish nomenclature.

Perhaps the first matter that needs to be emphasized is Jesus' primary title as expressed in the Gospels, namely, *the Christ*. *Christ* is a title derived from a Greek term designating a person who has been anointed for a particular task, such as a priest (e.g., Exod 28:41) or a king (e.g., 1 Kgs 1:39). The Hebrew counterpart is $m^e\check{s}iah$, from which we get the word, *messiah*. In both Greek and Hebrew, the verbal form indicates the process of anointing (with oil) and the nominal form refers to the recipient of that anointing as an *anointed one*, in Hebrew *Messiah* and in Greek *Christ*. Strictly speaking, an Israelite messianic king who in the future will rescue and restore Israel is not a concept central to the Hebrew Bible / Old Testament. An *anointed one* is never used of a person destined as a future savior or redeemer for Israel.[9]

Nevertheless, there are Old Testament texts that feature a Davidic royal figure who will play a decisive role in Israel's future. For example, in Isa

---

9. De Jonge, "Messiah," 777.

9:1–6 (Eng. 9:2–7) Israel will be led from darkness into light with the birth of a child who will one day occupy David's throne and rule over his kingdom. Likewise, in Isa 11:1–9, using a botanical image, a *shoot*, or a *branch* from the *stump* of Jesse will emerge, ushering in eventually a Spirit-induced ideal age characterized by harmony and unity. Jesse, of course, was David's father. In Mic 5:1–3 (Eng. 5:2–4), Bethlehem will be the birthplace of a member of Judah who will be a ruler in Israel. Again, David is descended from Judah. Similarly, in Jer 23:5–6, a *righteous branch* from David's line will reign as king, eventuating in Judah's salvation.[10] These and other references to David, who was most assuredly anointed and in time granted kingship over Israel in perpetuity (1 Sam 16:13; see also, 2 Sam 7:1–17), are said to be fulfilled by Jesus throughout the New Testament.[11] These references do not use the messiah terminology specifically. Nevertheless, these are clearly indirect allusions to a period that will feature rule by a royal figure who had been anointed.

It is fair to say that the four Gospels elaborate considerably on Jesus' appearing as Israel's *Messiah* or *Christ*. Indeed, it would not be a stretch to argue that this idea was basic to the minority of Jews who were convinced that Jesus of Nazareth *was* Messiah/Christ. A few other Jewish groups did have messianic expectations and a figure that they identified as that messiah, but this was never mainstream to the Jewish religious experience.[12] At the same time, the belief that Jesus was the Christ saturates the New Testament. For example, all three Synoptic Gospels feature Jesus asking his disciples what the word on the street was about his identity. Though various answers to that question are mentioned, Peter, perhaps representing the disciples, comes up with the correct answer, namely, that Jesus is the Christ (Matt 16:13–20; Mark 8:27–30; Luke 9:18–22). In the Fourth Gospel, Andrew points out to his brother, Simon Peter, that "we have found the Messiah (which means Christ)" (John 1:41). In the same Gospel, Jesus is identified as the Christ by the Samaritan woman at the well and by Martha, Lazarus' brother (John 4:29; 11:27). Indeed, at the conclusion of the Fourth Gospel the narrator provides the reason for writing the Gospel in the first place: "that you may believe that Jesus is the Christ, the Son of God, and that believing you may have life in his name" (John 20:31).[13]

---

10. De Jonge, "Messiah," 780.

11. See Spina, "Son of Jesse," 171–95.

12. De Jonge, "Messiah," 781–87.

13. Though this verse is obviously specific to John, in the final canonical form of the New Testament it is legitimate to see this text as alluding to the purpose of all four Gospels.

It is not necessary to rehearse all the instances of the term *Christ* in the Gospels to make this point. However, what is most significant for present purposes is that, as much as anything else, assigning to Jesus the title of *Christ/Messiah* keeps him inexorably and intricately connected to Israel as God's elect people. An anointed ruler, an anointed leader, or an anointed king has to have a people! In Jesus' case, that people was named Israel.

Another feature that associates Jesus closely with Israel as a people is the symbolism of his calling twelve disciples, corresponding to the twelve tribes of Israel. The three Synoptic Gospels stress throughout that Jesus elected these twelve disciples quite deliberately.[14] This number is accented even when it is clear that other disciples were following Jesus as well (e.g., Mark 4:10; Luke 8:1-3). Even the Gospel of John, which depends on sources quite different from those on which the Synoptics depended, notes Jesus' having twelve disciples (John 6:67, 70, 71; 20:24).[15] Jesus' calling of twelve disciples was a prophetic speech-act or sign-act underscoring that his whole ministry had enormous implications for Israel. Illustrating a prophetic word with symbolic actions was common among prophets (e.g., Exod 32:19-20; 1 Kgs 22:11; Jer 13:1-7). In Jesus' interactions with the *twelve*, in effect he is providing concrete evidence that he is leading *Israel* in a different direction from that being offered by rival Jewish religious movements.[16]

Though not a speech-act *per se*, Jesus being frequently associated with various synagogues also accents Jesus' relationship with Jews/Israelites. Often, Jesus is said to be teaching or preaching in synagogues (Matt 4:23; 9:35; 13:54; Mark 1:21, 39; 6:2; Luke 4:15, 44; 6:6; 13:10; John 6:59; 18:20). On occasion, Jesus heals people or performs exorcisms in synagogues (Matt 12:9-13; Mark 1:23-27; 3:1-5). As well, Jesus made important announcements about his ministry in the synagogue (Luke 4:16, 20, 28, 33, 38, 44). Equally, Jesus was not reticent to criticize certain actions that he thought were reprehensible for Jews/Israelites who worshipped in synagogues (Matt

---

14. Matt 10:1-2, 5; 11:1; 19:28; 20:17; 26:14, 20, 47; Mark 3:14, 16; 4:10; 6:7; 9:35; 10:32; 11:11; 14:10, 17, 20, 43; Luke 6:13; 8:1; 9:1, 12; 18:31; 22:3, 47.

15. Arguably the earliest reference to Jesus having had twelve disciples is in 1 Cor 15:5, where Paul points out that Jesus appeared to Cephas and (subsequently?) the twelve. Some suggest that this means that Paul knew nothing of the tradition about Judas' death.

16. In Jesus' time Israel was being pulled in different directions depending on the political, religious, and theological outlook of those who were committed to Israel's survival. For example, the *Essenes* had separated from the temple cultus, because they viewed those in charge as corrupt. *Zealots* were mostly zealous for torah observance, but at least some of these were adamantly against Roman occupation or Jews who had accommodated to Roman rule. In time, being a Zealot took on a more political nuance (see Rhoads, "Zealots," 1044-45).

6:5-6; 10:17; 23:6, 34; Mark 12:38-40; 13:9; Luke 11:43; 12:11; 20:46-47; 21:12). Finally, Jesus sometimes ministers to people who are connected to a synagogue (Mark 1:29-32; Luke 7:1-10; 8:41). None of this is surprising for Jesus of Nazareth since, *as was his custom* (*kata to eiōthos autō*), he often was found in the synagogue (Luke 4:16).

The announcing of the coming kingdom of heaven/God, which is prominent in the Synoptic Gospels, also has Israel as its focus. Both John the Baptizer and Jesus himself made this proclamation central to their public ministry (e.g., Matt 3:2; 4:17; Mark 1:14-15; 4:11, 26, 30; 9:1; Luke 4:43; 7:28; 8:1).[17] Even in John, where the kingdom of heaven/God is not a motif, Jesus is reported to have mentioned it when Nicodemus came to see him (John 3:3, 5). The kingdom of heaven/God has nothing to do with the afterlife. It is a cipher for the upcoming reign of Israel's God. This explains why *all Judea* and *all the region about the Jordan* went to John the Baptizer, confessed their sins, and were baptized (Matt 3:5-6). We are to understand that these were Jews/Israelites who were responding to John's preaching. Also, when Pharisees and Sadducees came themselves to be baptized, the Baptizer had a scathing rebuke ready for them (Matt 3:7-10). Again, this soon-to-arrive kingdom involved Israel and Israel's God. It was not a generic summons to all people. John's and Jesus' invitation was directed to Jews/Israelites and demanded amendment of life in preparation for this reign of the Israelite God.

For present purposes, we need not rehearse various interpretations about the nature of this approaching kingdom of heaven/God. Suffice it to say that, regardless of the nuances of various ways of thinking about this, it was primarily and fundamentally about Israel and Israel's God. This is why a commitment to Jesus apart from participation in Israel, God's elect people, makes little sense. According to this theme in the New Testament, what God was doing in Jesus of Nazareth, had finally to do with Israel and the very reason for their divine election in the first place. Though John's Gospel does not emphasize at all the coming of the kingdom of heaven/God, Jesus had no trouble telling the Samaritan woman at the well that "salvation is from the Jews" (John 4:22). In this instance, "Jews" is simply shorthand for

---

17. References to the *kingdom of God* are found in Matt 12:28; 19:24; 21:31, 43; Mark 1:15; 4:11, 26, 30; 9:1, 47; 10:14, 15, 23, 24, 25; 12:34; 14:25; 15:43; Luke 4:43; 6:20; 7:28; 8:1, 10; 9:2, 11, 27, 60, 62; 10:9, 11; 11:20; 13:18, 20, 28, 29; 14:15; 16:16; 17:20, 21; 18:16, 17, 24, 25, 29; 19:11; 21:31; 22:16, 18; 23:51. References to the *kingdom of heaven* are exclusive to Matthew: 3:2; 4:17; 5:3, 10, 19, 20; 7:21; 8:11; 10:7; 11:11, 12; 13:11, 24, 31, 33, 44, 45, 47, 52; 16:19; 18:1, 3, 4, 23; 19:12, 14, 23, 24 (variant); 20:1; 22:2; 23:14; 25:1.

"Israelites." Of course, anything that has to do with Israel cannot logically exclude Israel's God and that God's imminent reign.

Jesus' constant appeal to Jewish Scripture, the Hebrew Bible, has to be brought into this discussion. Jewish Scripture—the Scripture that contained the torah, that told the Israelite story, that features prophets and wisdom material, etc.—is the only Scripture that Jesus read, quoted, and considered authoritative. From time to time, he would debate Jewish interlocutors about interpretation, which was an ordinary Jewish activity. But at no time did he cast doubt on these scriptures. Instead, he affirmed the Jewish scripture (Matt 5:17–20), quoted it when necessary (Luke 4:1–13), commended its contents (Mark 10:19), and saw it as testifying to his own work and mission (Luke 4:16–21; 24:27; John 5:46). Jesus is portrayed throughout the Gospels as knowing the Jewish Scripture, citing it, recommending it, debating its meaning, alluding to it, using its stories illustratively, and the like. In that, he was engaging in a quintessential Jewish activity. Again, these Jews were what Israelites were called in Jesus' era.[18]

Paul's Botanical and Legal Adoption Metaphors

The book of Acts and the Pauline letters clearly feature Paul as most responsible for the mass inclusion of gentiles into the nascent church and therefore the Israelite story.[19] There is an ironic aspect to Paul's efforts in that he was

18. I believe that even the so-called antitheses found in Matthew's Gospel (5:21–48) need to be reconsidered. Most Christians, scholars included, believe that Jesus is *correcting* the Jewish Bible here and, in the process, substituting a more palatable ethic. However, on form critical grounds, scripture is never introduced anywhere in the New Testament with language like, "you have heard that it was said," or similar language. I argue that Jesus is challenging certain interpretations of the Jewish Scripture rather than the Scripture itself.

19. Non-Israelites were also part of Israel prior to the Jesus movement, though it is impossible to know how large a group this constituted. But at the textual level, in the Hebrew Bible / Old Testament there are some indications that becoming part of Israel was neither impossible nor necessarily uncommon. Judah, the ancestor of David, for example, fathered children with Tamar, a Canaanite (Gen 38). Joseph married the daughter of an Egyptian priest (Gen 41:45). A Midianite woman married Moses (Exod 2:21). Solomon, of course, famously married everyone (1 Kgs 11:1–2)! Other non-Israelites became part of the community regardless of status, like Rahab, a Canaanite prostitute (Josh 2), or Naaman, a Syrian military officer (2 Kgs 5). The episode featuring an elaborate ruse on the part of the Gibeonites is yet another example (Josh 9). Of course, the story of Jonah features every last man, woman, and child who lived in Nineveh, a city in Assyria, acknowledging Israel's God. Even the cattle wore sackcloth (Jonah 3:6–9)! As well, there are prophetic texts that indicate inclusion of gentiles into Israel, in a sense fulfilling the promise YHWH made to Abraham (Gen 12:3; see also Isa 19:24–25; 25:6–8; 45:22–25; 55:5; 56:6–8; 60:3, 11; Zech 2:16 [Eng. 2:11]; 14:16; see

so negative in his perception of the character of at least some Jewish religious expression, which he viewed as hopelessly legalistic.[20] At the same time, according to Paul what God had done in and through Jesus the Christ obviously involved Israel, the very community he excoriated. Despite the apostle's negative assessment of Israelite/Jewish religious practice as he saw it, not to mention the rejection of Jesus as ushering in the messianic age, he still viewed Israel ultimately as the "Israel of God" (Gal 6:16). Jews, quite obviously, then, and now, would reject legitimately and see as condescending Paul's claim that Israel will be *saved* regardless of persisting unbelief. But the larger point to be made is that for Paul the existence of the church apart from Israel is inconceivable.[21] Though Paul saw Israel as a "broken branch" and consequently temporarily alienated from God, he insisted that God's promises to Israel were finally *irrevocable* (Rom 11:29; *ametamelēta*). This conviction on the apostle's part led him to develop two significant metaphors that support gentile inclusion into Israel as the elect people of God.

The first metaphor was a botanical one, in which Israel is construed as an olive tree (Rom 11:17; cf. Jer 11:16; Hos 14:6). Gentiles, viewed as a "wild olive shoot" were grafted into this tree, thus being nourished by the tree itself. Paul underscores the fact that the *root* (= Israel) supports the *shoot* (= gentiles), not the other way around (Rom 11:18). Once the graft takes, as it were, it will be indistinguishable from the tree itself, according to Paul's logic. Paul in this passage also makes certain that no boasting on the part of gentiles is appropriate. This is due to the priority of Israel as God's elect. Gentiles are without question part of the elect community of Israel, yet it must never be forgotten that Israel's election came first.

The second metaphor is that of legal adoption into a family. Paul makes this argument in the Letter to the Galatians (4:1–7). In a sense, this metaphor is mixed, combining a child heir who is waiting for the moment when family assets will be available and a child awaiting adoption into a family. The complexity of these two slightly different metaphors is increased by the fact that Paul is writing to both Jews and gentiles, but not always making clear which group he has in mind. Some scholars argue that the apostle uses different pronouns for the two groups, but this is not consistent in the

---

also Christiansen, "Nation," 1044–49).

20. Given the polemic nature of the New Testament generally, Jewish opponents to the Jesus movement are often depicted simplistically. However, Sanders has demonstrated from his historical studies the complexities and highly nuanced features of Jewish religious expression in the first century CE. Of course, judging Jews as mainly religiously legalistic and morally obtuse is a caricature. See *Paul and Palestinian Judaism*; *Jesus and Judaism*; *Jewish Law from Jesus to Mishnah*.

21. Karrer, "Paul's Last Journey to Jerusalem," 75.

letter.[22] Logically, Jews are analogous to the child waiting for the father's will to be read so that access to family wealth will be possible. Conversely, gentiles are symbolized by a child who has no biological relationship to the family but nonetheless becomes a full-fledged daughter or son. Interestingly, both children were previously enslaved by "the elemental spirits of the universe" (*ta stoicheia tou kosmou*), but now are free in their new families by adoption. Thus, regardless of being a Jew once under the law or a gentile formerly existing outside of Israel, the Israelite *family* is now *home*. Interestingly, the word *adoption* (as sons) (uiothesian) is even applied to Jews in this mixed metaphor (Gal 4:5). In any case, both Jews *and* gentiles are either heirs or finally adopted, respectively.

Thus, even the apostle Paul, who is so steadfastly opposed to Jewish religious expression that he saw as fundamentally, irredeemably legalistic, and devoid of grace, still saw the Jews as representative of Israel and therefore legitimately expected God's promises to this elect people in the future (Rom 11:29). Gentiles, too, could become part of this *Israel of God* via grafting and adoption.

To summarize, the New Testament presents Jesus of Nazareth as inextricably and intimately related to Israel as the elect people of God. This is why seeing the church as figured by Israel is hardly idiosyncratic, notwithstanding the church's growing gentile composition and vilification of Jews as a religious group. As well, because the promises made to Israel originally were irrevocable (Rom 11:29) Judaism—Rabbinic Pharisaic Judaism, as it exists to this day despite its several iterations—has every right to see itself as figured by Israel. Most would not view Judaism seeing itself as figured by canonical Israel as either unusual or arrogant. My argument is that the church's seeing itself as figured by canonical Israel as well should not be seen as unusual or arrogant either. Instead, I argue, it is requisite.

THE UNITY AND DISUNITY OF THE CHURCH IN THE NEW TESTAMENT

Dealing with what the New Testament says about the church's unity and disunity is an enormously complex task. Clearly, that is beyond the scope of this book. Nevertheless, the New Testament's juxtaposing an almost idealistic portrayal of the church's unity alongside depictions of the church's struggles with disunity is instructive. I will cite only the broad outlines of the New Testament's treatment of this phenomenon. As well I will leave aside the subject of the origins of the church. Instead, I will be content to

22. Cousar, *Galatians*, 91–92.

deal with this topic in terms of *groups* who believed that Jesus of Nazareth was Israel's Christ which eventually *became* a church, a community that was distinct from the synagogue. In this light, it might be worth mentioning how often the Greek version of the Jewish Scriptures uses *ecclesia/church*, to translate *qāhāl*, a common word in the Hebrew version of Jewish Scripture meaning *community* or *congregation*.[23] Also interesting in this regard is that the term *synagogue* is a *Greek* compound noun despite over a two thousand year association with Jews. In any case, we turn now to the church's unity or disunity according to the New Testament.

Jesus' most famous prayer is surely the so-called Lord's Prayer (Matt 6:7-13; Luke 11:1-4). But Jesus' prayer in the Gospel of John, in which he prays for the unity of those who follow him arguably warrants a solid second place (John 17:20-26). The first part of that prayer seemed to focus on his immediate disciples (John 17:1-19), as evidenced by his allusion to Judas' betrayal (John 17:12). In the second part of the prayer, he includes those who believe in him through *their* (i.e., the disciples') word (John 17:20). When Jesus includes these prospective believers, he prays that they will be *one*, just as he and the Father are *one* (John 17:21). It is hardly an overstatement to suggest that this prayer has been the foundation on which all subsequent ecumenical efforts of the church have been built.

At first, the prayer appears quite straightforward, even simple. On reflection, though, questions emerge. Precisely *how* are Jesus and the Father *one*? Does this speak to a unity of purpose or mission? Did Jesus have in mind *essence*, something that theologians in centuries to come would conclude? If the latter, then how could those who follow Jesus possibly be unified in the same manner? Perhaps Jesus is praying only for unity of basic belief or foundational ethics? That is, what beliefs and behaviors are required to be held in common so as to constitute a people, a community, or a church? Even as we are struck by the implications of Jesus' prayer, we realize that it is at the same time simple and complex.

Since there is scant amplification in the text, we have to be satisfied with inferences. For example, regardless of how diverse the people who believe in Jesus may be, they are to be *somehow* unified. Differing cultures, differing languages, differing nationalities, and differing ethnicities are presumably not to be decisive. Despite such differences, those who believe in Jesus will be fundamentally unified. This unity need not involve conformity.

23. E.g., Deut 4:10; 9:10; 18:16; 23:2-3; 31:30; Josh 9:2; Judg 20:2; 21:5; 1 Kingdoms 17:47; 19:20; 1 Chr 13:2; 28:2; 29:1; 2 Chr 1:3; 6:3; 7:8; 10:3; 20:5; 23:3; 28:14; 29:23; 30:2; 2 Esd 2:64; 10:1, 8, 12, 14; Neh 5:7, 13; 7:66; 8:2, 17; 13:1; Jdt 6:16, 21; 7:29; 14:6; Job 30:28; Pss 21(22):23, 26; 25(26):5, 12; 34(35):18; 39(40):10; 67(68):26; 88(89):6; 106(107):32; 149:1; Prov 5:14; Sir 15:5; 21:17; 23:24; 24:2; 26:5; 38:33; 39:10; 44:15; 50:13, 20; Mic 2:5; Joel 2:16; Lam 1:10; 1 Macc 2:56; 3:13; 4:59; 5:16.

Still, a basic belief and ethic would presumably be required. It would seem that Jesus prayed that those who followed him be at least unified in basic beliefs, goals, and a common mission. He had announced that the kingdom of heaven/God was at hand. Those who followed him should most certainly work to foster this kingdom. Perhaps other inferences are possible. But the main point is this: As the Gospel of John presents Jesus, the unity of his followers—soon to be a church—is an extremely important issue. Jesus' prayer made clear how crucial unity was to him. Indeed, absent this unity, the world will have little reason to believe that he (i.e., Jesus) was sent by God (John 17:23).

At least one New Testament author described the unity of the early group of believers in who Jesus was and what he had accomplished in striking terms.[24] This community, now consisting of three thousand people, devoted themselves to apostolic teaching, fellowship, common meals, and a vibrant prayer life. These believers witnessed many wonders performed by the apostles. They participated in communal living by a radical sharing regimen. Possessions and goods were sold, with the proceeds distributed to anyone who needed them. As well, they attended temple together, ate together, and were collectively thankful. This manner of living was regarded favorably by all the people. Due to this favorable reception, their numbers increased dramatically (Acts 2:41–47).

This same author elaborated on this form of living by describing in more detail the selling of property for the good of the whole. The *company* (*plēthous*) of those who believed were of *one heart* and *soul*. These people had no problem in regarding their possessions as belonging to the whole community. Such communal behavior meant that no one lacked anything. Wealthy people in this collective sold their possessions for the benefit of everyone else. They brought the proceeds of these sales to the apostles, who then distributed to anyone who had a need. Underscoring this incredible communal largess, we learn that a man by the name of Joseph—otherwise known as Barnabas—sold a field and, to mimic the communal process experienced by this group of believers, brought the money derived from the sale to the apostles (Acts 4:32–37).

Passages like these have sometimes been interpreted as a form of communism practiced by early followers of Jesus and his apostles. Illustrating how seriously this group took this intentional communal living, an episode immediately following details how a married couple, Ananias and Sapphira,

---

24. Viewed historically, the author of Acts probably did not know of Jesus' prayer for unity since it occurs in the Gospel of John. But in terms of the *canonical* structure of the present New Testament, at the literary level it is permissible to see descriptions found in Acts as explicating material in the Four Gospel tradition.

withheld *some* of the proceeds they got when they sold property. According to Peter, once the couple made the sale, all of the proceeds were to be given for the community's use. Withholding any amount was apparently forbidden. Violating this communal rule, Ananias died on the spot upon hearing Peter's rebuke. A little later Sapphira also died, as Peter predicted, when she lied about the amount she and her husband received for the sale. Everyone who heard about this stunning event became fearful (Acts 5:1-11).

The unity experienced by this community of believers in Jesus was ideal; indeed, it was virtually utopian. Nevertheless, soon cracks in the system developed. The episode involving Ananias and Sapphira was one illustration of such a crack. Other difficulties surfaced, too. As the community grew in numbers, one segment, the Hellenists (people who spoke Greek?) complained about the Hebrews (people who spoke Aramaic?) because widows—an especially vulnerable group—belonging to their contingent were neglected in the daily distribution (Acts 6:1). However, this problem was addressed by appointing people who would deal with the issue. The eventual resolution allowed those designated as preachers to continue their work and not have to be distracted by quotidian matters (Acts 6:2-6). This strategy seemed to have succeeded, at least for a while (Acts 6:7).

Still, in the chronology of Acts, in time this marvelous unity could not prevent other forms of division. Peter struggled with the prospect of eating foods that were ritually unclean according to Scripture (Acts 10). A so-called *circumcision party* complained about Peter's having table fellowship with people who had not been circumcised (Acts 11:1-2). These difficulties were faced, dealt with, and apparently solved, at least temporarily (Acts 11:3-18). Of course, the most consequential dispute took place when Paul and Barnabas argued vehemently with those who were still insisting on circumcision as requisite for following Jesus (Acts 15:2). This led to a meeting being held in Jerusalem to settle the matter once and for all (Acts 15:4-35). Though this issue was resolved with something of a compromise, the issue persisted as, for example, Paul's Letter to the Galatians made clear. Perhaps a full-blown division in this early group of believers had not yet come about according to Acts, but issues that had the potential of undermining unity were impossible to ignore.

The New Testament epistles provide a window for seeing some of the other fractures that are starting to come to the fore in the Acts narrative.[25] The apostle Paul wrote his first letter to the church at Corinth primarily

25. It is important to keep in mind that I am treating the New Testament from a canonical perspective, rather than a historical one. In that sense, it does not matter that, for example, Acts was written *after* Paul's letters. For an excellent treatment from a historical perspective, see Vischer et al., *Unity of the Church*.

to address the developing factions that had arisen and were threatening to become more divisive. It is difficult to know precisely which theological trajectories are in play when Paul complains that people are identifying with different proponents: Paul himself; Apollos; Cephas; Christ (!) (1 Cor 1:11–13). Though scholars have attempted to describe these groups in detail, no consensus has emerged. Regardless, this is a serious enough issue to justify Paul's letter, replete with admonitions and counter arguments. For example, Paul chastises this church for its immaturity and jealousy (1 Cor 3:1–3). Evidently, disputes had arisen over various functions that people had had in various church activities (1 Cor 3:4–9). Such disputes, though, were only part of the problem. Immoral behavior was also an issue (1 Cor 5:1–5). Even those who were not themselves behaving immorally nevertheless were associating with others who were (1 Cor 5:9–13). As the letter develops, the apostle brings up one matter after another. It was doubtful that every issue had the potential to divide the church significantly. Still, Paul thought it was necessary to use the metaphor of the human body to warn against individual body parts denouncing other body parts as not belonging (1 Cor 12:1–31). As well, the apostle's famous chapter on love (1 Cor 13) was thought necessary precisely because those at Corinth were not expressing the love that was to be the mark of a church committed to Jesus the Christ. Putting the matter sharply, the Corinthian church seemed at the time of the apostle's writing anything but unified in a meaningful sense.

In the Letter to the Galatians, the apostle Paul addresses one of the most vexing issues that confronted the church, at least from his vantage point. That issue had to do with those who continued to hold on to features of Jewish religious expression that Paul thought were incompatible with the message he had preached. In this letter he took on the so-called *Judaizers*. For Paul, these were people who believed in Jesus as the Christ but thought such faith did not preclude obedience to Jewish religious law as embodied in the torah. For present purposes, we will not cite pros and cons of Paul or his detractors' respective arguments. Of more immediate concern is whether this dispute presented a serious challenge to the unity of the fledging church.

Without question, the language the apostle uses to counter his opponents underscores how seriously he regarded this matter. Paul refers to those to whom he is writing as having *deserted* (*metatithesthe*) rather than, say, having disagreed with, him (Gal 1:6). Their position is not a minor difference of theological opinion. Rather, it represents *another gospel* (*heteron euangelion*). This is why the apostle minces no words. For him, what he is up against is nothing short of a *perversion* (*metastrepsai*) of the gospel of Christ (Gal 1:7). For an offense so grave, the apostle believes imprecations are appropriate. More than once in this letter he says that any promoting a belief that keeping the law is necessary should be cursed (*anathema*) or are already under a *curse* (*kataran*). Christ has redeemed Jews and gentiles from the curse of the law by taking on the curse on himself (Gal 1:8-9; 3:10, 13). Having no reticence to employ intemperate language, Paul calls his implied interlocutors *stupid*, asking who it was that bewitched them (Gal 3:1).

This was no coffeehouse theological debate that the apostle was having. For him, the stakes could not have been higher. Paul reminded the Galatians that he had had the temerity to oppose Cephas (= Peter) to his face over this matter (Gal 2:11). In Paul's eyes, Cephas/Peter stood *condemned* (*hoti kategnōsmenos ēn*). Cephas was not the only one who had to deal with Paul's ire. As well, Paul did not hold back from criticizing James, Jesus' own brother and leader of the Jerusalem church. According to Paul, some in James' camp made Cephas uncomfortable for eating with gentiles even though he had no trouble doing that previously (Gal 2:11-12). The apostle even supplied the details of his conversation with Cephas (Gal 2:14-21). Can there be any question that Paul thought without reservation that he simply could not lose this argument? For the apostle, this issue was at the heart of the gospel.

For Paul, people taking the path that included keeping the Jewish law would end up being severed from Christ and falling from grace (Gal 5:4). *Circumcision*, by which Paul has in mind not only the actual physical act but also a way of referring to torah observance generally, is simply irrelevant (Gal 5:6). The only law that those in the church needed to keep is loving one's neighbor as oneself (Gal 5:14). Anything else is extraneous. Unless the people to whom Paul is writing are convinced by his argument, the dispute might lead to the community's dissolution in the form of members of the congregation devouring one another (Gal 5:15). To summarize, for Paul this issue is an attack on the very foundation of the church, threatening not only disunity but possible destruction.

The Epistle of James has to be understood relative to the argument Paul put forth in Galatians and elsewhere as well. It shows how powerful were the centrifugal forces with which the early church had to contend. Though the differences between the position advocated in James and the position advocated in the Pauline material have sometimes been overdrawn, the fact that there are significant differences cannot be denied. When Paul can say that justification happens "apart from works of law" (*choris ergōn nomou*) while the letter of James asserts that "faith apart from works is dead" (*pistis chōris ergōn nekra estin*), those statements are not easily reconciled (Rom 3:28; Jas 2:18, 20, 26). Arguably, the writer of the Epistle of James either caricatures Paul's argument or comes close to it (Jas 2:18). At the same time, the apostle Paul and the writer of James have entirely different understandings of faith and works. Indeed, they are reflecting differing theological streams of Christian tradition.[26] Paul sees Israel's efforts to obey the law/torah as disjunctive with living in the Spirit and by the grace effected by Jesus' death and resurrection. However, the author of James sees an unbroken line of continuity between an obedient Israel and the obedience called for by those who believe in Jesus as Israel's Christ. Originally, this letter was addressed to Jews who believed in Jesus but have been dispersed (Jas 1:1). Now, as part of a canon, it is addressed to everyone, even gentiles who have become metaphorically part of dispersed Israel. However, before the New Testament canon was fixed, this letter evinces fault lines in the early community that believed in Jesus.

The tensions between those who saw themselves as members of the church who were aligned with Pauline thought as opposed to those who were aligned with the thought found in the Epistle of James were real. Many so-called Jewish Christians as well as some gentiles originally enamored with Jewish religious expression, and therefore nascent Judaism, often attended synagogue, tried to be observant of the law, kept Jewish festivals, worshipped on the Sabbath, and the like. Christian officials for at least a couple of centuries into the Common Era rebuked Christian congregations—or subgroups of them—for precisely such activities.[27] This did not mean that the church was split per se. Incipient *denominations*, an anachronistic term for this period, were not hermetically sealed from each other. At the same time, tensions were evident, serious ones, in this community that could lead subsequently to more substantial divisions.[28]

In sum, the New Testament presents Jesus as praying for the unity of his followers, a prayer surely indicating that Jesus felt such a prayer was necessary. Early on, as depicted in Acts, the unity of those believing in Jesus was idealistic, if not utopian. But the New Testament letters reveal challenges to the church's unity; that unity was challenged before Acts concluded its story. Granted, the New Testament documents provide no evidence to suggest that the fledgling Christian community was hopelessly divided. Nevertheless, disunity was a besetting problem for the church. By no means could the unity of the fledgling community be taken for granted. Achieving unity remained a task, an arduous task. In that sense, from the very beginning those who were following Jesus mirrored Israel, its figure, in its proclivity

---

26. Childs, *New Testament as Canon*, 440-41.

27. See Dunn, *Partings of the Ways*, xx.

28. I do not regard the entities that were eventually judged as too far afield theologically to ever be part of catholic Christianity as germane to my discussion. *Gnosticism* would be an example of such an outside group.

to divide. Neither Ezekiel's vision of Judah's and Israel's future reunification (Ezek 37:15–23) nor Jesus' prayer that his followers be *one* have yet to be realized.

FINAL REFLECTIONS

As we reflect on the implications of this study for the Christian church, we need to keep in mind the following: (1) descriptions of division in Israel are persistent and prominent throughout the Old Testament—this was no secondary matter; (2) because the New Testament in comparison covers a much narrower time frame, it depicts division in the church primarily as a *potential* problem; nevertheless, the struggles it had to deal with were substantial and jeopardized unity in the long term. Sometimes, the unity that was achieved in this or that circumstance was at best fragile; (3) canonical Israel is a figure for the church (= Christianity), no less than it is a figure for the synagogue (= Judaism).

Implications for the Church as Being Figured by Canonical Israel

Relative to the third item, namely, that canonical Israel is a figure for the church, we need to deal with this in both general and more specific terms. That is, what difference would it make were the church to take seriously that it is figured by Israel? Certainly, it would involve not only a recognition but a new appreciation of its Jewish origins. But something more compelling is being called for that transcends correcting historical amnesia. Something much more robust theologically and practically should derive from such a shift in thinking. Several matters are worth considering.

One, the church needs to reassess its relationship to and appropriation of the Old Testament. Formally, virtually all Christian churches, regardless of tradition or denominational affiliation, acknowledge that the Old Testament is part of its sacred scriptural canon. Informally, however, the Old Testament often is relegated to an inferior position, especially when compared to the New Testament. This is the case, notwithstanding appreciation and appropriation for some sections such as the Psalms, selected material from the Prophets, and the story that makes up *salvation history*. However, when Christians realize that reading about Israel in the Old Testament is not about *them* but *us*, a radical change of perspective is possible. Instead of seeing the Old Testament as background, as prefatory, as preliminary, as secondary, exclusively promissory, or predictive, and the like, it might be seen as a veritable vehicle of revelation.[29] No New Testament writer thought the new community of Jesus' followers needed a new scripture. This new community already *had* scripture: the Jewish scripture. That is why every New Testament author, in one way or another, tried mightily to convince readers that what God had done in and through Jesus was "according to the Scripture" (1 Cor 15:3). Should not Christians have the same respect for and trust in these biblical texts as the authors of the New Testament had? Also, realizing and accepting that the Jewish Scripture was Jesus' Bible should call into question Christian negative postures about that section of the Christian Bible.

Two, because gentiles—which now constitute most of the Christian community—have been grafted into the Israelite olive tree and adopted into the Israelite family, when they read about the Israelite ancestors they are reading about *their* ancestors. As Christians, when we read about Israel's deliverance from Egyptian bondage, we have to accept that as *our* story. When we read Isaiah, Jeremiah, Amos, or Hosea we are paying attention to *our* prophets. Proverbs, Job, and Ecclesiastes constitute *our* canonical wisdom tradition. The Old Testament is *our* scripture, *our* tradition, and *our* story. That is at least minimally the result of the grafting and the adoption process. Additionally, in the context of this book, especially, when we read about divisions in Israel throughout biblical narratives should we not realize that we are reading about not only *our* past but something also that speaks to *our* contemporary ecclesial divisions?

Three, when Christians have paid attention to the Old Testament, they have typically gravitated to texts focusing on God's love, grace, goodness, and mercy. That is all to the good. But if we are figured by Israel, we dare not avoid texts that accent divine judgment. Divine judgment on Israel is virtually central to the Old Testament, even though judgment is never YHWH's final stance. Why is it that we think that Israel was under God's judgment, and rightly so, but that the church, which is figured by Israel, is somehow exempt from divine wrath? Is this because of a superficial interpretation of the apostle Paul? That is, Israel was under *law* and therefore susceptible to divine punishment whereas the church is under *grace* and therefore exempt from divine punishment. That is a spurious reading, in my judgment. The grace of God that was manifested in Christ is not something brand new in the divine economy. Jesus did not introduce God's love and grace. Instead, he was an example, extension, and, most importantly, incarnation of the deity who was already known for being loving and gracious. Israel experienced grace, for instance, in the election of the ancestors and by being

---

29. See Seitz, *Character of Christian Scripture*.

rescued from Egyptian bondage, not to mention in countless other ways. But receiving God's grace does not immunize against judgment. When one belongs to Israel, one is part of a community that has covenanted with God to believe certain things and act in certain ways. When Israel persisted in violating the agreement they had with God, eventually punishment became necessary. It was not an ultimate punishment, but it was at times severe. Has the church ever been guilty of so violating its commitments to God that judgment is appropriate? Why are Christians so arrogant and oblivious of their own *collective* sin that they dismiss even the possibility of divine censure? If we had nothing to do with Israel, we would still be liable for communal sins. Being figured by Israel surely means that we cannot rejoice in God's graciousness and simultaneously be confident that we are not liable to divine judgment.

Any fair presentation of the history of the Christian church for the two millennia it has existed cannot ignore the sins it has *collectively* committed. In my judgment, it is a specious argument that the church *as such* cannot sin, only its individual members can.[30] That would be a church unrelated to its actual worldly existence. The church, as it is *on the ground*, so to speak, is where evaluation of its morality has to focus. As a matter of fact, the church *has* sinned, sometimes grievously. A number of those past sins have been particularly egregious. Christians have to answer for the Crusades, the Inquisition, the Pogroms against Jews, the treatment of so-called heretics when possessing not only ecclesial authority but also political power, and other similar perfidies. This list of communal sins committed by the church in the past could easily be expanded.

Granted, the church has also done a great deal of good in these last two thousand years. Its positive impact on culture in so many areas cannot be fairly denied. The contemporary church, in its many guises, continues to be a positive force in a variety of cultures. While that is a reason for Christians to be pleased and even thankful, that circumstance does not absolve the church's sins or provide an excuse for it to be blind to the many past sins that it has committed.[31]

At the same time, it would be the height of hypocrisy not to admit that there are many sins for which the church is responsible in the modern period as well. The church's sins cannot be relegated to the past. In the American context, for example, racism in a variety of forms continues to

30. Radner, *Brutal Unity*, 163.
31. See Dickson, *Bullies and Saints*. In the 2022 Erasmus Lecture, Anthony Fisher listed a catalogue of positive contributions made by the Roman Catholic Church over the last two millennia. Other Christian communions can make similar claims as well. See Fisher, "The West," 22–23.

plague society. When slavery ended, and after the unspeakable carnage of the American Civil War that was required to eliminate that vile institution, *Jim Crow* laws were implemented by a white majority, most of whom were self-confessed Christians. These laws precipitated dreadful treatment of black citizens. As well, in addition to laws that were explicitly discriminatory and oppressive, white citizens terrorized and intimidated black people without having to worry about facing any consequences. Thus, a social, political, and religious context was created that allowed, for example, white lynch mobs to carry out scores of extralegal executions with impunity.[32] This relatively recent past continues to infect the general American culture with a lingering racism that still operates implicitly and explicitly.[33] Again, many members of the Christian church have been either all too silent in the face of continuing racial injustice or have participated willingly in it. The unpalatable truth of the matter is that Christians supported and benefitted from slavery, went to war to preserve the institution, and later established a segregated society that violated not only constitutional ideals but standard Christian virtues as well. If there were no other sins that required the church's repentance, this one by itself demands sober evaluation.

Another terrible stain on the church's soul has been its historic treatment of Jewish people. What began as an intramural religious and theological debate between Jews, soon eventuated into a polemic encounter that involved vitriolic accusations between a largely gentile group and an exclusively Jewish one. Before long, religious disagreement devolved into outright hostility. Again, at first this was primarily rhetorical hostility, but soon became increasingly behavioral. In time, animosity against Jews was based primarily not on religious grounds, but simply because Jews were Jews. Once Christianity became the dominant religion in both Western and Eastern Europe, Jews became not only a minority but a severely persecuted minority. Following Jesus of Nazareth, himself a Jew, meant little for Christians who saw no contradiction between their commitment to the church and their treatment of Jews, whether they were religious or not. Arguing with Jews for religious and theological reasons eventually metastasized into unadulterated virulent anti-Semitism. Since Adolf Hitler and the Nazi party was responsible for the Holocaust in World War II, it has been all too convenient to place all the blame on them for what happened to millions of Jewish people. However, if it had not been for centuries of anti-Semitic propaganda, policies, attitudes, official and unofficial actions, and old-fashioned disdain and hatred, all of which took place in populations

32. See Cone, *The Cross and the Lynching Tree*.
33. See Wallis, *America's Original Sin*.

that often were predominantly Christian, Hitler would not have found that anti-Semitic ground so easy to cultivate.[34] Indeed, in the period of time that encompasses World War II, many countries had actual policies that prevented Jews attempting to flee German persecution from finding asylum. Even countries that did not have formal barriers often had individuals in key offices that were so anti-Semitic that they made sure that Jewish calls for help were ignored. Again, these were countries that were at least demographically mostly Christian. To be sure, many Christians either recoiled because of this depravity or did what they could to mitigate it. But for the most part, these were exceptions. Given that grim reality, is that not a sufficiently deplorable sin for which the church needs to be deeply and humbly repentant?

Another grievous sin that the church has committed comes under the heading of colonialism. Historians, Christian or not, as well as Christian theologians have been concerned about this area, but for the most part it is not a feature of popular thinking in the church. Nevertheless, colonialism has been a dominant aspect of world history for the last few centuries. When one thinks of the standard colonial powers, Britain and France come readily to mind. But these two countries were not the only ones whose policies were defined by colonial expansion. Spain, Belgium, Portugal, the Netherlands, and America (once itself a colony) were also colonial powers. Indeed, Richard Overy argues that World War II is best explained by the efforts expended by Germany, Italy, Russia, and Japan to become colonial empires in their own right.[35] That is, modern states wanting to establish their own empires eventually went to war with modern states who were protecting the empires they had already established. Excepting Japan, most of these colonial countries, or aspiring colonial countries, were considerably if not predominantly Christian demographically, culturally, and sometimes formally in terms of *established* Christian churches. It hardly needs to be pointed out that the ideology that supported the colonialism in which these nation-states engaged the last several centuries was based on beliefs of cultural and racial superiority. These ideas were often stated forthrightly and quite explicitly. How might one reconcile concepts of cultural and racial superiority with Christian theology and ethics? How could orthodox Christian tradition become so distorted as to permit using that tradition to justify the colonial efforts of this or that so-called *Christian nation*? The question seems to be entirely rhetorical. At the communal level, along with sins of

34. Overy, *Blood and Ruins*, 226.
35. Overy, *Blood and Ruins*.

racism and anti-Semitism, should not colonialism be added to the list of sins that the church needs to confess?

In this context, perhaps this is one of the areas where a renewed appreciation of the Old Testament would be most beneficial. The prophetic tradition in the Old Testament was a form of ongoing and pervasive Israelite self-criticism. Indeed, it is remarkable that the community canonized the prophetic material since it seldom is flattering to Israel as God's elect community. Plus, the prophetic tradition is central to the Old Testament in its Hebrew form. The central part of the Hebrew Bible is called Prophets; it comes in two sections. The first section, the Former Prophets, consists of materials narrated in Joshua, Judges, Samuel, and Kings. All of these narratives are told from a prophetic, that is, a self-critical perspective. The second section, the Latter Prophets, consists of Isaiah, Jeremiah, Ezekiel, and the Book of the Twelve (= Minor Prophets). The prophetic material pulls no punches in calling into account Israel's penchant to violate their divinely initiated covenant agreements. To be sure, the prophetic material never concludes with divine judgment as the final word. The prophets offer hope for Israel's future. Still, one cannot skip the judgment oracles and go straight to the restoration oracles. For Christians, that would be like celebrating Easter while ignoring Good Friday. The point to be emphasized is that, as the church is figured by Israel, the prophetic tradition has something indispensable to say to that church in every generation. Christians dare not appropriate prophetic hopefulness while ignoring prophetic censure.

Four, since the church is figured by canonical Israel, as intimated, by no means can it afford to ignore the several stories featuring division in God's elect community according to the Old Testament, the longest section of Christian scripture. The reason for this is simple. Division has been one of the worst features of the church. Granted, some of the older divisions seem to have waned. Hostility between Protestants and Roman Catholics, for example, has not only lessened but has yielded to civil, even amiable, discussions between the two groups at a number of levels. In the twentieth century great ecumenical efforts were made. Even though results of these efforts have been largely disappointing in terms of final, lasting arrangements, the efforts themselves were noteworthy. Loyalties to one Protestant denomination and corresponding suspicions about other denominational identities have almost disappeared. That situation, however, may be related to the fact that differences among denominations are increasingly seen as irrelevant. Notwithstanding, not only is the church no closer to a meaningful unity than in previous eras, a case may be made that it is not only still divided but continues to multiply divisions.

Five, a final benefit to the church's reevaluating its previous desultory appropriation of the Old Testament would be recovering the use of the divine name. This would affect not only the church's attitude toward and relationship with Judaism but would have profound implications for Christian theology. That divine name, of course, is the Tetragrammaton, the four-letter distinctive name of the Israelite deity: YHWH (see Exod 3:13–18). As the church was in the process of forming, YHWH as a viable personal name played almost no role. There were at least two reasons for this.

One is that the Greek versions of the Jewish Bible were the primary texts consulted by the early followers of Jesus of Nazareth, including writers of materials that eventually became the New Testament. These Greek versions, conventionally referred to as the Septuagint, translated *kyrios, lord*, to render YHWH. Modern translations typically emulate this practice by translating YHWH with the word *Lord*, very often in small capital letters. However, *Lord* is a title, not a personal name. The enormous significance of the ubiquitous use of the Israelite God's personal name in the Old Testament / Jewish Bible therefore is either greatly diminished or lost altogether.[36]

A second reason that the church did not factor in the Israelite God's personal name is that by the time of the Jesus era the name YHWH had become an ineffable name. That is, the name was considered so mysterious, so holy, and so awe-inspiring that pronouncing the name aloud was seen to be grossly inappropriate or even blasphemous. Jews no longer pronounced the name in the synagogue liturgy during worship. The sacred Tetragrammaton is sometimes alluded to in the New Testament, but with circumlocutions or titles (e.g., Mark 14:61–62). When Jesus teaches his disciples to pray only a title is used—*Our Father*—even though the prayer begins with the petition that God's name be *hallowed* (e.g., Matt 6:9). In any case, were the church to take seriously its relationship to canonical Israel, its figure, as well to a renewed relationship to Judaism the recovery of YHWH, the sacred personal name of God that is used throughout the three-quarters of the Christian Bible, the Old Testament, would surely yield to immeasurable benefits.[37]

---

36. The name YHWH appears almost seven thousand times in the Old Testament / Jewish Bible in its Hebrew version.

37. See the impressive work of R. Kendall Soulen, who emphasizes that God's promises to Israel have never been cancelled, that the church needs to recover YHWH, the God of Abraham, Isaac, and Jacob, and the God who became incarnate in Jesus of Nazareth, and that the Tetragrammaton has an important role in explicating the Trinity and in unifying the Old and New Testaments. *Irrevocable*; *The God of Israel and Christian Theology*; *The Divine Name(s)*.

ONE, HOLY, CATHOLIC AND APOSTOLIC CHURCH

The claim that the church is *one* derives from the Nicene Creed, which most Christians recite as part of their regular worship. Some traditions do not make this recitation part of their weekly liturgy, but nevertheless accept this creed as a summary of their basic belief system. A relatively small minority pay little attention to the Nicene Creed, or any other creeds for that matter, because of a strict *sola scriptura* stance that regards any non-biblical statement as dubious.[38] Still, many in the latter group would not have any difficulty in acknowledging the essential truth of the creedal claim that there is "one, holy, catholic, and apostolic church," though they would want to make sure that the word *catholic* did not begin with an uppercase letter!

Few Christians would challenge the claim that the church was *holy*, for it came about by divine action; that the church is *catholic* or universal, in that it spans the globe; and that the church is *apostolic*, because of the role played by Jesus' immediate disciples in its formation. But the confession that the church is *one* at best expresses an aspiration. At worst, it is a vacuous, perhaps even hypocritical assertion.

Though usually painted with broad brush strokes, the major divisions experienced by the church over the centuries are well known.[39] The differences among the larger groups—the Roman Catholic church, the Anglican communion, the Orthodox tradition, Protestantism—representing *the* church, and the difficulty that they have had in having meaningful discussions with each other let alone settling differences, are well known, too, and basically accepted as realities with which Christians have to cope. Little has been significantly altered in a divided church despite great expenditures of energy by the so-called Ecumenical Movement in the last century.[40] Pope John Paul II, when he published *Ut Unum Sint* (= "That they may be One") in 1995, contributed substantially to the topic of unity in the church. Over twenty-five years later, the church seems no closer to unity. Even happy expressions of concord between various Christian iterations, for all the good will they have manifested, have done relatively little in the way of structural change.

---

38. This phrase comes out of the Protestant Reformation. Ironically, in a sense Protestantism promised to promote unity by adhering only to Christian Scripture. Five hundred years later there seems to be no limit to the number of Protestant denominations. The cynical joke that Protestantism made church division a sacrament is *not* a joke!

39. See Noll, *Turning Points*.

40. See Dulles, "Saving Ecumenism from Itself"; Root, "Ecumenical Winter?"

Of course, many of the schisms that the church has experienced now seem like ancient history in public consciousness. Unless one happens to be a church historian or a historical theologian, these ecclesiastical issues do not preoccupy ordinary Christians. The rift between Eastern and Western Christianity, the Protestant Reformation, as well as splits that occurred among churches and within denominations due to epochal political events, like the American Civil War, the French Revolution, World War I and II, and the like, are safely ensconced in the foggy past. At the same time, though, most Christians who pay any attention at all to the church in general or their own local church in recent times are quite aware that the church is not moving toward unity; instead, it continues to multiply divisions.

For example, as I write in 2023, the Episcopal Church in America and the American United Methodist Church are both dealing with matters that undermine unity in one way or another. United Methodists are attempting to divide without hostility and a complete loss of Christian brotherly and sisterly affection. Already that process has run into trouble. The Episcopal Church in America has settled in its own mind matters touching on human sexuality but is at odds with other members of the worldwide Anglican Community over the same issues. This is especially the case with Anglicans located elsewhere, such as Africa. Other denominations, or even so-called parachurch organizations (like colleges, universities, or seminaries), face enormous challenges over these same matters. There is little wonder that various obituaries are being written about a variety of Christian groups, denominations, or institutions.[41] Whether these obituaries are premature or "greatly exaggerated" only time will tell.

No matter how often Christians recite the Nicene Creed about the church's being *one* or sing hymns extolling the church's unity, the unpalatable truth is that the church is not even close to being *one*. And, there is precious little evidence that suggests that this divided condition will end any time soon. As already noted, despite Ezekiel's vision, Jesus' prayer, or the wondrous intentional communal living as portrayed in Acts, the church was not, then, or now, one.

If the church, in its guise of being figured by canonical Israel, actually makes time to read the stories of Israel's proclivity to divide, it will recognize, sadly, the familiarity of the issues raised by these narratives. There are arguments over religious symbols and whether they are to be seen as positive or negative, as we saw in the story about the big altar in Joshua 22. Both sides were suspicious of each other from the outset, even though both sides were composed of bona fide Israelites. Then again, there are jealousies that

---

41. See Leithart, *End of Protestantism*; Yancey and Quosick, *One Faith No Longer*.

arise when one segment of Israel feels slighted by another segment of Israel, as the story of Deborah and Jael indicated (Judg 4–5). Equally, sometimes the rawest grabs for power, rooted in violence, are manifested in Israel, as was the case with Abimelech (Judg 9). As well, on occasion terrible division was the result of meanness and inconsideration, not to mention impulsive behavior, confused commitments, or intemperate language, as we witnessed in the Jephthah narrative (Judg 10–12). Again, there are times when both groups in a dispute are so lacking in common decency or so prone to depravity, divine judgment on the whole group seems justified, as indicated in the story of the Levite's concubine (Judg 19–21). Also, even a story in which Israel starts as divided but ends up being unified cannot be said to be a positive development without remainder, according to the story when David consolidates his power (2 Sam 1–5). At least, the unity achieved only lasted for a couple of generations. Of course, when Absalom revolts against his father, David, we observe the tragic consequences of a community mirroring familial conflicts (2 Sam 12–19). And, Sheba's revolt illustrates what happens when the communal fabric that had been torn has been hastily and therefore poorly stitched together (2 Sam 20). Finally, when we come to Israel's *Great Schism*, we realize that it had been moving inexorably in this direction for years, even centuries (1 Kgs 12). Israel's proclivity to divide had been progressing up to that time. Is it any wonder that Israel's prophets spoke to this issue (see chapter 10)?

In the end, these are depressing, even dystopian, stories. As well, they offer little in the way of remedy for disunity. They do provide a context for ecclesial reflection on its continuing disunity, but little more. It seems like a complete failure of nerve to fall back on the claim that unity will be achieved when the kingdom comes in full force. But after two thousand years of disunity, and experiencing a time when divisions continue to be multiplied, what else might one say? Ezekiel's vision remains unfulfilled. Jesus' prayer remains unanswered. Seeing the church as it was depicted in Acts 2 and 4 seems a fantasy. In this situation, any unity at all that the Christian church can achieve, and however minimal that unity might be, should be regarded as praiseworthy but terribly insufficient.[42]

Still, perhaps we give in too easily to despair over this matter. Even when Israel was hopelessly divided, YHWH was involved in one way or another in *every* Israelite iteration. Rarely did YHWH opt for one faction to the complete exclusion of another. Furthermore, quite often the division that Israel experienced was orchestrated by God. Ironically, Israel's many

---

42. See the important study that underscores the difficulty of achieving solidarity and unity, in Radner, *A Brutal Unity*.

divisions were on occasion simultaneously a function of sin *and* divine punishment. Add to this equation the fact that God is sometimes said to be committed primarily to a *remnant* of Israel in the future.[43] Who exactly makes up this *remnant*? Only God knows! Perhaps that is a point that we need to reconsider. Wheat and tares are growing simultaneously (Matt 13:24–30). Only at harvest time will separation be possible. Sheep and goats are being distinguished (Matt 25:31–46). Both are equally surprised at the final verdict. That is at the same time frightening and emboldening. If God never abandoned completely a divided Israel, dare we say that God has abandoned a divided church, even one that continues to multiply divisions? To me, the answer to that question is obvious.

---

43. See Meyer, "Remnant," 669–71.

Bibliography

Arnold, Patrick M. "Mizpah." In *Anchor Bible Dictionary*, edited by David Noel Freedman, 4:879–81. New York: Doubleday, 1992.
Avery-Peck, Alan J. "Oral Tradition (Judaism)." In *The Anchor Bible Dictionary*, edited by David Noel Freedman, 5:34–35. New York: Doubleday, 1992.
Baker, Robin. "Double Trouble: Counting the Cost of Jephthah." *Journal of Biblical Literature* 137.1 (2018) 29–50.
Barth, Karl. *Church Dogmatics, IV.1, The Doctrine of Reconciliation*. Translated by G. W. Bromiley. Edinburgh: T. & T. Clark, 1956.
Bird, Phyllis. "'To Play the Harlot': An Inquiry into an Old Testament Metaphor." In *Gender and Difference in Ancient Israel*, edited by P. Day, 75–94. Minneapolis: Fortress, 1989.
Bluedorn, Wolfgang. *Yahweh versus Baalism: A Theological Reading of the Gideon-Abimelech Narrative*. Supplements to the Journal for the Study of the Old Testament 329. Sheffield: Sheffield Academic, 2000.
Childs, Brevard S. *The New Testament as Canon: An Introduction*. Philadelphia: Fortress, 1984.
Christiansen, Duane L. "Nations." In *The Anchor Bible Dictionary*, edited by David Noel Freedman, 4:1037–49. New York: Doubleday, 1992.
Clements, Ronald E. "Baal-Berith of Shechem." *Journal of Semitic Studies* 13 (1968) 21–32.
Cone, James H. *The Cross and the Lynching Tree*. Maryknoll, NY: Orbis, 2011.
Cousar, Charles B. *Galatians*. Atlanta: John Knox, 1982.
Davis, Ellen. *Opening Israel's Scriptures*. New York: Oxford University Press, 2019.
Dickson, John. *Bullies and Saints: An Honest Look at the Good and Evil of Christian History*. Grand Rapids: Zondervan, 2021.
Dulles, Avery (Cardinal). "Saving Ecumenism from Itself." *First Things* 178 (December 2007) 23–27.
Dunn, James. *The Partings of the Ways*. 2nd ed. London: SCM, 2006.
Earl, Douglas S. *The Joshua Delusion? Rethinking Genocide in the Bible*. Eugene, OR: Cascade, 2010.
———. *Reading Joshua as Christian Scripture*. Journal of Theological Interpretation Supplement 2. Winona Lake, IN: Eisenbrauns, 2010.
Endris, Vince. "Yahweh versus Baal: A Narrative-Critical Reading of the Gideon/Abimelech Narrative." *Journal for the Study of the Old Testament* 33.2 (2008) 173–95.

Fisher, Anthony. "The West: Post- or Pre-Christian." *First Things* 330 (February 2023) 19–26.
Hauser, A. J. "Two Songs of Victory: A Comparison of Exodus 15 and Judges 5." In *Directions in Biblical Hebrew*, edited by E. R. Follis, 265–84. JOSTSS 40. Sheffield, UK: Sheffield Academic, 1987.
———. "Unity and Diversity in Early Israel, Before Samuel." *Journal of the Evangelical Theology Society* 22.4 (December 1979) 289–303.
Hulst, A. R. "Der Jordan in den alttestamentlichen Überlieferungen." *Oudtestamentische Studiën* (1965) 162–88.
Jonge, Marinus de. "Messiah." In *The Anchor Bible Dictionary*, edited by David Noel Freedman, 4:777–78. New York: Doubleday, 1992.
Karrer, Andreas. "Paul's Last Journey to Jerusalem." In *Unity of the Church in the New Testament and Today*, translated by James E. Crouch, edited by Lukas Vischert et al., 73–76. Grand Rapids: Eerdmans, 2010.
Leithart, Peter J. *The End of Protestantism: Pursuing Unity in a Fragmented Church.* Grand Rapids: Brazos, 2016.
Linafelt, Todd. "Private Poetry and Public Eloquence in 2 Samuel 1: 17–27: Hearing and Overhearing David's Lament for Jonathan and Saul." *Journal of Religion* 88 (2008) 497–526.
Malamat, Abraham. "Charismatic Leadership in the Book of Judges." In *Magnalia Dei: The Mighty Acts of God in Memory of G. Ernest Wright*, edited by Frank Moore Cross et al., 152–68. Garden City, NY: Doubleday, 1976.
Mendenhall, George E. "The Shady Side of Wisdom: The Date and Purpose of Genesis 3." In *A Light Unto My Path: Old Testament Studies in Honor of Jacob Myers*, edited by H. N. Bream et al., 319–34. Gettysburg Theological Studies 4. Philadelphia: Temple University Press, 1974.
Meyer, Lester V. "Remnant." In *The Anchor Bible Dictionary*, edited by David Noel Freedman, 5:669–71. New York: Doubleday, 1992.
Nogalski, James D., and Marvin A. Sweeney, eds. *Reading and Hearing the Book of the Twelve.* Atlanta, GA: Society of Biblical Literature, 2000.
Noll, Mark A. *Turning Points: Decisive Moments in the History of Christianity.* 2nd ed. Grand Rapids: Baker, 1997, 2000.
Novak, David. "From Supersessionism to Parallelism in Jewish-Christian Dialogue." In *Jews and Christians: People of God*, edited by Carl E. Braaten and Robert W. Jenson, 108–10. Grand Rapids: Eerdmans, 2003.
Oeste, Gordon. "Butchered Brothers and Betrayed Families: Degenerating Kinship Structures in the Book of Judges." *Journal for the Study of the Old Testament* 35.3 (2011) 295–316.
Overy, Richard. *Blood and Ruins: The Last Imperial War, 1939–1945.* New York: Viking, 2021.
Peterson, Anthony R. *Behold Your King: The Hope of the House of David in the Book of Zechariah.* Library of Hebrew Bible / Old Testament Studies 513. New York: T. & T. Clark, 2009.
Polzin, Robert. *Moses and the Deuteronomist: A Literary Study of the Deuteronomic History.* New York: Seabury, 1989.
Radner, Ephraim. *A Brutal Unity: The Spiritual Politics of the Christian Church.* Waco, TX: Baylor University Press, 2012.

Redditt, Paul L., and Aaron Schart, eds. *Thematic Threads in the Book of the Twelve.* Berlin: de Gruyter, 2003.
Rendtorff, Rolf. "Christliche Identität in Israels Gegenwart." *Evangelische Theologie* 55 (1995) 3–12.
Rhoads, David. "Zealots." In *The Anchor Bible Dictionary*, edited by David Noel Freedman, 6:1043–54. New York: Doubleday, 1992.
Root, Michael. "Ecumenical Winter? The Ecumenical Movement Has Stopped Moving." *First Things* 286 (October 2018) 33–39.
Rottzoll, Alexandra, and Dirk U. Rottzoll. "Die Erzählung von Jiftach und seiner Tochter (Jdc 11, 30–40) in der mittelalterlich-jüdischen und historisch Bibelexegese." *Zeitschrift für die alttestamentliche Wissenschaft* 115 (2003) 210–30.
Ruether, Rosemary Radford. *Faith and Fratricide: The Theological Roots of Anti-Semitism.* Crossroad; New York: Seabury, 1974.
Sanders, E. P. *Jesus and Judaism.* Philadelphia: Fortress, 1985.
———. *Jewish Law from Jesus to Mishnah.* London: SCM Press, 1990.
———. *Paul and Palestinian Judaism.* London: SCM Press, 1977.
Schneider, Tammi J. *Judges. Berit Olam: Studies in Hebrew Narrative and Poetry.* Edited by David W. Cotter. Collegeville, MN: Liturgical, 2000.
Schulte, Hannelis. "Beobachtungen zum Begriff der Zônâ im Alten Testament." *Zeitschrift für die Altestamentliche Wissenschaft* 104 (1992) 255–62.
Seitz, Christopher R. *The Character of Christian Scripture: The Significance of a Two-Testament Bible.* Grand Rapids: Baker, 2011.
Sonderegger, Katherine. *That Jesus Christ Was Born a Jew: Karl Barth's "Doctrine of Israel."* University Park, PA: Penn State University Press, 1992.
Soulen, R. Kendall. *The Divine Name(s) and the Holy Trinity: Distinguishing the Voices.* Vol. 1. Louisville, KY: WJK, 2011.
———. *The God of Israel and Christian Theology.* Minneapolis: Fortress, 1996.
———. *Irrevocable: The Name of God and the Unity of the Christian Bible.* Minneapolis: Fortress, 2022.
Spina, Frank Anthony. "The 'Face of God': Esau in Canonical Context." In *The Question for Context and Meaning: Studies in Biblical Intertextuality in Honor of James A. Sanders*, edited by Craig A. Evans and Shemaryahu Talmon, 3–25. Biblical Interpretation 28. Leiden: Brill, 1997.
———. *The Faith of the Outsider: Exclusion and Inclusion in the Biblical Story.* Grand Rapids: Eerdmans, 2005.
———. "In but Not of the World: The Confluence of Wisdom and Torah in the Solomon Story (I Kings 1–11)." *Asbury Seminary Theological Journal* 56.1 (2001) 17–30.
———. "The Irony of Reading the Book of Joshua as Christian Scripture." In *Orthodoxy and Orthopraxis: Essays in Tribute to Paul Livermore*, edited by Douglas R. Cullum and J. Richard Middleton, 27–43. Eugene, OR: Pickwick, 2019.
———. "Israel as a Figure for the Church: The Radical Nature of a Canonical Approach to Christian Scripture." In *The Usefulness of Scripture: Essays in Honor of Robert W. Wall*, edited by Daniel Castelo, Sara König, and David Nienhuis, 3–23. University Park, PA: Eisenbrauns, 2018.
———. "Israelites as *Gērîm*, 'Sojourners,' in Historical and Sociological Perspective." In *The Word of the Lord Shall Go Forth: Essays in Honor of David Noel Freedman in Celebration of His Sixtieth Birthday*, edited by Carol Myers and Michael O'Connor, 321–35. Winona Lake, IN: Eisenbrauns, 1983.

———. "Moses and Joshua: Servants of the Lord as Purveyors of the Word." In *Go Figure! Figuration in Biblical Interpretation*, edited by Stanley D. Walters, 65–92. Princeton Theological Monograph Series. Eugene: Pickwick, 2008.

———. "The Son of Jesse: Is the Story of David and Goliath a David and Goliath Story?" In *My Name Is Frank and That's Who I Am: Essays in Honor of Frank H. Thompson*, edited by Gary L. Hunter, 171–95. Greenville, IL: Greenville College, 2015.

Trible, Phylis. *Texts of Terror: Literary Feminist Readings of Biblical Narratives*. Philadelphia: Fortress, 1984.

Vischer, Lukas, et al., eds. *Unity of the Church in the New Testament and Today*. Translated by James E. Crouch. Grand Rapids: Eerdmans, 2010.

Wallis, Jim. *America's Original Sin: Racism, White Privilege and the Bridge to a New America*. Grand Rapids: Brazos, 2016.

Wong, Gregory T. K. "Song of Deborah as Polemic." *Biblica* 88 (2007) 1–22.

Yancey, George, and Ashlee Quosick. *One Faith No Longer: The Transformation of Christianity in Red and Blue America*. New York: New York University Press, 2021.

Zimmerli, Walter. *Ezekiel 1: A Commentary on the Book of the Prophet Ezekiel, Chapters 1–24*. Translated by Ronald E. Clements. Hermenia. Philadelphia: Fortress, 1979.

Index of Biblical References

[following the canonical order of the Hebrew Bible]

Genesis

3	115
3:6	115
8:20	17fn9
12–50	2, 3, 12
12:1–3	1, 151
12:2	3
12:3	166fn19
12:5–7	12
12:6	35
12:7–8	17fn9
13:4	17fn9
13:7	3, 15fn8
13:8–12	3
13:18	17fn9
15:18–21	12, 12fn4
15:18	12
17:8	12
17:15–21	3
17:16	3
18:16—19:29	142
19:1–38	3
19:30–38	13
22	58fn5
22:9	17fn9
25:1	34
25:23	3
25:24–26	13
25:29–34	3
26:25	17fn9
27:1–45	4
27:41	4
28:2	4
28:3	3
29:13–14	4
29:15	4
29:18	4
29:23	4
29:25–30	4
29:29	34
29:31–35	5
30:1–8	5, 34
30:3–8	34
30:9–13	5
30:14–21	5
30:22–24	5
30:25–43	5
31:1–3	5
31:9–13	5
31:17–19	5
31:19	5
31:22–24	5
31:33–35	5
31:36–50	5
31:51–54	5
32:3–8	6
32:9–12	6
32:13–20	6
32:28	13
33:1–4	6
33:9–11	6
33:20	17fn9

Genesis (*continued*)

34	67
34:2	35
34:16	3
34:20	35
34:22	3
34:24	35
34:25–29	35
34:25–26	67
34:25	35
34:27–29	67
34:27	35
34:30–31	6
34:30	67
35:4	36
35:6	3
35:10	13
35:22–26	34
35:22	6, 34
36:1	13
36:2	35fn8, 142
36:5	142
36:6–8	3
36:8	13
36:19	13
36:31	3
36:41	142
36:42	13
37:1	35
37:2	6, 34
37:3–4	6
37:4	6
37:5–11	6
37:12–14	36
37:17–20	6
37:22	6
37:25–28	7
37:29	7
38	166fn19
38:2	7
38:3–5	7
38:6	7
38:7	7
38:8–9	7
38:9–10	7
38:11	7
38:14	7
38:15–19	7
38:20–23	7
38:24	7
38:25–26	7
41:45	166fn19
42:21–22	7
42:36–38	6
44:16	7
46:32	15fn8
48:4	3
48:19	3
49:4	7
49:5–7	67
49:7	7
49:8	7
49:27	7

Exodus

	2, 141
1:9	2
2:1–10	67
2:11	2
2:21	166fn19
2:23	2
2:25	2
3:7	2, 144
3:8	12fn4
3:10	144
3:13–18	181
3:17	12fn3
5:1	144
6:4	12fn3
6:25	18fn10
7:4	144
7:16	144
7:26 [Eng. 8:1]	144
9:7	15fn8
12:8	12fn4
12:17	12fn4
12:19	67
12:49	67
13:5	12fn3, 12fn4
13:11	12fn3
15	28
17:8	78
17:11	78
17:13	78
17:14	79

… INDEX OF BIBLICAL REFERENCES 193

17:15	79	14:25	14
22:20[Eng. v.21]	68	14:39–45	14
22:21[Eng. v.22]	68	18:6	67
23:23	12fn4, 35fn8	18:23–24	67
23:28	12fn4, 35fn8	18:23	67
27:21	142fn3	20:1	14
28:41	162	20:22–23	14
28:43	142fn3	21:1–3	14fn6
29:45–46	144	21:4	14
31:1–11	120	21:21–22	15
31:6	142	21:23	15
32:1–6	130	21:24–25	15
32:7–10	14	21:31–32	15
32:11–12	144	21:33–35	15
32:19–20	164	22–24	15fn7, 55
32:25–28	67	24:17–24	15fn7
32:29	67	24:20	79
33:2	12fn4, 35fn8	24:25	55
34:11	12fn4, 35fn8	25	18
38:21	67	25:7	18fn10
		25:11	18fn10

Leviticus

		32:1–5	15
5	19fn11	32:6–7	15
14:34	12fn3	32:8–13	16
18:3	12fn3	32:14–15	16
18:21	57	32:16–19	16
18:24–30	57	32:16	16
25:38	12fn3	32:20–23	16
		32:24–27	16
		32:28–32	16

Numbers

		32:33–42	16
1:47	67	34:1–15	13
1:50	67	35	67
1:53	67	35:33–34	58fn6
3:5–10	67		
13:1–2	13	**Deuteronomy**	13fn5
13:2	12fn3	1:7	12fn3
13:17—14:38	16	1:16	32fn2
13:17–33	13	2:4–5	13
13:28–29	12fn4	2:4–8	3
13:29	79	2:9–19	13
14:1–3	14	2:12	13
14:4–10a	14	2:22	3, 13
14:6–10	13	4:26	13fn5
14:11–12	14	6:4	1
14:20	14	6:14	122fn4
14:21–38	14	7:1	12fn3, 35fn8

Deuteronomy (*continued*)

8:19	122fn4
10:9	67
11:24	12
11:30	12fn3
11:31	13fn5
12:10	13fn5
12:12	67
12:31	57
16:9–14	68
16:18	32fn2
17:9	32fn2
17:12	32fn2
17:14–20	119
18:1	67
18:6–7	67
18:9–10	57
19:17	32fn2
19:18	32fn2
20:1–20	79
20:16–18	9fn1
20:17	12fn4
21:2	32fn2
23:7	3, 13
25:2	32fn2
25:17	35fn8, 79
25:19	79
26:11	68
26:12	68
26:13	68
27:2	13fn5
27:4	13fn5
27:12	13fn5
30:18	13fn5
31:13	13fn5
31:25	67
32:47	13fn5
32:49	12fn3
33:8–11	67

Joshua 9, 35, 136fn1, 180

1:1–3	12fn3
1:2–5	35
2	9fn1, 13, 166fn19
3:3	67
3:10	12, 12fn4, 35fn8
7–8	10fn1
7:1–12	18
9	9fn1, 166fn19
9:1–2	35fn8
9:1	12fn4
9:7	35fn8
11:3	12fn4, 35fn8
11:19	35fn8
12:8	12fn4, 35fn8
13:1–7	10
13:8–12	10
13:15–32	10
14–21	9
18:7	10, 67
20:1–6	36
20:7	36
21	10
21:21	36
21:43–45	9, 35
21:43	10
21:44	10
21:45	10
22	9, 13, 21, 183
22:1–34	2
22:1–6	10
22:1	11
22:2–3	10
22:4	10, 11, 16
22:6	10
22:7–9	17
22:7	10, 11, 16
22:8	11
22:9	11, 16
22:10	18
22:11	18
22:12	18
22:13–14	18
22:16–18	18
22:19	19
22:20	18
22:22	19
22:23	19
22:26–27	20
22:28	20
22:29	20
22:30	20
22:31	21
22:32–33	21
22:34	21

INDEX OF BIBLICAL REFERENCES 195

23–24	119	3:12–30	32fn1
23:4–5	10	3:12	33, 48, 50
23:12	119	3:14	48
24:1	36	3:15–30	33
24:3	12fn3	3:15	33, 33fn3, 48, 50, 51
24:11	12, 12fn4, 35fn8	3:30	33, 38, 48, 61
24:19–24	36	3:31	32fn1, 33, 34fn7
24:25	36	4–5	2, 23, 32fn1, 184
24:32	36	4:1–16	33
		4:1–3	24
Judges	2, 24, 29, 30, 31, 32,	4:1	33, 48, 50
	33, 34, 35, 50, 62,	4:3	48, 50
	74, 75, 136fn1, 180	4:4–5	24, 32
1:1–20	35	4:4	33, 48
1:1	23	4:6–7	24
1:2–19	23	4:6	48
1:2	74	4:8–9	25
1:21–36	23	4:9	27
1:21	35	4:10	25
1:27	35	4:11	25
1:29	35	4:12–14	25
1:30	35	4:15–16	25
1:31–32	35	4:17	25, 26
1:33	35	4:18	26
1:34–36	35	4:19	26
2:1–5	36	4:20	26
2:3	35	4:21	26, 27
2:4	24	4:22	27
2:11—3:6	24	4:23–24	27
2:11–16	32, 63	4:23	48
2:11–15	33, 35	5	27, 28, 29
2:11–13	36	5:1	27
2:11	24, 50	5:12	27
2:12	122fn4	5:13	27
2:16	33, 33fn3, 51	5:14–15	29
2:17	33, 33fn3	5:15de	29
2:18	33, 33fn3, 51	5:16–17	29
2:19	33, 33fn3, 122fn4	5:18	29
2:21–23	35	5:23	29
3:3	35fn8	5:24	30
3:5	12fn4	5:25	30
3:7–11	32fn1	5:26	30
3:7	33, 48, 50	5:27	30
3:9–10	51	5:28	30
3:9	33, 33fn3, 48, 50	5:29–30	30
3:10	33, 55	5:31	31, 38, 61
3:11	33, 38, 61	6–8	32fn1

Judges (continued)

Reference	Pages
6:1–6	47
6:1	33, 47, 50
6:7	47, 50
6:8	47
6:11	51
6:14	33, 47
6:15	33, 47
6:31	33
6:34	33, 55
6:35	48
6:36	33, 48
7:2	33, 48
7:7	33
7:14	48
7:15	48
7:23	48
8:1	58
8:2–4	59
8:22	33, 36, 48
8:23	37, 38
8:23–27	37
8:27	34, 48
8:28	33, 38, 48
8:30	34, 35
8:31	34
8:33–34	33
8:33	38, 50
9	2, 32, 184
9:1	37, 47
9:2	38
9:3	38
9:4	38
9:5	39, 47
9:6	32
9:7	39
9:8–9	39
9:10–11	39
9:12–13	40
9:14–15	40
9:15	46
9:16–20	40
9:16	40
9:20	46
9:21	40
9:22–24	41
9:22	32, 40, 49
9:23	41, 49
9:25	41, 44
9:26	42
9:27	44
9:28	44, 45
9:29	42, 44
9:30	44, 45
9:31–33	45
9:34	45
9:35–36	45
9:37–38	45
9:39–41	45
9:40	46
9:42–44	46
9:45	46
9:46	46
9:47	46
9:48–49	46
9:49	46
9:50	46, 47
9:51	46
9:53	46
9:54	47
9:55	49
9:56	47
9:57	47
10–12	184
10:1–2	32fn1, 34fn7
10:1	33, 48
10:2	33, 48
10:3	33, 48
10:3–5	32fn1, 34fn7
10:6	33, 48, 50
10:7–9	48, 50
10:7	51
10:10–15	48
10:10	50
10:11–12	51
10:12	33
10:13–15	55
10:13–14	60
10:13	33, 51, 56
10:14	33, 51
10:15	48fn18, 51
10:16	51, 53, 54, 55
10:17—12:7	32fn1
10:17	51
10:18	51, 52

INDEX OF BIBLICAL REFERENCES

11–12	2	13–16	32fn1
11:1	52	13:1	33, 49
11:2	52	13:5	33, 49
11:3	52, 53fn2, 59	13:25	33
11:4–5	48	14:6	33, 55
11:4	52	14:19	33, 55
11:6	53	15:14	33, 55
11:7	52	15:20	33
11:8	53	16	63
11:9	53	16:31	33, 49, 63
11:10	54	17	24
11:11	53, 54	17:6	63, 70, 74
11:12	54	18:1	63, 74
11:13–27	48	19–21	2, 62, 184
11:13	54	19:1	63, 69, 74
11:14	54	19:2	64
11:15	54	19:3	64
11:16–17	54	19:4	65
11:18	54	19:5	65
11:19–20	54	19:6	65
11:21–22	54	19:7	65
11:23	55	19:8	65
11:24	55	19:9	65
11:25	55	19:10	65
11:26	55	19:11–12	65
11:28	55	19:12	69
11:29	33, 55, 59, 60	19:13	65
11:30–31	56	19:14–15	66
11:32–33	56	19:14	66, 69
11:35	57	19:16–17	66
11:36	58	19:16	69
11:37	58	19:18	66, 69, 73
11:39	58	19:19	68
11:40	58	19:20–21	68
12:1	58	19:22–25	72
12:2–3	59	19:22	69
12:2	33	19:23	69
12:3	33fn3	19:24	70
12:4	59	19:25	70, 72
12:5	60	19:26	70, 71, 72
12:6	60	19:27	71
12:7	48	19:28	71
12:8–10	32fn1, 34fn7	19:29	71
12:8	48	20:1	71, 72
12:11–12	32fn1, 34fn7	20:2	71
12:11	48	20:3	71, 72
12:13–15	32fn1, 34fn7	20:4	72
12:13	49	20:5	72

Judges (continued)

20:6-7	72
20:8-10	72
20:8	72
20:11	72
20:12-13	73
20:14	73
20:15-17	73
20:18	73, 74
20:19-21	73
20:22-23	73
20:23	74
20:24-25	73
20:26-28	74
20:28	74
20:29-48	75
20:47	75
21:1	75
21:2-3	75
21:4	75
21:5	75
21:8-9	75
21:10-11	75
21:12	75
21:13	75
21:19	76
21:20-21	76
21:22	76
21:25	63, 70, 74, 76

1 Samuel

	90, 136fn1, 180
2:27-34	38
3	78
4:11	38
4:18	38
7:15	38
8:1-9	38
8:3-4	78
8:5	78
8:6-7	78
10:1	77
12:12	78
13	78
13:13-14	78
15	85
15:1-9	79
15:10-11	78, 84
15:10	78, 79
15:17-29	84
15:35	78
16:1	78
16:3	163
16:6-7	78
16:13-14	42
16:13	77, 82, 90
16:14-23	81
16:21-23	42
18:1	81
18:3-4	81
18:6-9	81
18:10-11	42, 81
18:12-15	81
18:16	81
18:17-30	81
18:20-29	85
18:20	86
18:21-27	86
19:1	81
19:2-10	81
19:9-10	42
19:11-17	81, 86
19:18-24	81
20:1-29	81
20:13-17	88
20:30-31	81
20:32-42	81
23:2	82
23:4	82
23:6-14	82
23:17	82
24:3-7	80
24:6	80, 81
24:8-15	80
24:10	80, 81
24:20	82
25	85
25:3	43
25:38	82
25:43	85
25:44	85, 86
26:9-12	80
26:9	80, 81
26:11	80, 81
26:12	82
26:13-16	80

26:16	80, 81	2:22–23	83
26:23	80	2:24	84
27:3	85	2:25	84
27:8–9	79	2:26	84
27:8	79	2:27	84
28:6	82, 90	2:28	84
28:17	82	2:29	84
30:5	85	2:30	84
31	79fn2	2:31	84
31:4–6	79	2:32	84
31:11–13	82	3:1	84
		3:2–5	85, 92
2 Samuel	136fn1, 180	3:6	85
1–5	2, 77, 184	3:6–10	85
1:1	77	3:7	85
1:3–4	79	3:11	85
1:4	79	3:12	85
1:5–10	80	3:13–14	85
1:8	79	3:14	86
1:11–12	80	3:15–16	86
1:13–14	80	3:17–21	87
1:13	79	3:17–19	89
1:15	80	3:17–18	86
1:16	80	3:19	86
1:18	80	3:20–21	86
1:19–27	80	3:22	86
1:19	80	3:23–26	87
1:20	80	3:26	87
1:21	80	3:27	87
1:23	80	3:28–29	87
1:24	80	3:30	87
1:25	80	3:31	87
1:25b–26	80	3:32–34	87
1:27	80	3:32	87
2:1	82, 84	3:35–37	87
2:2–4a	82	3:38–39	87
2:2	85	4:1	87
2:4b–7	82	4:2–3	88
2:8–9	83	4:4	88, 109fn3
2:9	85	4:5	88
2:10–11	83	4:6	88
2:12–13	83	4:7	88
2:13	83	4:8	88
2:14–16	83	4:9–12	89
2:17	83	5:1	89
2:18–20	83	5:2	89
2:21	83	5:3	89
		5:5	89

2 Samuel (continued)

Reference	Page
5:6–10	65
5:6–9	89
5:10	89
5:11	89
5:12	89
5:13–16	90
5:19	90
5:20–21	90
5:22–25	90
6:16–23	86
7:1–17	163
8:3–6	124
8:3–4	12
8:16	95, 116
9:1–8	109
9:10	88
10:15–19	124
11:1–22	91
11:6–25	92fn1
11:21	47
12–19	184
12:1–6	95, 110
12:1–4	91
12:1	91
12:5–6	91
12:7–12	92
12:7	91
12:10	92
12:11–12	92
12:12	103
12:13–14	92
12:14	92
12:19	92
12:26–31	116
13–19	2
13	92
13:1–14	92
13:1	92
13:2	92–93
13:3	93
13:4	93
13:5–14	93
13:15	93
13:16	93
13:17	93
13:18–19	93
13:20–22	93
13:23–29	92, 94, 116
13:30–33	94
13:34–36	94
13:37–39	95
14:1–24	116
14:1	95
14:2–3	95
14:4–7	95
14:8–11	95
14:12:13	95
14:14	95
14:15–17	96
14:18–20	96
14:21–24	96
14:25–27	96
14:28	96
14:29–32	96
14:33	96
15:1–6	116
15:1	97
15:2–3	97
15:4–6	97
15:6	108
15:7–9	98
15:10–11	98
15:12	98, 100
15:13	98
15:14	98
15:16	98, 102
15:17–18	99
15:19–22	99
15:19	99
15:23	99
15:24	99
15:26	99
15:27–29	99
15:30	99
15:31	100
15:32	100
15:34–36	100
15:34	103
15:37	100
16:1–4	108
16:1	100
16:2	100
16:3	100
16:4	101

INDEX OF BIBLICAL REFERENCES

16:5–8	108	18:29–30	106
16:5–6	101	18:31	106
16:8	101	18:32	106
16:9	101, 108	19	112
16:10	101	19:1 [Eng. 18:33]	107
16:11	101	19:2–5 [Eng. 19:1–4]	107
16:12	101	19:6–7 [Eng. 19:5–6]	107
16:13	102	19:8–9 [Eng. 19:7–8]	107
16:15	102	19:10 [Eng. 19:9]	107
16:16	102	19:11 [Eng. 19:10]	107
16:17–19	102	19:12–13 [Eng. 19:11–12]	107, 108
16:20–23	85	19:14 [Eng. 19:13]	107, 113, 116
16:20	102	19:15 [Eng. 19:14]	108
16:21	102	19:16 [Eng. 19:15]	108
16:22	102, 113	19:17 [Eng. 19:16]	108
16:23	102	19:20 [Eng. 19:19]	108
17:1–2	103	19:21 [Eng. 19:20]	108
17:3	103	19:22 [Eng. 19:21]	108
17:4	103	19:23 [Eng. 19:22]	108
17:5	103	19:24 [Eng. 19:23]	108, 109fn3
17:7	103	19:25 [Eng. 19:24]	109
17:8–10	103	19:26 [Eng. 19:25]	109
17:11–13	103	19:27–28 [Eng. 19:26–27]	109
17:14	104	19:29 [Eng. 19:28]	88, 109
17:15	104	19:30 [Eng. 19:29]	109
17:16	104	19:32 [Eng. 19:31]	109
17:17	104	19:33 [Eng. 19:32]	109
17:20	104	19:34–39 [Eng. 19:33–38]	110
17:21	105	19:40 [Eng. 19:39]	110
17:22	105	19:41 [Eng. 19:40]	110
17:23	105	19:42–44 [Eng. 19:41–43]	111
17:24	105	19:42 [Eng. 19:41]	110
17:25	105	19:43 [Eng. 19:42]	110
17:26	105	19:44 [Eng. 19:43]	110
17:27–28	105	20	2, 112, 184
18:1–2	105	20:1	112, 114fn2, 116, 117, 129
18:3	105	20:2	112
18:5	105	20:3	113
18:6–7	105	20:4	113
18:8	106	20:5	113
18:9–15	116	20:6	113, 114fn2
18:9	106	20:7	113
18:11	106	20:8	113
18:12–14	106	20:9	113
18:13	106	20:10	113, 114fn2
18:14–15	92, 106	20:11	113
18:24–27	106	20:12–13	114
18:28	106	20:13	114fn2

2 Samuel (*continued*)

20:14	114fn1
20:15	114
20:16	114
20:17–18	114
20:19	115
20:21	115
20:22	115, 116
20:23	116
20:24	116
20:25–26	116
21:5	109fn3
21:7	88, 109fn3

1 Kings

	136fn1, 180
1–3	116
1–2	118
1:8	118
1:39	162
2	115
2:6	115
2:7	110
2:9	115
2:13–25	118
2:19–22	85
2:46c	118
3	118, 123
3:1	118, 122
3:2	119
3:3–4	119
3:4	119
3:5–13	119
3:13	118
3:14	119
3:16–28	119
4:1–6	119
4:6	120
4:7–19	119
4:7	118
4:20—5:1 [Eng. 4:20–21]	119
4:20	118
4:29–34	118
5:1 [Eng. 4:21]	12, 118
5:2–8 [Eng. 4:22–28]	119
5:9–11 [Eng. 4:29–31]	119
5:12–13 [Eng. 4:32–33]	119
5:14 [Eng. 4:34]	119
5:15—7:51 [Eng. 5:1—7:51]	120
5:20–25 [Eng. 5:6–11]	120
5:26 [Eng. 5:12]	120
5:27 [Eng. 5:13]	120
6:1–10	118
6:11–12	123
6:14–36	118
6:38	120
7:1	120
8:22–53	120
8:56–61	120
8:61	120
8:65	12
9	123
9:1–9	120
9:22	120fn3
9:24	120, 122
10:1–5	121
10:4–5	118
10:4	118
10:5	121
10:9	121
10:10	121
10:11–12	121
10:13	121
10:14–22	121
10:23	121
10:24–25	121
10:26–29	121
11	77, 121
11:1–2	122, 166fn19
11:2	122
11:3	34, 122
11:4	122
11:5	55fn3, 122
11:6	122
11:7	55fn3, 122
11:8	122
11:9–10	123
11:9	123
11:11–12	123
11:12	123
11:13	123
11:14	123
11:15–17	123
11:19	123
11:20	123
11:21	124

11:22	124	13:3	132
11:23	124	13:4	132
11:24	124	13:5	132
11:25	124	13:6	132
11:26	124	13:7	132
11:27	124	13:8	132
11:28	124	13:9	132
11:29	124	13:10	132
11:30	125	14:1–20	132
11:31–32	125	14:7–11	134
11:33	125	14:21–24	134
11:37	125	14:30	133
11:38	125	15:11–13	134
11:39	125	15:14	119
11:40	125	15:14a	134
12	2, 118, 184	15:14b–15	134
12:1	46, 126, 130fn6	15:16–24	133
12:2	126	15:16	133
12:3	126	15:27–28	133
12:4	126, 127	15:29	134
12:5	126	16:8–10	133
12:6	126	16:11–12	134
12:7	127	16:15	134
12:8	127	16:18	134
12:9	127	16:21	134
12:10	127	22:1ff.	133
12:11	128	22:11–12	125fn5
12:13–14	128	22:11	164
12:13	128	22:19–23	42
12:15	128	22:43	134
12:16	117, 129	22:43cd	134
12:17	129	22:44	133
12:18	120fn3, 129	22:46	134
12:19	129		
12:20	129	**2 Kings**	136fn1, 180
12:21	130	3:2	134
12:24	130	3:3	134
12:25	130	3:6–8	133
12:26–27	130	5	166fn19
12:28	130	9:6–10	134
11:29–37	132	9:14	133
12:30	131	9:24	133
12:31–32	119	9:27–28	134
12:31	131	9:30–33	134
12:32	131	10:1–10	134
12:33	131	10:11	134
13:1	131	10:28	134
13:2	119, 131		

2 Kings (continued)

10:29	134
10:31	134
12:2–3	134
12:20–21	133
14:3–4	134
14:8–14	133
14:18–20	133
15:3–4	134
15:10–11	133
15:23–25	133
15:30	133
15:34–35	134
16:1–4	134
18:1–8	135
19:15–19	135
19:20–34	135
21:1–9	135
21:19–23	133
21:24	134
22:1ff.	131
23:21–23	135
23:26–27	135

Isaiah   136fn1, 137fn2, 138, 139, 141, 176, 180

1–39	137fn2
1:1	137
9:1–6 [Eng. 9:2–7]	162–63
9:20 [Eng. 9:21]	137
10:11	137
11:1–9	163
11:10	137
11:11	137
11:12	137
11:13	137
11:16	137
19:24–25	166fn19
25:6–8	166fn19
27:6	137
40–45	137fn2
42:6	159
43:1	137
44:1	138
44:3	138
44:5	138
45:22–25	166fn19
49:6	159
55:5	166fn19
56–66	137fn2
56	138
56:1–7	138
56:6–8	166fn19
56:7	138
56:8	138
60:63	166fn19
60:11	166fn19
63:10–19	138
64	138
64:10–11	138
65	138
65:1–16	138
65:17	138
65:18–25	138
65:18–19	138
66:23	138

Jeremiah   136fn1, 139, 141, 176, 180

2:23	122fn4
3	139
3:6–10	139
3:11	139
3:12–13	139
3:18	139
4:1	139
5:11	139
11	139
11:2	139
11:3–5	139
11:10	139
11:16	167
11:17	140
13:1–7	164
16:14–15	140
21:1	36
23	140
23:1–6	140
23:5–6	163
23:7–8	140
23:13–15	140
30	140
30:3	140

30:4–9	140	23:32–35	143
30:22	140	23:36–49	143
31	140	34	143
31:1	140	34:1–6	143
31:5–6	140	34:7–10	143
31:8	140	34:11–16	143
31:9	140	34:23–24	143
31:18	140	34:25–31	143
31:20	140	34:26	143
31:27	141	34:30	144
31:31	141	34:31	143
31:35	141	37	144
31:36	141	37:4	144
31:37	141	37:5–6	144
32	141	37:7–10	144
32:38	141	37:11	144
32:44	141	37:13	144
38:1	36	37:14	144
50:17	141	37:15–23	175
50:18	141	37:16	144
50:19	141	37:17	144
50:20	141	37:19	144
50:33	141	37:21	144
		37:22	144
Ezekiel	136fn1, 141, 142, 143, 145, 175, 180, 183, 184	37:23	145
		37:24–28	145
		47:13–14	145
16	142	47:15–23	145
16:49–51	142	48:1	145
16:53–58	142	48:2	145
20	142	48:3	145
20:1–44	142	48:4	145
20:13	142	48:5	145
20:27	142	48:6	145
20:30	142	48:7	145
20:31	142	48:8–14	145
20:39	142	48:23	145
20:40	142	48:24	145
20:44	142	48:25	145
23	142	48:26	145
23:1–4	142	48:27	145
23:5–7	143		
23:8	143	**Hosea**	145, 145fn8, 146, 176
23:9–10	143		
23:11	143	1:2–5	145
23:12–16	143	1:6–7	145
23:19–21	143	2:1–2 [Eng. 1:10–11]	146

Hosea (continued)

4	146
4:15	146
4:16-19	146
5:5	146
5:8-14	146
6:4	146
6:5	146
8:14	146
12:1 [Eng. 11:12]	146
12:3 [Eng. 12:2]	146
12:10 [Eng. 12:9]	142fn3
14:4-7	146
14:6	167

Amos 146, 147, 148, 176

1:1—2:5	146
1:2	146
2:4-5	148
7:10-13	146
7:13	146
7:15	147
7:16-17	147
9:11-15	147, 148
9:11	147
9:11-12	147
9:12	147
9:13	147
9:14	147
9:15	147

Jonah

3:6-9	166fn19

Micah 148

1:5	148
4:1-2	148
4:3-4	148
4:6	148
4:7	148
4:8	148
4:10	148
4:11	148
4:13	148
5:1-3 [Eng. 5:2-4]	163
5:2 [Eng. 5:3]	148

5:4-5 [Eng. 5:5-6]	148
6:4-5	148
6:16	148
7:8	148
7:14	148
7:18	149
7:20	149

Zephania

1:1	149
1:7	149
2:9	149
3:8-29	149
3:13	149
3:14	149
3:15	149

Zechariah 149

2:2 [Eng. 1:19]	149
2:14 [Eng. 2:10]	149
2:15 [Eng. 2:11]	149
2:16 [Eng. 2:11]	166fn19
8:8	149
8:13	149
8:22	149
8:23	150
9:7	150
9:9	150
9:10	150
10-11	150fn10
10:6	150
10:10	150
11:4-14	150
14:1-21	150
14:16	166fn19

Psalms

47:9 [Eng. v8]	36
78	150fn10
78:67	150fn10
78:71	150fn10
93:1	36
96:10	36
97:1	36
99:1	36
105:11	12fn3

106:37–38	57	5:3	165fn17
146:10	36	5:10	165fn17
		5:17–20	158, 166
Job	176	5:21–48	166fn18
		5:19	165fn17
Proverbs	176	5:20	165fn17
		6:5–6	164, 165
		6:7–13	169
Ruth		6:9	181
1:2	36	7:21	165fn17
1:3	36	8:11	165fn17
2:3	36	9:35	164
4:3	36	10:1–2	164fn14
4:9	36	10:5	164fn14
		10:6	153
Ecclesiastes	176	10:7	165fn17
		10:17	165
Ezra		11:1	164fn14
8:6	43fn12	11:11	165fn17
9:1	12fn4	11:12	165fn17
		12:9–13	164
		12:28	165fn17
Nehemiah		13:11	165fn17
9:8	12fn4	13:24–30	185
9:24	12fn3	13:24	165fn17
		13:31	165fn17
		13:33	165fn17
1 Chronicles		13:44	165fn17
1:32	34	13:45	165fn17
1:52	142	13:47	165fn17
3:20	142	13:52	165fn17
		16:13–20	163
2 Chronicles		16:19	165fn17
8:7	12fn4	18:1	165fn17
		18:3	165fn17
Matthew	157, 160, 162	18:4	165fn17
1:1–17	157	18:23	165fn17
1:16	159fn7	19:12	165fn17
1:20–21	157	19:14	165fn17
2:1–2	157	19:23	165fn17
2:3–8	157	19:24	165fn17
2:12–18	157	19:28	164fn14
3:2	165, 165fn17	20:1	165fn17
3:5–6	165	20:17	164fn14
3:7–10	165	21:9	160
4:17	165, 165fn17	21:15	160
4:23	164	21:31	165fn17
		21:43	165fn17

INDEX OF BIBLICAL REFERENCES

Matthew (*continued*)

22:2	165fn17
23:6	165
23:14	165fn17
23:34	165
25:1	165fn17
25:31–46	185
26:14	164fn14
26:20	164fn14
26:47	164fn14
27:11	160
27:29	160
27:37	160
27:42	160

Mark 160, 160fn8

1:14–15	165
1:15	165fn17
1:21	164
1:23–27	164
1:29–32	165
1:39	164
3:1–5	164
3:14	164fn14
3:16	164fn14
4:10	164, 164fn14
4:11	165, 165fn17
4:26	165, 165fn17
4:30	165, 165fn17
6:2	164
6:7	164fn14
8:27–30	163
9:1	165, 165fn17
9:35	164fn14
9:47	165fn17
10:14	165fn17
10:15	165fn17
10:19	166
10:23	165fn17
10:24	165fn17
10:25	165fn17
10:32	164fn14
11:11	164fn14
12:34	165fn17
12:38–40	165
13:9	165
14:10	164fn14
14:17	164fn14
14:20	164fn14
14:25	165fn17
14:43	164fn14
14:61–62	181
15:2	160
15:9	160
15:12	160
15:17–19	160
15:20	160
15:26	160
15:32	160
15:43	165fn17

Luke 157, 159, 160, 160fn8, 162

1:11–17	158
1:26–33	158
1:54–55	158
1:67	158
1:68–69	158
1:72	158
1:76–79	158
2:21–24	158
2:25–26	159
2:31	159
2:36	159
2:37	159
2:38	159
3:23–38	159
3:23	159fn7
3:38	159
4:1–13	166
4:15	164
4:16–21	166
4:16	164, 165
4:20	164
4:28	164
4:33	164
4:38	164
4:43	165, 165fn17
4:44	164
6:6	164
6:13	164fn14
6:20	165fn17
7:1–10	165
7:28	165, 165fn17
8:1–3	164

INDEX OF BIBLICAL REFERENCES 209

8:1	164fn14, 165, 165fn17	24:27	166
8:10	165fn17		
8:41	165	**John**	160fn8, 161, 164, 169
9:1	164fn14	1:41	163
9:2	165fn17	3:3	165
9:11	165fn17	3:5	165
9:12	164fn14	4:22	165
9:18–22	163	4:29	163
9:27	165fn17	5:46	166
9:60	165fn17	6:59	164
9:62	165fn17	6:67	164
10:9	165fn17	6:70	164
10:11	165fn17	6:71	164
11:1–4	169	11:27	163
11:20	165fn17	17:1–19	169
11:43	165	17:12	169
12:11	165	17:20–26	169
13:10	164	17:20	169
13:18	165fn17	17:21	169
13:20	165fn17	17:23	170
13:28	165fn17	18:20	164
13:29	165fn17	18:33	161
14:15	165fn17	18:36	161
16:16	165fn17	18:37	161
17:20	165fn17	18:39	161
17:21	165fn17	19:2	161
18:16	165fn17	19:3	161
18:17	165fn17	19:5	161
18:24	165fn17	19:14	162
18:25	165fn17	19:15	162
18:29	165fn17	19:19	162
18:31	164fn14	19:21	162
19:11	165fn17	19:22	162
20:46–47	165	20:24	164
21:12	165	20:31	163
21:31	165fn17		
22:3	164fn14	**Acts**	166, 170fn24, 171, 174
22:16	165fn17	2	184
22:18	165fn17	2:41–47	170
22:47	164fn14	4	184
23:2	161	4:32–37	170
23:3	161	5:1–11	171
23:11	161	6:1	171
23:37	161	6:2–6	171
23:38	161	6:7	171
23:51	165fn17	10	171
24:19–20	161	11:1–2	171
24:21	161		

Acts (continued)

11:3–18	171
11:26	153
15:2	171
15:4–35	171
26:28	153

Romans 166

3:28	173
11:17	167
11:18	167
11:29	167, 168

1 Corinthians 166

1:11–13	172
3:1–3	172
3:4–9	172
5:1–5	172
5:9–13	172
12:1–31	172
13	172
15:3	176
15:5	164fn15

Galatians 166, 167, 171, 172

1:6	172
1:7	172
1:8–9	173
2:11–12	173
2:11	173
2:14–21	173
3:1	173
3:10	173
3:13	173
4:1–7	167
4:5	168
5:4	173
5:6	173
5:14	173
5:15	173
6:16	167

James 173, 174

1:1	174
2:18	173
2:20	173
2:26	173

1 Peter

4:16	153

THE SEPTUAGINT (LXX)

Deuteronomy

4:10	169fn23
9:10	169fn23
18:16	169fn23
23:2–3	169fn23

Joshua

9:2	169fn23

Judges

20:2	169fn23
21:5	169fn23

1 Kingdoms (=1 Samuel)

17:47	169fn23
19:20	169fn23

1 Chronicles (=1 Paralipomenon)

13:2	169fn23
28:2	169fn23
29:1	169fn23

2 Chronicles (=2 Paralipomenon)

1:3	169fn23
6:3	169fn23
7:8	169fn23
10:3	169fn23
20:5	169fn23
23:3	169fn23
28:14	169fn23
29:23	169fn23
30:2	169fn23

INDEX OF BIBLICAL REFERENCES

2 Esdras (=Ezra and Nehemiah)

2:64	169fn23
10:1	169fn23
10:8	169fn23
10:12	169fn23
10:14	169fn23

Nehemiah

5:7	169fn23
5:13	169fn23
7:66	169fn23
8:2	169fn23
8:17	169fn23
13:1	169fn23

Judith

6:16	169fn23
6:21	169fn23
7:29	169fn23
14:6	169fn23

1 Maccabees

2:56	169fn23
3:13	169fn23
4:59	169fn23
5:16	169fn23

Psalms

21(22):23	169fn23
21(22):26	169fn23
25(26):5	169fn23
25(26):12	169fn23
34(35):18	169fn23
39(40):10	169fn23
67(68):26	169fn23
88(89):6	169fn23
106(107):32	169fn23
149:1	169fn23

Proverbs

5:14	169fn23

Job

30:28	169fn23

Sirach

15:5	169fn23
21:17	169fn23
23:24	169fn23
24:2	169fn23
26:5	169fn23
38:33	169fn23
39:10	169fn23
44:15	169fn23
50:13	169fn23
50:20	169fn23

Lamentations

1:10	169fn23

Micah

2:5	169fn23

Joel

2:16	169fn23

Isaiah

57:14	159
57:18	159

www.ingramcontent.com/pod-product-compliance
Lightning Source LLC
Chambersburg PA
CBHW031359230426
43670CB00006B/589